Hazrat Inayat Khan

SOCIAL GATHEKAS

Selected titles from Sulūk Press and Omega Publications

The Art of Being and Becoming
by Hazrat Inayat Khan

The Ecstasy Beyond Knowing: A Manual of Meditation
by Pir Vilayat Inayat Khan

The Hand of Poetry: Five Mystic Poets of Persia
by Hazrat Inayat Khan and Coleman Barks

Mastery through Accomplishment
by Hazrat Inayat Khan

The Message in Our Time:
The Life and Teachings of the Sufi Master
Pir-O-Murshid Inayat Khan
by Pir Vilayat Inayat Khan

Mingled Waters:
Sufism and the Mystical Unity of Religions
by Pir Zia Inayat-Khan

Saracen Chivalry:
Counsels on Valor, Generosity and the Mystical Quest
by Pir Zia Inayat-Khan

The Sufi Message of Hazrat Inayat Khan
Centennial Edition
Volume I: The Inner Life
Volume II: The Mysticism of Sound
Volume III: The Art of Personality
Volume IV: Healing and the Mind World

The Complete Works of Pir-o-Murshid Hazrat Inayat Khan series
in cooperation with the Nekbakht Foundation

For a complete list of titles please visit
www.omegapub.com

SOCIAL GATHEKAS

SUFI WISDOM ON SOCIAL HARMONY AND SERVICE

HAZRAT INAYAT KHAN

Sulūk Press
Richmond, Virginia

Published by Sulūk Press
an imprint of Omega Publications, Inc.
Richmond, Virginia
www.omegapub.com

Cover design by Sandra Lillydahl

This edition is printed on acid-free paper that meets ANSI standard X39-48.

Author: Inayat Khan (1882–1927)
Title: Social Gathekas: Sufi Wisdom on Social Harmony and Service
includes foreword, preface
biographical note, glossary
Subject: Sufism

Library of Congress Control Number: 2020948971

Printed and bound in the United States of America

ISBN 978–1–941810–35–4 hardcase
ISBN 978–1–941810–39–2 paper

Contents

Foreword

HAZRAT Inayat Khan (1882–1927), the Indian poet-philosopher, musician, and mystic, to this day continues to be celebrated as a radiant representative of India's contemplative life and meditative mysticism in their Sufi mode and method—that is, in a characteristically world-embracing rather than world-renouncing system such as can be found to predominate in other Indian systems of notable value. Indeed, the relevance of his theory and teachings would appear to have increased and expanded with time, and enthusiasm for his message of spiritual liberty has continued unabated.

The depth of his mystical perception, the breadth of his philosophical vision and religious universalism, and the poetic charm of his evocative and allusive style continue to be admired by those who come in contact with his work. His preferred way of communicating—of both developing his insights and conveying them to others—was through lectures and oral teachings, most of which were carefully recorded by those close to him. This spontaneity in approach is part of the abiding charm of his Sufism; it was with him from his very first lectures and practical illustrations of Indian classical music that he gave all over India as a young man, and then throughout the United States and Europe in the years before and after the Great War. In this way, his Sufism forever retained the Indian musical expert's mastery of improvising elaboration, with all the freshness and drive of new discoveries within familiar contexts.

As background for his life's work in Sufism, it is well to keep in mind Hazrat Inayat Khan's fondly repeated remark: "Sufism was born intellectually in Arabia, devotionally reared in Persia, and spiritually completed in India."

It is a fortunate initiative at this time to bring together Inayat Khan's discourses on topics relating to social values. The main portion of these had been assembled and issued to his *murids* (followers) as the "Social Gathekas" (or "Songbook on Social Subjects"). Some of the texts have appeared in print before, most notably in the thirteen Sufi Message volumes of the Pallandt edition brought out between 1960 and 1967 and revised in the 1990s. To be sure, the Sufism of Hazrat Inayat Khan in its social dimension does not aim at formulating a specific ideology or anything resembling such, anymore than his religious philosophy seeks to convey a set of religious beliefs! The latter's familiar and essential refrain of "love, harmony, and beauty" renders in characteristically poetic style the psychological notions of will, balance, and focus—the three essentials of Inayat Khan's Sufi tuition.

If anything, Hazrat Inayat Khan's very Indian Sufism seeks to establish such balance and a harmonious relationship between all such differing idealisms and their all-too-often contentious positions. And in so doing, it may in certain contexts veer to one or another of such sets of ideas more markedly for the time deemed required for meeting on common ground.

For it is the moral, psychological, and spiritual level from which all socially defined values, whether religious or ideological, are—and should be—regarded. This requires an advanced point of view, presupposing self-discipline and objectivity without loss of sensibility or sympathy. It involves "a training of the view," which also happens to be Hazrat Inayat Khan's own favorite general description of his Sufism.

The fact that Sufism mostly aims at being world-embracing naturally means that civilized and cultural values, personal and social standards, are an integral part of its spiritual vision and

practical attitudes, of its teachings and trainings in mystical contemplation and attainment—for "who worships God and despises man, worships in vain."

It is this depth of insight and embrace of cultural, personal, and social differences—of multiculturalism, if you will—that renders the present collection of addresses and discourses of singular interest in our time. The *Social Gathekas* constitute a veritable treasure house of perceptions and perspectives, "human and divine," to inspire and illuminate the aspiring traveler on the challenging spiral pathway of "the inner life."

Just concentrate, contemplate, meditate, and realize!

Shaikh-al-Mashaik Mahmood Khan Youskine

Preface

FUNDAMENTAL to the mystical vision of life is the insight that the whole universe forms a single body. From this perspective, everything is related to everything else within a complex and dynamic pattern of interconnectedness. One who discerns this all-encompassing moiré of unity-in-multiplicity discovers the self in the other and the other in the self. The mode of living that results from this discovery is a gentle and refined manner. Hazrat Inayat Khan's teachings on kinship are a profound introduction to this way of seeing and being. Here, simply spoken, is the answer to the problem of the day.

Pir Zia Inayat Khan

Acknowledgments

Many thanks to Halim Bruno Knobel for the original inspiration for this volume, as well as for his dedicated and careful compilation of the text from its authentic source material. Many thanks are also due to Anne Louise Wirgman, Director, Nekbakht Foundation in Suresnes, France for all the initial editing and corrections. Thanks also to Cannon Labrie who provided additional skilled editorial assistance.

Our deepest gratitude goes to Shaik-al-Mashaik Mahmood Khan who supported this work in friendship.

Sandra Lillydahl, editor

Social Gathekas

1

Sufism Not Pacifism

VERY often the Sufi message, in its form of beneficence, is taken to be what they call in these days pacifism; and those who are unfavorable to the idea of pacifism explain it as being peace at any price. Sufism does not teach that.[1] Sufism does not mean goodness, kindness, or piety; Sufism means wisdom. All things in life are materials for wisdom to work with, and wisdom cannot be restricted to any principles. Among Sufis there have been great souls who were kings or in the position of a beggar. Saints and workers, commanders, generals, business people, statesmen and women, prophets—in all different walks of life the Sufis of different ages have practiced Sufism. This shows that no one can point out with a finger that this particular belief or tenet is a Sufi doctrine. There are two things: sound and notes. Notes point out the degree of the sound, but sound is all notes, not any note in particular. So it is with Sufism: it is all beliefs and no belief in particular. There is no action that the Sufi calls right or wrong, for every action can become right and can become wrong—it depends upon the use or abuse of the action, its fitness or unfitness. Right or wrong depends upon the attitude and situation, not the action. This naturally gives the Sufi tolerance toward another, and makes Sufis ready to forgive another and unwilling to form an opinion about the action of another person.

This attitude keeps the Sufi far removed from saying that peace is good or war is good. The Sufi will say war is good at the time of war, peace is good at the time of peace.

1. Lecture given in 1922, date and location are unknown.

But then you will say that if all things are right in their proper place, then Sufism has nothing to do with life. In answer to this I will say that there is one principle mission of Sufism, and that is to dig the ground under which the light of the soul becomes buried. This is the same as the teaching of Christ, who has said that no one should cover one's light under a bushel, and also to raise your light on high.[2]

The condition of the world today is such that humanity has become abnormal in these days. Humanity is not only frightened at badness, but also at goodness; humanity does not dread only war, but also peace; humanity is not only tired of enmity, but also of friendship; humanity does not only suspect an adversary today, but even one's own brother or sister. It seems as if the mind of the world were not only tired, but ill. It seems as if humanity has had a nervous breakdown. Humanity, individually or collectively, does not know its life's purpose or goal. The Sufi message warns humanity to know life better and to achieve freedom in life; it warns humanity to accomplish what it considers good, just, and desirable, and before every action, to note its consequences by studying the situation, by judging one's own attitude, by studying beforehand the method which one adopts to act in life.

It is true that Sufism does not only guide those who are religious, mystical, or visionary; but the Sufi message gives to the world the religion of the day, and that is to make one's life a religion; to turn one's occupation, one's profession into religion; to make one's ideal a religious ideal. Sufism has as its object the uniting of life and religion, which, so far, seem to have been kept apart. Think, when once a week a person will go to church and all the other days of the week a person will devote to business, how can anyone benefit by religion? Therefore, the teaching of Sufis is to make everyday life into a religion, that every action in life may have some spiritual fruit.

2. Matthew 5:15.

The method for world reform that different institutions have adopted today is not the method of the Sufi Movement. We think that if ill is contagious, good must be more so. The depth of every soul is good. Every soul is searching for good, and, by the effort of individuals who wish to do good in the world, much can be done—even more than what a materialistic institution can do. No doubt, for the general good there are political and commercial problems to be solved, and little can be done in that direction before several difficult problems have been solved. But that must not debar individuals from progress, for it is the individualistic progress through the spiritual path that alone can bring about the desired condition in the world.

2

Our Work in the Line of Kinship

IN working in the line of kinship, our main object is to bring about a better understanding among the different classes, followers of different religions, and people of different races and different nations.[1] But by this we do not mean to mix them up. If that were our idea, it would have been quite a different thing again. We want to let the farms of wheat be farms of wheat; on the farms where rice grows, let rice grow; where there are woods, let there be woods; where there are gardens, let there be gardens. All things are necessary; our ideas have not reached to the extreme of cooking all things in one dish. We do not wish to stretch the fingers of the hand so as to make them all even, for their natural size is the proper size for them; our imagination of equality has not yet reached that idea. Our only motive is that the East and West, North and South, instead of turning their backs on each other, may turn their faces to each other. We do not wish that all people in the world should have the same occupation or the same religion or the same education or the same customs and manners; nor do we think that all classes must become one class, which is impossible. We wish that all classes may blend with each other, and yet that every individual may have an individual expression in life.

All nations may have their peculiarities, their individuality; but at the same time they may exchange goodwill and friendly feelings toward each other. Different races may have their own

1 Lecture given in Suresnes, France, August 5, 1922.

customs and manners and their own ideas, but at the same time may understand each other. The followers of different religions may belong to their own religions, but at the same time may become tolerant toward each other.

Therefore, our idea of kinship is not in any way extreme. The motive is not to change humanity, but to help humanity on toward its goal. People may belong to one church, and yet they often fight with one another. It would be just as well that they belong to different churches and yet understand each other and respect each other's religion and tolerate one another. People may belong to one institution and disagree—then what is the use of that institution? It is not at all the mission of our order[2] to make the whole humanity as the followers of one special order, but to give to humanity what God has given us, that we may serve in God's cause.

2. The Sufi Order was the general name of the organization in 1922. In October 1923 the name officially changed to the Sufi Movement, and the Sufi Order name was then used for the activity of the esoteric school at that time.

3

Optimism and Pessimism

I SHOULD like to speak this afternoon on the subject of optimism and pessimism.[1] Optimism represents the spontaneous flow of love; also optimism represents trust in love. This shows that it is love, trusting love, which is optimism. Pessimism comes from disappointment, from a bad impression of some hindrance in the path. Optimism gives a hopeful attitude in life, where pessimism sees darkness in one's path. No doubt sometimes pessimism shows conscientiousness and also cleverness; and pessimism also shows experience. But in point of fact, can we be conscientious enough if we only thought what difficulties we had before us in our life? It is trust that solves the problem in the end.

Very often the wise have seen that cleverness does not reach far; it goes so far and there it stands, for cleverness is a knowledge that belongs to earth. As to experience, what is humanity's experience? One is only proud of one's experience in life until one has seen how vast is the world. In every line of work and thought there is a new amount of experience that is needed; the further one has the experience, the less one realizes that one has none.

The psychological effect of optimism is such that it helps to bring success, for it is by the optimistic spirit that God has created the world. Therefore, optimism comes from God, and pessimism is born out of the heart of humanity. From what

1. Lecture given in Suresnes, France, August 6, 1922.

little experience of life a person has, one finds this will not be done, this will not succeed, that will not go, that will not come right. For the ones who are optimistic, if it does not come right in the end, it does not matter; they will take their chances.

And what is life? Life is an opportunity. To the optimistic person this opportunity is a promise, and for the pessimistic person this opportunity is lost. It is not that the Creator helps to lose it, but it is humanity itself that withdraws from the possibility to take it. Many in this world prolong their illness by giving way to pessimistic thought. Mostly you will find that with those who have suffered for many years from a certain illness, the illness becomes so real to them that its absence seems to them unnatural. They believe that illness to be their nature, and its absence is something they do not know; and in that way, they keep that illness in themselves.

Then there are pessimistic people who think that misery is their share in life: they are born to be wretched, they cannot be anything else but unhappy; heaven and earth are against them. In fact, they are against themselves, and their pessimism is their misfortune. One's life depends on what one concentrates upon. If one concentrates upon one's misery, one cannot be other but miserable. With a certain habit or a certain nature that people do not approve in themselves, they think they are helpless before it because it is their nature, it is their own. Nothing is one's nature except that which one makes oneself. As the whole nature is made by God, so the nature of each one is made by oneself. And as the Almighty is powerful enough to change its nature, so one has the power, if one only knew it, to change one's own nature.

Among all the creatures of this world, humanity is most entitled to be optimistic, for humanity represents God on earth: God as judge, as creator, and as master of all creation. So one is master of one's own life, master of one's affairs, if only one knew it. Someone with an optimistic view will help another drowning in the sea of fear or disappointment; but on the contrary, pessimists, if someone comes to them ill or downhearted by a hard life, will pull that person down and let that person sink with them. Therefore, on the side of one there is life; on the side of the other there is death. One is climbing toward the top of the mountain; the other is going to the depth of the earth. Is there any greater helper in one's sorrow, in misfortune, at moments when every situation in life seems dark, than that spirit of optimism that knows it will be right? Therefore, it will not be an exaggeration if I said that the very spirit of God comes to humanity's rescue in the form of the optimistic spirit.

Friends, it does not matter how hard is the situation in life, how great the difficulty may be; it all can be fought with, it all can be surmounted. But what matters is that if one's own pessimistic spirit is weighing one down low, then already one has gone down below the waters. Death is preferable to being weighed down in one's misery by a pessimistic spirit. Therefore, the greatest reward that there can be is the spirit of optimism, and the greatest punishment that could be given to someone for their worst sins is the spirit of pessimism. Verily, hopeful is the one who in the end will succeed.

4

HARMONY

I WOULD like to speak on the subject of harmony this afternoon.[1] It seems that what makes beauty is harmony; beauty in itself has no meaning. A certain object that is called beautiful at a certain place and time is not beautiful at another place or another time. And so it is with thought, speech, and action. That which is called beautiful is only at a certain time and condition that makes it beautiful. Therefore, if one could give a true definition of beauty, it is harmony. Harmony is the combination of colors, harmony is the drawing of design or line that is called beauty. At the same time, a word, a thought, a feeling, an action that creates harmony is productive of beauty.

Now the question is, from where comes the tendency to harmony, and from where comes a tendency to disharmony? The natural tendency of every soul is toward harmony, and the tendency toward disharmony is an unnatural state of mind or affair. And the very fact that it is not natural makes it void of beauty. The psychology of humanity is that we respond to harmony and inharmony, both. People cannot help it, because naturally they are made so; mentally and physically, they respond to all that comes to them, harmonious or inharmonious. And the teaching of Christ, "Resist not evil,"[2] is a hint not to respond to inharmony. For instance, a word of kindness, of sympathy, an action of love and affection, has a response; but

1. Lecture given in Paris, December 18, 1922.
2. Matthew 5:39.

at the same time, a word of insult, an action of revolt or hatred creates a response too, and this response creates more inharmony in the world. By giving a way to inharmony, one allows inharmony to multiply.

At this time, when one sees in the world the greatest unrest and discomfort pervading all over—where does it come from? It seems that it is the ignorance of the fact that inharmony will create inharmony and will multiply the inharmony. People have a natural tendency that, if they see they are insulted, they think the proper way of answering is to insult the person still more. By this they get a momentary satisfaction to have given a good answer, but they do not know what they have done by their good answer. They have given a response to the power that was given by another, and these two powers, being negative and positive, create more inharmony.

"Resist not evil" does not mean receive evil unto yourself. "Resist not evil" only means this: do not send back the inharmony that comes to you, just like a person playing tennis would throw back the ball with the racket. But at the same time, it does not suggest that you receive the ball with open hands. The tendency toward harmony must be like a rock in the sea. Through the wind, through the storm, the rock stands in the sea. And the waves come with all their force, and yet the rock is still, stands and bears it all, letting the waves beat against it.

By fighting with inharmony one increases it; by not fighting it one does not give fuel to the fire that would rise for destruction and would cause destruction. But no doubt the wiser you become, the more difficulty you have to face in life, because every kind of inharmony will be directed to you for the very reason that you will not fight it. But at the same time you must know, with all that difficulty, that you have helped that disharmony—which would have otherwise multiplied—to be destroyed. It is not without advantage, for every time you stand against inharmony you increase your strength, although outwardly it may seem a defeat. But one conscious of the increase of one's power will never admit that it is a defeat. After time has passed, those against whom one has stood firm will realize that it was their defeat.

Life in the world has a constantly jarring effect, and the finer you become the more trying it becomes to you. And the time comes that when people are sincere and good-willing, kind and sympathetic, the worse life becomes for them. But if they are discouraged in it, they go under. If they kept their courage, then you find it was not disadvantageous in the end, because their power will someday increase to that stage, to that degree that their presence, their word, their action, will control the thoughts and feelings and activities of all. For they will get that heavy rhythm, the rhythm that will make the rhythm of everybody else follow it. This is the attribute that is called in the East the quality of the mastermind. But in order to stand firm against the inharmony that comes from without, one must first practice to stand firm against all that comes from within, from one's own self. For our soul itself is more difficult to control than the others. And when one is not able, and one has failed to control oneself, it is most difficult to stand against the disharmony without.

Now the question is, what is it that causes inharmony in oneself? It is weakness—physical weakness or mental weakness, but it is weakness. Very often, therefore, one finds that it is bodily illness that causes inharmony and causes inharmonious tendencies. Besides, there are many diseases of the mind that the scientist of today has not yet found. Today in the world there are two things. One thing is that a person who is too ill perhaps is considered as an insane person. And then there are all other illnesses that are not counted at all. These people are counted among the sane people, and as notice is not taken of the defects that are of the diseases of the mind, people never have a chance to notice them within themselves. They are constantly finding fault with others. If they are in an office, if they are in a good position, if they are at home, everywhere they cause inharmony. Nobody knows it, for to be treated as insane, they must first be called insane.

The health of the mind is a question so little thought about these days. In point of fact, as there are more solicitors, more lawyers, more barristers, more courts, and more judges, so there come more cases. Consequently prisons increase, and what is the outcome? After people have gone to prison and come back, they have forgotten where they were. They go again in the same path, for the disease is not found out. At the court a person is judged, but it is not found out what is the matter psychologically, what is the matter, what caused that person to do this. One can find in these prisons thousands of people. There is something the matter with their minds, and if for a thousand years they were kept in prison, they would not improve. Nothing but injustice is given to them by putting them in prison. It is just like putting a person in prison because that person's body is ill.

The cause of every discomfort and of every failure is inharmony. And what would be the most useful thing at the present moment in education? To give the sense of harmony, to develop it in children. It will not be so difficult as it appears to be, to bring harmony to their notice. What is necessary is to point out to the youths the different aspects of inharmony in different aspects of life's affairs.

The work of the Sufi message, a message that is of love, harmony, and beauty, is to waken the consciousness in humanity of the true nature of love, harmony, and beauty. And the training that is given to those who become initiated in the inner school is to cultivate these three principal things, which are the principal factors in human life.

5

Happiness

DOES happiness depend upon the conditions of life or upon our outlook on life?[1] It is a question that is very often asked, and it is most difficult to answer. Many with philosophical knowledge will say that the material world is an illusion and its condition a dream, but yet there are very few who can make themselves believe it. To know a thing interiorly is a very different thing from practicing it. It is most difficult in the world to rise above the effect of conditions. No doubt, to rise above conditions there is only one thing that helps, and that is a change of outlook on life; and this change is made practicable by the change of attitude. In the language of the Hindus, life in the world is called samsara. It is pictured as life in a mist. One thinks and says and does and feels, and yet does not know fully why. If a person knows one reason for it, there is another reason hidden behind that a person does not know. Very often condition in life shows a picture of captivity; often it seems as if one had to walk between the water and a pit. And to rise above conditions one needs wings, which everyone has not got. The wings are attached to the will: one wing is independence, the other is indifference. Independence wants a great deal of sacrifice before one can feel independent in life. Indifference against one's nature of love and sympathy is like cutting one's heart asunder before one can practice indifference through life. No doubt, when once the will is able to spread its wings, then one sees the conditions of life far removed, one stands

1. Lecture given in Suresnes, France, August 20, 1922.

above all conditions that make humanity captive. There is no difficulty that cannot be surmounted sooner or later, but even if one has achieved something one desires in life, there is something else in life that seems to be unfinished. And so if one went from one thing to another, achieving all one desires, the objects of desire will multiply, and then there will never be an end to one's desire.

The more one has to do in life, the more difficulties one must meet. If one is far away from the life of the world, then one's life is purposeless. The more important the task, the more difficult to accomplish. And so every evening follows the day and goes on until eternity. For a Sufi, therefore, it is not only the patience to bear all things, but it is necessary to see all things from a certain point of view that can relieve a person for that moment from difficulty and pain.

Very often it is the outlook on life that changes the whole life of a person. It can turn hell into heaven, it can turn sorrow into joy. When one looks from a certain point of view, every little pinprick feels like a sword piercing through one's heart. If one looks at the same thing from a different point of view, the heart becomes sting-proof; nothing can touch it. All things that are thrown at one as bullets, drop down without having touched one.

What is the meaning of walking upon the water? Life is symbolical of water. There is one who becomes drowned in the water, there is another who swims in the water, but there is another one who walks upon it. The one who is so sensitive that, after having one little pinprick, is unhappy all the day and the night, is someone of the first category; and one who gives and takes back and makes a game of life is the swimmer. People do not mind if they receive a knock, for they derive their satisfaction by being able to give a knock in return. But those whom nothing can touch are in the world and yet above the world. They are the ones who walk over the water. Therefore life is under their feet, their joy and sorrow both. Truly independence and indifference are the wings which enable them to fly.

6

THE MISSION OF SUFISM TO THE WORLD

THE Sufi Movement has two missions to perform in the world: one is a duty to individuals searching after truth, and the next duty is to bring about a better understanding among people.[1] Therefore, these two missions depend on each other for their fulfillment. Without the progress of individuals, the progress of humanity is difficult; without the progress of humanity in general, the progress of the individual also is difficult. The Sufi Movement is not political, because beyond politics is the mystic idea of the Sufi. In all ages in the past the spiritual message was given by the prophets, for the words of God come to humanity by the mediumship of a mystic. When the law is fallen into the hands of worldly intellectual people, it will always prove imperfect. By *law* is meant the hidden law of life and of nature, not only rules and regulations for a government. It wants seeing further than the average eye to see the actual condition of life that those interested in life cannot see, for they cannot help being partial when there is a question of their own interest.

The principal thing that the Sufi message has brought to the world is tolerance for all faiths existing in the different parts of the world and followed by different people. This can be done by giving the idea of the one truth that stands as the stem of religion, and that all different faiths are its branches. The true religion to a Sufi is the sea of truth, and all different faiths are as its waves. The message of God comes from time to time, as tides in the sea; but what remains always is the sea, the truth.

1. Lecture given in Suresnes, France, June 23, 1922.

Those who consider another on the wrong track are themselves also not on the right track, for the one who is on the right track finds every road leading to the same goal, sooner or later.

The Sufi mission does not make converts to a certain faith, exclusive to all faiths. A convert to the Sufi Order means a convert to all faiths of this world, bound by no particular faith. Faith, to a Sufi, is a freeing ideal, not a captivity. The Sufi mission looks upon the whole humanity as one body, and all races as different parts of this body, all nations its organs, the people as the particles that make this body; and the spirit of this body is God. As the health and happiness of the body depends upon each particle being in good condition, so the happiness and peace of the whole world and the people therein depend upon the condition of one another. The Sufi mission does not invite people to believe in superstitions, to take an interest in wonder-workings, or to increase power, or to investigate phenomena. Its main object is the same that Christ has taught: love your neighbor.[2]

To individuals the Sufi mission has a different duty. The murshid, as a physician, first treats the murids in order to make them better able to realize where they are, what they are, what they want to do, and how they must work to accomplish it. What is worthwhile and what is not worthwhile, the murshid explains to the murid. And it is not only study, but it is the exercises that the murshid gives now and again as a prescription for the murid. But still more important is the contact of the murshid. A moment's conversation with the murshid is more helpful than a whole year's study of books in the library, for the murshid is a living book. The object of the murshid is to kindle in the heart of the murid the divine spirit that is humanity's heritage. There is no particular discipline nor a particular faith that is forced upon murids. All murids are free to think for themselves. The murshid's whole idea is to liberate the soul of the seeker after truth.

2. Matthew 22:39.

7

Sufism

SUFISM comes from an Arabic word *saf*, which means a "purifying process."[1] All the tragedy in life comes from the absence of purity, and what does purity mean? Purity means to be natural; the absence of purity means to be far from being natural. Pure water means that no substance, such as sweet or sour or milk or any other substance, is mixed with it. Sterilized water means water made purer; in other words, natural. Sufism, therefore, is the process of making life natural. You may call this process a religion, a philosophy, a science, or mysticism, whatever you may. It is true that all the religious teachers who have come in this world from time to time have brought this process of purity in the form of a religion. It is therefore that Christ has said, "I have not brought you a new law, but I have come to fulfill the law."[2] It is not a new process; it is the same old process that the wise of all ages have given. If there is anything new given in it, it is the form in which it is put to suit a certain period of the world. Now, in this present period of the world, it is given in its present form.

A person thinks perhaps that by spirituality it is meant that one must learn something which one did not know before, or one must become extraordinarily good, or one must attain some unusual powers, or one must have experiences of a supernatural kind. None of these things Sufism promises, although

1. Lecture given in Suresnes, France, July 23, 1922.
2. Matthew 5:17.

nothing in the path of the Sufis is too wonderful for them. All the abovesaid things and even more are within their reach, yet that is not the Sufis' aim. By this process of Sufism, one realizes one's own nature, one's true nature. And thereby, one realizes human nature; and by the study of human nature one realizes the nature of life in general. All failures, disappointment, and sorrow are caused by the lack of this realization. All success, happiness, and peace are acquired by the realization of one's own nature. In a few words, Sufism means to know one's true being, to know the purpose of one's life, and to know how to accomplish that purpose. Many say out of disappointment, "I shall perhaps never be successful in my life," not knowing the fact that humanity is born to do what it longs to do, and success is natural, failure is unnatural. If people are themselves, the whole world is their own; if they are not themselves, then even this self does not belong to them. Then they do not know what they are, where they are, why they are here on earth; then one is less useful to oneself and to others than a rock.

It is in self-realization that the mystery of the whole life is centered. It is the remedy of all maladies; it is a secret of success in all walks of life; it is a religion and more than a religion. And at this time when the world is upset, this message conveys to the world the divine message. What is wrong with humanity today is that it is not itself, and all the misery of the world is caused by this. Therefore, nothing can answer the purpose of humanity save this process of sages and of the wise of all ages, which leads souls to self-realization.

8

What the World Needs Today

THE unrest that one finds throughout the world, the difficulties among nations, hatred existing among people for one another, a cry of misery that is coming more or less from all sides, commercial catastrophe, political problems—all this makes one wonder what may be done to find a solution for the general cry of humanity.[1]

What is done today is that the different institutions are trying to extinguish the fire burning here and there, but that can never solve the problem of the world. The first thing that should be remembered is that all activities of life are connected with one another, and if one thing is arranged, another thing goes wrong. It is just like a person who is ill, who needs sleep and good diet. If a person has sleep, without a good diet it will not do that person good; nor will a good diet without sleep help. While wanting to straighten up commercial difficulties, political problems creep up; while considering social questions, moral difficulties manifest to view. Therefore, in wanting to serve humanity in the work of reconstruction—which is the duty and responsibility of every sensible soul, whatever be their rank or position or qualification in life—first this question must be studied: What will be the remedy for all the maladies that manifest on the surface of life today? There is one principal thing, and that is the changing of the attitude of humanity, which alone can help in all directions of life. And that attitude can be

1. Lecture given in Suresnes, France, July 16, 1922.

changed by a moral, spiritual, and religious advancement. The work that the Sufi message has to accomplish is in this particular direction.

The Sufi message is no new religion, no particular system, but it is a method of changing the attitude in life that enables humanity to have another outlook on life. The chief thing that the Sufi Movement will try to avoid is sectarianism, which has divided humanity in all ages of the world's history. The Sufi message is not opposed to any religion, faith, or belief; on the other hand, it is a support of all religions, it is a defense for religions that are attacked by the followers of other religions. At the same time, the Sufi Order provides humanity with the religion that is, in reality, all religions. The Sufi Order is not supposed to take the whole of humanity in its arms, but the service of the whole of humanity is the fulfillment of the Sufi mission. The Sufi Order, therefore, does not stand as a barrier between its members and their religious faith, but as an open door leading to the heart of their faith. The members of the order are messengers of the divine message to the followers of the church or the sect to which they belong. The work of the Sufi Order is not to collect all the rainwater in its own tanks, but to work and make a way for the stream of the message to flow, supplying water for all the fields of the world.

The work of the Sufi mission is sowing. Reaping we shall leave to humanity to do, for the fields do not belong to our particular order; all the fields belong to God. We who are employed on this farm of the world do the work we must do and leave the rest to God. Success we do not trouble about, and for those who strive for it, let them seek some other direction. Truth alone is our success, for lasting success is truth.

9

Different Points of View

THERE are two different points of view open to all things in the world: liberal and conservative.[1] And each of these points of view gives a person the sense of satisfaction, because in both there is a certain amount of virtue. When one looks from the conservative point of view at one's family, one becomes conscious of family pride and acts in every way to keep up the honor and dignity of one's ancestors. One follows the chivalry of the ancestors, and by looking at the family from this point of view, one befriends and protects those who belong to the family, whether worthy or unworthy. In this way one helps to keep up a flame that has been lighted, perhaps for years, by holding it in hand through life as a torch to guide one's way. When, from a conservative point of view, one looks at one's nation, it gives the feeling of patriotism, which today is the substitute for religion in the modern world. There is no doubt a virtue in the way that one begins to consider one's whole nation as one family. It is not for one's own children that one cares, but also the children of the nation. People give their lives when occasion arises to defend their nation and the dignity, the honor, and the freedom of their people.

Therefore, the conservative spirit is the individualizing spirit, which is the central theme of the whole creation. It is this spirit that has been functioning as the sun; if not, it was the all-pervading light. And it is the power of this spirit working in nature

1. Lecture given in Suresnes, France, July 30, 1922.

that keeps many branches together on one stem and several leaves together on one branch. It is again this spirit working in someone's body that keeps the hands and feet together, thus keeping them an individual entity. But there is always a danger of this spirit, if increased, producing congestion. When family pride is too much, one lives only in pride, forgetting one's duty toward humankind and not recognizing something that unites one with others beyond the limited circle of the family. When this congestion is produced in a nation, it results in all kinds of disasters, such as wars and revolutions with violence and destruction. The nightmare that humanity has recently experienced[2] has been the outcome of a world congestion produced by the extremity of this same spirit. This shows that it is not true that virtue is one thing and sin another thing. It is the same thing that was once virtue that becomes sin. Virtue and sin are not actions. It is the condition, it is the attitude which prompts one to a certain action; and it is the outcome of an action that makes it a sin or a virtue.

Life is a movement, and death is the stopping of the movement; congestion stops it, circulation moves it. The conservative spirit is useful as far as it is moving; in other words, it is broadening itself. Those who were once proud of their family, after having done their duty to their people, if they take the next step to help citizens and the third step to defend their nation, they are progressing onward. Family pride and patriotism are, no doubt, virtues, for they lead a person from one thing to another that is better.

Congestion comes when one is set in one's own interest. If family makes one so absorbed in its pride and interest that nobody else exists in the world, or when one thinks of one's own people alone and nothing else interests one, then others do not exist for one. In that case patriotism becomes a veil over the eyes, making one blind so as not to be able to serve others or one's own. In selfishness there is an illusion of profit, but in the

2. World War I.

end, the profit attained by selfishness proves to be worthless. Life is the principal thing to consider, and true life is the inner life, the realization of God, and the consciousness of one's spirit. When the human heart becomes conscious of God it turns in the sea, and it spreads and extends the waves of its love to friend and foe, spreading further and further till it attains perfection.

The Sufi message is not necessarily the message of pacifism; it does not teach us to make peace at any cost and at every cost. It does not condemn family pride or patriotism, it does not even preach against war. The message is to make people conscious of the words of Christ where he says: "We live, move, and have our being in God,"[3] and to realize it and to recognize the kinship of humanity in the realization of God. And the natural consequence of this will bring about the spirit of kinship and equality, and will result in preparing the outer democracy and inner aristocracy that is in the nobility of soul, whose perfection is hidden in the supremacy of God.

3. Acts 17:28.

10

THE JOURNEY TO THE GOAL

BELOVED Ones of God, my subject this evening is the road to the goal.[1] Before proceeding on my subject, I should like to say that there are two different stages in human evolution, and these two different stages may be very well called the minor and the major stage. In Hindu Puranic symbology, these two characters are called the younger and the elder brother or sister.

There is a stage of childhood when the child only knows what it wants and is only happy when it gets it, no matter what may be the consequences. That minor stage of soul is when one in reality desires only what one can see, hear, perceive, touch; beyond that one does not care. One wants only what is desirable, one does not wish anything else. And the major state is when someone has experienced life more or less, has known pleasure and pain, enthusiasm and disappointment, and knows the variability of life; only then has one reached the stage of majority. The minor and major do not depend upon a certain age, nor do they depend upon a particular education; no, they depend upon inner life. When one has gone into life as far as one could go, and when one has passed the limit of the minor state, then one arrives at the major state. In the East there is a custom that has become a kind of religious etiquette: not to wake someone who is asleep but to let that person sleep well. If this is not done it is considered a crime. In other words, you must treat

1. Lecture given in the Netherlands, September 6, 1921.

the world according to nature and not go against nature. Do not force someone in the minor state into the major; one must first sleep well before one can awake.

Now, about progress for the spiritual path, there are two different characters on the spiritual path. The first are those who say, "Yes, I would like to go on this path, but where shall I arrive?" They want to know all about it before traveling this path, and if their friends are going with them. And if not, they are not ready to go either, because they are not sure of the way, will not go alone, and want to know when and where they will arrive, and if it is safe to journey on that particular path. When they travel on the path, they look back and try to look forward, asking: "Shall I reach the goal? Is it really the right path?" A thousand times doubt comes, fear comes; they look back, forward, around. If others could only tell them how far they have journeyed. They are restless, wanting to know how far they are from the goal. They, therefore, are children still, although they have a desire to journey. For these people there are toys: the mystical hints for mental research keep them busy. They may look on the map of the journey to see where they go.

Now we are coming to the conditions of the major path. About this character the Bible says: "Unless the soul be born again, it will not enter the kingdom of God."[2] In the first place, if I were to say what the journey is and its object, the answer would be that the whole creation was purposed for this journey, and, if it were not for this purpose, there would be no creation at all. And before any take the journey, they practice in some form or other, in play, how they will make this; but they have not yet started in reality. For instance, some desire to be rich and devote all their time, their energy, their life, their thoughts to that object; and, so to speak, they journey to that goal. If some people desire power, they work for that and get it. If they want position, they use all their strength to reach this goal naturally, in a playing way. The proof of this is that every

2. See John 3:3.

activity of which they are in pursuit to attain the thing desired brings them to desire something else. If they are rich, they want to be famous; if they are famous, they want something else; if they have one thing, they strive for another and are never satisfied. It shows that humankind, externally busy in the pursuit of worldly things, is not satisfied in its soul but has a constant yearning in the soul for something more, which keeps people uneasy. A very good explanation is that which Rumi, a great Sufi teacher of Persia, gives us in his book, the *Masnavi*. There he says, "What is it, in the flute made of reed, that appeals to your soul, that goes through you, pierces your heart?" And the answer is that it is the crying of the flute, and the reason for its crying is that it once belonged to the plant of the earth, from which it was cut apart. Holes were made in its heart. It longs to be back and united with its source, its origin. And so the soul feels a longing for its origin. In another place in his book, Rumi says so it is with all who have left their original country for a long time. They may roam about and feel very pleased with all they see, but there will come a moment when a strong yearning is in their hearts for the place where they were born.[3]

One sees that those in the world who have really suffered, who have been disappointed, are brokenhearted and do not wish to tell anybody of their experiences, don't want any company but wish to be alone. And it is then as if there was someone waiting with open arms, awaiting that soul as a child comes to its mother. This shows that there is, somewhere, a consoler greater than any in the world, a friend dearer than anyone in the world, a protector stronger than any earthly one. Knowing that the world is not to be depended upon, they look for that great one in themselves.

A friend who is a friend in life and after death, in pleasure and pain, in richness and poverty, one on whom you can always depend, who always guides aright, who gives the best advice—that friend is hidden in your own heart. You cannot find

3. See *Masnavi*, book 1.

a better one. Who is this friend? Humanity's own being, the true inner being. That friend is the origin, source, and goal, the final goal of all. But the question arises: What if that friend is one's own being? Why then call it a friend? Why not call it oneself? The answer is that no doubt, in point of fact, this friend is really one's own being; but when compared with the present realization of the greater self, one finds oneself smaller than a drop in the ocean. One cannot very well call that friend oneself until one has forgotten one's own self, until one is no more oneself. Until and unless one has arrived at the state of perfection, one had better be quiet rather than insolent in talking about that which one has not yet become.

All occult schools, all over the world, prescribe, as the first lesson, quietude: no discussion, no dispute, no argument. The conditions for those on the path are altogether different from those of the outer world. The true knowers of life have kept their lips closed about that subject, and no method has been more successful and profitable than the method of the prophets of all lands who give humankind the first lesson of love for God. Of course, religious authorities of different times have kept humanity ignorant of the knowledge of God and have only given it the belief in God.

Absence of knowledge has made people of reason rebel against that which they could not understand. There remained no link between knowledge and understanding, and that is how the reign of materialism came to the world, a reign that is still spreading around. In such times of materialism there comes chaos in the world; all is confusion and unrest. All wish to do good but do not know how. Such times Sri Krishna has called the decay of dharma, when spirit has gone and form only remains.[4] No doubt warning comes in time as an intuition to the soul; but in the intoxication of the time, the mist is so great that the message is not heard, not understood, not received until the messenger has disappeared.

4. See Bhagavad Gita 4:7.

Now, coming to the journey, what is the manner and the method of it? We see that when a person rises above all things of the world—such as power, wealth, possession, all that gives pride and vanity—there comes a desire in the heart, a remembrance of the origin of the perfection of love and peace. No one in the world can pretend to have arrived at this stage, because every moment of one's life speaks louder of what one really is than of what one says.

A person's first tendency toward humanity is a loving attitude, a charitable attitude to such an extent that forgiveness leads every action in life. A person shows patience in actions, tolerance to humanity, and considers that each is at a stage of evolution and cannot be expected to act better than that point of evolution permits. One does not make one's own law and want others to follow it; one follows the law for all. When a person's attitude is a loving attitude, a tendency to serve, to forgive, to tolerate, a reverence for all—good and bad, young and old—then that person begins the journey. To explain what path this is, there is no better symbol for it than the path of the cross. No one without courage, without strength of will, and without patience can go on this path. When one has to live among people of all natures, one must make one's own character soft as a rose and make it finer, so that no one can be hurt by the thorns. Two thorns cannot harm each other. The thorns can hurt the rose, but the rose cannot tear the thorns. Think what the life must be of the rose between two thorns. The journey begins with a path of thorns, and one must go barefoot. It is not easy to be tolerant, always to be patient, to refrain from judging others, and to love one's enemy. It is a dead individual who walks on this path, one who has drunk the bowl of poison. The beginning of each path is always difficult and uninteresting, hard for everybody. Ask the violinists about the first days when they practice the scales and cannot even form the tones; often they have not patience enough to go on till they can play so well that they are satisfied.

The first part of the path is permanent strife, a struggle with life; but as one approaches the goal, the path gets easier. The distance seems larger, but the path is easier, the difficulties less. The journey is achieved first by realizing in oneself: What am I? Am I body, mind, or what else am I? Do I originate from earth or from somewhere else?

As soon as one has started on the journey, one's lower nature rises up. All the follies and weaknesses want to drag one down to earth, and the struggle of breaking these chains requires the strength of a Samson. Then comes the struggle between beauty in matter and spiritual beauty. Beauty in form is more realistic; spiritual beauty is hidden in mist until one comes to a stage where spiritual beauty becomes the beauty that is shining with light. Another struggle is that when people have acquired knowledge, power, and magnetism, they are conscious of having a greater power than others, of knowing more than others, that they can do more than others. To use those faculties rightly is another struggle. One must not pride oneself on these accomplishments. There is an enemy who starts with travelers on the journey and never leaves them: pride and spiritual egotism. It stays as long as an individual is on the path.

Think of the temptation, on having received inspiration and power, when one can think, "I can do and know and understand more than you." That is a constant struggle till the end, and every moment one falls and tumbles down. Only the steady travelers will persist in rising up every time, as without patience they may lose the path. Those who journey on this path will get help, as Christ said, "First seek the kingdom of God, and all things will be given to you."[5]

The goal is the important thing, and the right attitude of the soul toward it, and not the things you meet on the path. The inner circle of the Sufi school, which is now presented to the Western world, is meant as a guidance on this path. Nobody in the world can carry a person on this path. The only thing is that

5. Matthew 6:33.

a little advice can be given by those who have journeyed on the path to those who really wish to travel it.

Thank you for your kind sympathy and response. God bless you.

11

World Reconstruction 1

BELOVED Ones of God, my subject this evening is world reconstruction.[1] Especially after the war[2] and the pain that the world has experienced, people are beginning to think on the subject of reconstruction. But no doubt one looks at it according to one's own mentality, and in this way the ideas about the reconstruction of the world differ very much.

Considering the condition of the world as it is today, in the first place when one thinks of the financial condition that is most essential for order and peace, it is so confused and has become so difficult to solve that it seems that there are many, with their intellect and brain and understanding, who are helpless before this most difficult problem. No doubt there are many who will tell us that there is no other remedy for the betterment of humanity than the solution of the financial problem. But at the same time, it seems that the problem, the financial problem, is becoming everyday more and more difficult, and bringing nations and races and communities to a greater and greater destruction. And before this problem will be solved, it is no wonder if a great deal of damage will be done to many nations. And although intoxicated by the absorption in each one's own problems of life, humanity does not think enough about these things. Nevertheless, in the end, the world in general will realize the weakness and feebleness caused by this disorder and

1. Lecture given at the Salle de l'Athénée, Geneva, October 10, 1923.
2. World War I.

unbalanced condition of the financial problem of the world. The nations and the people who profit by the loss of other nations and people, for the moment may think that they are benefited; but in the end all will realize that we—the human beings, individuals, or as a multitude—all depend upon one another. For instance, if for the cause of one part of the body, the other part suffers, in the end it will prove an unbalanced condition, a lack of health in the physical body. What does health mean? Health means all the organs of the body in good condition, and so the health of the world means all nations, all people in good condition.

When one leaves this financial condition and comes to the problem of education, in spite of all the progress that has been made in the educational world, no one with thought will deny the fact that little children, whatever their ages, whatever their strengths and whatever work is given them to accomplish—it seems that in the enthusiasm of making education richer and richer, a kind of load has been put on the minds of the children. And what happens? It is like a dish which was meant to be ready after half an hour's cooking and that is made ready in five minutes' time. It is perhaps burnt, or it wanted a longer time. The children know too much for their age, which they do not require, which they do not value, which is a load to them, which is forced upon their minds. And how few of us stop to think of this question that childhood is kingliness in itself; that it is a gift from above that the children are growing; and that during the time of their growth they are unaware of the woes and worries and anxieties of life, the only days of experiencing the kingliness of life, the days when they should play, when they should be near to nature, when they should grasp what nature gradually teaches. Imagine then that childhood is devoted to study, study of material knowledge. And as soon as the children have grown, the burden of life is put on the shoulders of the youth—the burden of life which is becoming everyday heavier and heavier for the rich and poor. And the result of that is that there are parties, there is disagreement between labor and between capital, and life is full of struggle to which the children open their eyes and never have the time to be one with nature or to dive deep within themselves or to think beyond this life in the crowd.

When we leave the problem of education and come to the problem of nations, one becomes still more perplexed. The enmity and the hatred and the prejudice that exist between nations and nations, and the antagonism and the utter selfishness that is the central theme of communications and connection between nations show that the world is turning from bad to worse, and unrest seems to be all-pervading. There seems to be no trust between nations, no sympathy except their own interest. And what is the outcome of it? Its impression falls as a reflection, as a shadow upon the individual, touching individuals also in that egoism, in that selfishness.

And the only thing in the world that was meant to be the source, for taking refuge under it, was religion. But at the present moment, with the increase of ever-growing materialism and of overwhelming commercialism, religion seems to be fading away. A silent indifference seems to be increasing toward religion, especially in the countries foremost in civilization today. That being the condition, where could humanity find the solution of the problem of the day?

12

WORLD RECONSTRUCTION 2

NOW, looking at the question from a philosophical point of view, what is construction, and what is reconstruction? Construction is that which is already made. A child born is a construction.[1] But after a disorder in the health or in mind, there comes again a need of reconstruction. In the English language there is a phrase: to pull oneself together. The reconstruction of the world today means for the world to pull itself together. Education, the political, the social condition, the financial condition, religion, all these things that make civilization, seem to have dropped down, seem to have been scattered; and in order for these things to come together, the secret of life must be studied. What is the secret of healing power? The secret is to make oneself strong enough to pull oneself together. And that is the secret of the life of the mystic. The world has lost its health, and when one can picture the world as an individual, one can see what it is to lose one's health. It is just like illness in the life of an individual. And as for every illness there is a remedy, so for every disaster there is a reconstruction.

But now there are different ideas that people have. There is the pessimist who says: "Well, if the world has got to this state of destruction, who can help it? How can it be helped?" It is like an ill person who says, "Well, I have been so ill, I have so much suffered, that I do not care. How can I be well now? It is almost too late." In this way the ill person holds the disease

1. Lecture given at the Salle de l'Athénée, Geneva, October 10, 1923.

and keeps it, cherishes it, although the person does not like it. And then there is a curious person who is very astonished to see the newspaper; and sees that this money has gone up and that money has gone down; and sees that there is the probability of war, there may be another war; and also will excite friends at the dinner table. Some societies, some leagues must be formed, something definitely must be done. And in this way there are now so many societies and congresses formed and discussing, and so many more meetings, so many more discussions. But there seems to be no end to the discussions and disputes in order to find out the ways and means by which the conditions must be bettered.

I do not mean to say that any effort, in whatever form, made toward the reconstruction or toward the betterment of conditions is not worthwhile, however small. But what is most needed is for us to understand that religion of religions and that philosophy of philosophies that is self-knowledge. We shall not understand the life outside if we do not understand ourselves. It is in the knowledge of the self that is the knowledge of the world. The politician, the statesperson, however qualified, will dispute over things for years and years; they will never come to a satisfactory conclusion unless they understand the psychology of life and the psychology of the situation. And so the educators, year after year, will try a new scheme and will never come to a satisfactory conclusion unless they have the psychological knowledge of life, which will teach them the psychology of human nature that is the manner to solve the problem. What is today called psychology is not the one I mean. I do not mean by the word *psychology* what they call psychoanalysis. I call psychology the understanding of the self, the understanding of the nature and the character of the mind and the body.

Friends, what is health? Health is order. And what is order? Order is music. Where there is harmony, where there is rhythm, where there is regularity, where there is cooperation, there is harmony, there is sympathy. The health of mind, therefore, and the health of body depend upon the preserving of that harmony, upon keeping intact the sympathy that is going on in the mind and body. And remember that life in the world, and especially such as we live amidst the crowd, will try and test our patience every moment of the day. And it will be most difficult to preserve the harmony and peace that are called happiness, for what is the definition of life? Life means struggle with friends and battle with foes. It is all the time giving and taking, and it is most difficult in this to keep the symphony, to keep the harmony which is health and happiness.

Now, you will ask where we are to learn it. My friends, all education and learning and knowledge is acquired, but this one art is a divine art; and humanity has inherited it but, absorbed in the outer learning, has forgotten it. But it is an art that is known to the soul; it is one's own being, it is the deepest knowledge that an individual has in the heart. No progress, in whatever line, that a person will make will give the satisfaction that the soul is craving except this one, which is the art of life, the art of being that is the pursuit of the soul.

In order to serve the reconstruction of the world, the only thing possible and the only thing necessary is to learn the art of being—the art of life for oneself—and to be an example oneself before trying to serve humanity.

What is the Sufi Movement? What is Sufism? It is that art of which I have just spoken, the art by which that music and symphony of life can be preserved; and by that humanity can enable itself to become the proper servant of God and humanity.

13

Kinship 1

ONE can see the beginning of the spirit of kinship when one sees the flocks of birds flying in the sky together, when one sees the herds of animals in the forest together, and the swarms of little insects all living and moving together.[1] No doubt in humanity this tendency of kinship is pronounced, for humanity is not only capable of realizing the spirit of kinship but of fulfilling the purpose that is hidden in this natural tendency. What is called good or bad, right or wrong, sin or virtue—the secret behind all this diversity is one. And this secret is that all that leads to happiness is right, is good, and is virtuous. All that leads to unhappiness is wrong, is evil; and if there is any sin, it is that which may be called sin. When coming to the idea of kinship, it is not something that humanity has learned or acquired. It is something that is born in humanity, and according to the development of this spirit, humanity shows the unfoldment of its soul.

Coming to the great religions that have been given to the world—for instance, when we read in the Bible the words of Jesus Christ, what do we read? Love your fellow human being, love your neighbor, from the beginning to the end.[2] If there was any moral that the Master taught and repeated constantly, it was this moral: the moral of kinship. The different religions that are existing in the world, the followers of which are perhaps

1. Lecture given at the Salle de l'Athénée, Geneva, October 12, 1923.
2. Matthew 22:39.

millions and millions, if one studies their religion what is the central thing of it all? It is the one and same: kinship, love one another, serve one another, be sincere one to the other.

But as people are more capable of loving their friend, so they are more capable of hating their neighbor. The first tendency of kinship, of love, brings to them satisfaction, and happiness to the other. The other tendency of hating their brother or sister brings to them dissatisfaction, and unhappiness to the other. Kinship, therefore, is creative of happiness; and the spirit that is contrary to it is productive of sorrow. When we read the scriptures of great religions in this world—be it the Bible or Kabbalah or Qur'an, Gita or Buddhist scriptures—in some form or the other, in the manner best suited to the people to whom the religion was given, it was the same moral, the same symphony, and it was the same music that was performed before them. The great teachers of the world, whenever and whatever time they came to the world—were they especially engaged in giving mystical or occult teachings to the world, or were they engaged in discussing philosophical problems? Not at all. Though they were mystics, they knew philosophy, they knew occultism; but that was not the principal thing that they came to give. If ever they have done anything or given to the world anything, it was that simple philosophy that is never new to anyone. Even a child knows love one another, be kind, be sincere, be serviceable to one another.

And one might ask: When it is a simple thing and so simple that even a child knows it, what necessity is there that the great ones, the godly souls should have come and taught it? It is most simple and yet most difficult to live, and humanity does not accept any teaching from someone who does not live it. And if one accepts it, one will not hold it for long. Therefore they came with love from above to the world and lived that simple moral, that simple philosophy of kinship. The Mughal emperor of Hindustan who was a great poet—in history we read of his name, Ghasnavi[3]—writes that having been born in a palace and having reigned from the first day that I came on earth, I saw nothing but thousands and thousands of people bowing before me. But the day in my life when I learned the first lesson in love, my proud head bent and bowed and bent before every slave that was standing before me in attendance. And to those who were standing before me as my servants, I then felt that I was their slave. What does it show? It shows that the coldness of heart hardens one's feelings and closes one's eyes to the light that shows the path of kinship.

There are many relations, there are many connections in this world of blood and of law, but the great relationship is friendship. But what is the culmination of friendship? It is the culmination of friendship that is called kinship. Kinship means perfect friendship.

3. Mahmud of Ghazni (971–1030).

14

Kinship 2

BUT now comes a question, a question of how this kinship principle may be lived, how may it be practiced. It is most difficult to teach this principle to anyone.[1] The best way of teaching its principle is living it oneself. The parents, either father or mother, who show to their children, besides fatherly love and motherly tenderness, that kinship, that feeling of a sibling with their siblings—in this they can best express themselves to their children; and in this way the children are able to express their best to their parents. A father may be most kind, a mother may be most loving, but as long as he or she maintains the attitude of holding themselves as father, as mother, as something different from the children, the children grow to love them but will never look upon them as friends. The children look for friends somewhere else, because there is no kinship. And when we come to the teacher, a teacher may be respected by the pupils, the teacher may bear a great dignity before a pupil, but at the same time there cannot be established that communication of inspiration, of love, of sympathy, of understanding until the teacher has practiced with the pupil that manner of kinship. The great kings and generals for whom the soldiers have given, millions of them, their lives—this was not for the general; it was for kinship. No kings, no generals, no commanders, what-

1. Lecture given at the Salle de l'Athénée, Geneva, October 12, 1923.

ever be their order and position, have been able to own the hearts of those who followed them—never.

When we hear of the great ones—the prophets, the seers, the mystics—in what way have they treated their pupils, their disciples? The story of Jesus Christ is known to all, calling the fishermen to come and to sit and to talk together.[2] The Master never felt comfortable when they called him good, and he said, "Call me not good."[3] The whole idea was: "Consider me not superior to you, I am one of you." Think then of the picture of the Master washing the feet of his disciples.[4] What does it teach us? It all teaches us kinship. No miracle, no great power, no great inspiration, occult or mystical, can equal the phenomenon of that humbleness, of that fraternity, of that kinship with which the great ones have become one with all.

When, friends, we hear about the condition that humanity has passed through during the last few years,[5] and when we think what result has been achieved from all the prejudices and disagreement and inharmony that has come up between nations and between people, it seems that even now it is not lessening. The world seems to be going from bad to worse, the suffering in every way caused to humanity seems to have not yet ended. No doubt the life in the world is so intoxicating that humanity hardly stops to think about it. And the life, such as it is just now, has so many responsibilities that all people, rich or poor, are so absorbed in their affairs that they hardly have a moment to think of what is going on in the world. Nevertheless, illness is illness; the world is ill. Yes, people may neglect their illnesses and may engage their minds in something else, but if the illness is not attended to, that illness remains just the same. And when we see the cause of all that disaster, we may be able to find a thousand causes; and yet there is one principal cause, which is

2. See Matthew 4:19.
3. Mark 10:18.
4. See John 13:1–17.
5. World War I.

the lack of kinship. The absence of anything, one could have endured; but the world cannot be happy nor the order and peace of humanity attained in the absence of kinship—the kinship that can be learned and that all people have the facility of learning in life. Think of that master who is kind and who is loving to a servant, who considers the servant a brother or a sister; that master is blessed. Think of that family, a family in which two members, or three or four or five members, whatever be their relation, consider that idea of kinship in sharing with one another the pain and pleasure. How happy, how blessed that family will be. Think of a nation—whatever be its government, whatever be its constitution, if there was this spirit of kinship between the people of different position, of different ranks or occupation, how blessed that nation would be! From where does injustice come, from where does unfairness come? It all comes from the lack of kinship. Think of the conditions today: the courts full of cases, the prisons full of prisoners. How many disagreements between people, inharmony between nations is all caused by the lack of kinship.

Now, when we consider this question from a still deeper point of view, we shall find that in the spirit of kinship there is the way of illumination. People, perhaps who live by great principle or pray all day or meditate in the caves of the mountain—if they do not show the spirit of kinship, they do not do good to themselves or others, because kinship is the way to develop spiritually. It is not exclusiveness, it is not running away from the world that is the way of the real spiritual ones. It is to consider one's obligations; it is to keep by one's word, one's honor; it is to prove sincere in every little capacity that one may be working, faithful to friends, and true before everyone. These are the merits that, by themselves, develop when the spirit of kinship has become mature in humanity.

But when we come to the metaphysical point of view, we see that element attracts element. For instance, two streams of water will be attracted to one another. There will come a time that they will join together, but there will be efforts made by both to come together. Fire, starting from two ends of a certain line, will be attracted to the other flame that is coming from the opposite end; and they will meet and will become one. And so an artist is attracted to an artist, a thinker to a thinker, a scientist to a scientist, and the person of action to the person of action. It is not that they are attracted because there is the same element in them. No, no, but because there is a comfort, there is a happiness there in being attracted by the same element. Think of the joy when two people of the same thought meet together. It is greater than a joy, greater than a satisfaction; it is that happiness which is promised in heaven.

But behind all this world of various names and forms there is one life, there is one spirit: the spirit that is the soul of all beings. That spirit is attracted toward unity. It is the absence of that spirit that keeps it unhappy. Those who have just had some unpleasantness with a brother or with a sister, to them the food will be tasteless, the night without sleep, the heart restless, the soul under clouds. If one may ask, "What is the matter, what is closed before you?" they would give one answer if they knew; and that answer is that the sunshine has been covered by clouds. What does it show? It shows that we live not necessarily on food; our soul lives on love, the love that we receive, that we give and take. The absence of this is our unhappiness, and the presence of it is everything we need. There is nothing in the world that is a greater healing power, that is a greater remedy, a greater happiness than to be conscious of kinship and to be able to give that feeling to one's child, master, neighbor, friend.

The humble efforts made by the Sufi Movement in the service of God and humanity are toward kinship. In the form of devotion, in the form of philosophy, mysticism, or metaphysics, art or science, or in whatever form the Sufi Movement will present to the world is that ideal, the central theme of which is always kinship.

15

THE PROBLEM OF THE DAY

THERE has been a great upset in the world commencing from the time of the Reformation and culminating in the time of the Great War.[1] Today it seems there is a continual unrest; in all directions of life, in different departments of life, there is a great turmoil. In spite of all the progress that has been made during a number of years, civilization has, so to speak, not settled. The difficulty has been in the adjustment of new ideas of democracy to the foundation of aristocracy on which it was based. The outcome is felt now, after the war, more than before. There seems to be confusion and chaos rather than the understanding of living life to the best advantage. The reason is that the character of aristocracy and democracy is not understood by all people from the point of view of the mystic. As long as the law of understanding of this secret remains hidden, a thousand aristocracies or democracies will always fail in the end.

When we study nature, we find the model of life before us as a design to follow: the interdependence of stars and planets upon one another, and how they are sustained in the end by the magnetism of one another; how the light of the sun functions in the moon; and how the light of the sun reflects in all planets, and at the same time, how the planets differ in their light and character; and how every planet in the universe fulfills the scheme of nature. Call it aristocracy or call it democracy, theirs is a model of life that nature has produced before us.

1. Lecture given in Suresnes, France, July 8, 1923.

The word *aristocracy*, very often, when not understood becomes unpleasant to some ears. But the real meaning of aristocracy is not in the picture of its abuse, its degeneration. And what is democracy? Democracy is the fulfillment of aristocracy; in other words, democracy means complete aristocracy. And when aristocracy is not understood, then democracy is not complete. People are born in this world ignorant of the kingdom that is within themselves, and to attain to that kingdom within is the true aristocracy.

To recognize that kingdom in another is aristocracy, and to see the possibility of that kingdom in oneself and to try to fulfill that ideal in life is true democracy. Aristocracy means one king; democracy means all kings. But when one does not recognize one king, one cannot know all kings. The object of life is not in revolting against one more advanced than we are, and by this revolt to try to pull them down; that is not democracy. Democracy is to see the possibility of advancing to the same level of the other. This is the real democracy.

The question of the day must be studied by all sections of humanity and classes of humanity. It seems that, being absorbed in a more comfortable life, many have neglected their part in different works of life in home and outside, and there are leisured classes who are unaware of certain works that life demands. And the time has come when they meet with difficulties, because they find themselves more dependent on that which they have neglected, things that seemed beneath their idea of dignity.

Now the time has come when humanity is upset, and one class is going under another class. The place of the one class is being taken by another, and thus chaos is created. And the way out of it would be to imitate some of the ideas of olden times. If they are not imitated, perhaps life would become subtle in a certain way, but the whole of life would become hotel life, and there would be no more the joy and pleasure of experiencing the whole life. Difficulties will bring this about before long. In every district there will be some kind of hotel life, and so the culture and choice of the individual will become hampered. A person's individual choice will be sacrificed to the mechanism of living.

The method that may be followed was used in the ancient times by the Hindus, and even now, some of the methods exist among the Brahmins. A Brahmin may be in a very high position and very rich, but knows how to cook. I myself have seen the men in the house of the prime minister attend to the kitchen themselves. There is nothing in the home that they will not do. They were trained to sew, knit, weave, and cook, in keeping the house neat, decorating and painting it. All could be done by every person. No one possessed a horse who did not know anything of its care, independent of the groom. The perfection of life is not only perfecting oneself spiritually but in all different aspects of life. The one who cannot fulfill all life's needs is certainly ignorant of true freedom in life.

The more we study the problem of the day, the more we shall know that it is the distinction of life that has made people helpless. Into education should be introduced the spirit of providence, supplying all one's needs and arranging for oneself all that is necessary. The mechanical life of the day shows an incomplete progress. Imagine people in a factory, all day and every day, making part of one needle. Perhaps they do this for twenty years, and what do they know of life? Only how to make a needle. Perhaps the benefit goes to the head of the factory, but what about those who have devoted all their life in making one needle?

The secret of the ideal of progress in life is to become self-sufficient; the key to the secret of democracy is self-sufficiency. No doubt this is a vast subject, and it is difficult to explain all its aspects in a few words. But at the same time, spiritual perfection is the second step, and the one who has first made oneself self-sufficient is entitled to spiritual perfection in the end.

16

THE PRIVILEGE OF BEING HUMAN 1

HUMANKIND is so absorbed in this life's pleasures and pains that it hardly has a moment to think what a privilege it is to be human.[1] The life in this world is no doubt more pain than pleasure, and that which one considers pleasure costs so much that, by weighing it with its pain, it also becomes pain. And as humanity is so absorbed in its worldly life, it knows nothing but pain and complaint in life. And until people change their outlook on life, they cannot understand the privilege of being human.

There is one way of looking at this question, and that is: however unhappy people may be in their lives, if they were asked, "Would you prefer to be a rock or a human being?" they would rather suffer and be a human being than a rock. Whatever be the condition of life, if they were asked, "Would you rather be a tree than a human?" they would rather be a human being. And although the life of the birds and animals is so void of responsibility and troubles, and free in the forest, yet if people were asked if they would prefer to be one of the birds and animals and live in the forest, they would surely prefer to be a human being. This shows that when human life is compared to the different aspects of life, then it shows its greatness and its privilege; but when it is not compared with that life, it is then that humanity is discontented and its eyes are closed to the privilege of being human.

1. Lecture given at Collège de la Tour, Vevey, Switzerland, June 20, 1921.

Another thing is that people are mostly selfish, and all that interests them is concerning their own life. And not knowing the troubles of the lives of the others, they feel the burden of their life even more than the burden of the whole world. If one could only think in one's poverty that: "There are others who are poorer than me"; in one's illness that: "There are perhaps others whose suffering are perhaps greater than mine"; in one's troubles that: "There are others whose difficulties are perhaps greater than mine." Self-pity is the worst poverty. It overwhelms one, and one sees nothing but one's own troubles and pains; and it seems that one is the most unhappy person, more than anyone in the world. There is the story of a great thinker of Persia, Sa'di. He writes in the account of his own life that, "Once I had no shoes, and I had to walk in the hot sand, barefoot; and I thought how very miserable I was. And then I met a man who was lame, and it was very difficult for him to walk. I bowed down at once to heaven and offered thanks that I was much better off than the one who had not even his legs to walk." This shows that it is not the situation in life, but it is a person's attitude toward life that makes that person happy or unhappy. And even this attitude can make a difference between individuals to such an extent that one in the palace would be unhappy and the other in a humble cottage would be very happy. It is only this difference of the horizon that one sees. There is one person who only looks at the condition of that person's own life; there is another who looks at the lives of many people. It is this difference that is made by the horizon.

Besides this, it is the impulse that comes from within that has its influence on one's affairs. If there is an influence always working from within of discontent and of dissatisfaction in life, one finds its affects in one's affairs in life. For instance, a person impressed by an illness can never be cured by a physician or medicines. A person impressed with the thought of poverty will never get on in life.

A person who thinks, "Everybody is against me and everybody troubles me and everybody has a poor opinion of me," wherever such a person goes, that person will always find that it is so. There are many in the world in a business, in a profession—whatever be their occupation or profession, before they go to their work the first thought in their mind is: "Perhaps I shall not be successful." The teachers of humanity, in whichever period they came to the world, always taught humanity to learn, as the first lesson, faith. Faith in success, faith in love, faith in kindness, and faith in God. And this faith cannot be developed unless humanity is self-confident. It is very essential that human beings must learn to trust one another. If a person did not trust anyone, life will be hard for that person. If people doubted, if they suspected everyone they met, then the nearest people in the world, their closest relations, they will not trust; and it will even develop to such a state of distrust that they will even distrust themselves. But for those who trust another and do not trust themselves, that trust is profitless. Then those who trust another because they trust themselves have the real trust, and by this trust in themselves can make life happy in whatever condition they may be.

In the tradition of the Hindus an idea is very well known of the tree of the fulfillment of desires. There is a story told in India that a man was told that there was a tree of the fulfillment of desires, and he went in its pursuit. And after going in forests and mountains, he arrived in a place at last where, without knowing that there was the tree of the fulfillment of desires, he lay down and fell asleep. And before he went to sleep he was so tired that he thought what a good thing it would be if he had just now a soft bed to rest upon, a beautiful house with a courtyard around it and a fountain, people waiting upon him; and with this thought he went to sleep. And when he opened his eyes from sleep he saw that he was lying in a soft bed, and there was a beautiful house and there was a courtyard and there was a fountain and there were the people waiting upon him; and he was so astonished. He was very surprised at such a change, and he remembered that before going to sleep he had thought of it all. But then as he proceeded further on his journey, he happened to think on this subject and he found "The tree that I was looking for was that tree that I slept under," and it was the phenomenon of that tree that had accomplished this.

Now, friends, the interpretation of this legend is a philosophy in itself: that it is the individuals themselves who are the tree of their desire, and the root of this tree is in the heart of humankind. The trees and plants with their fruits and flowers, and the animals with their strength and power, and the birds with their wings are unable to arrive at this stage that humanity can attain; and it is through this that one is called human, which in Sanskrit means "mind." The trees in the forest await that blessing, that freedom, that liberation in stillness, in quietude; and the mountains and the whole nature seem to await that unfoldment, the privilege of which is given to humanity. Therefore, the traditions say that humanity is made in the image of God. You may say the most fitting instrument for the working of God is the human being. But according to the mystical point of view, you can also say that, for the means of experiencing the whole creation, the Creator takes the heart of a human being as the instrument. And this shows that no being on earth is more capable of happiness, of satisfaction, of joy, of peace than humankind. And it is a pity when a person is not aware of this privilege of being human, and that in this error, every moment such a person passes in life is a waste, and it is the greatest loss.

17

THE PRIVILEGE OF BEING HUMAN 2

HUMANITY'S greatest privilege in life is to become a suitable instrument of God.[1] And until one knows this, one has not realized one's true purpose of life. And the whole tragedy in this life of human beings is their ignorance of the fact that the moment they realize this, from that moment they live the real life, the life of harmony between God and humanity. When Jesus Christ said, "Seek ye first the kingdom of God and all these things shall be added unto you,"[2] this teaching was in answer to the cry of humanity: one crying "I have no wealth"; another crying, "I have no rest"; another crying, "My situation in life is difficult"; another crying, "My friends are troubling me"; another crying, "I want position, wealth." And the answer to all is: seek ye first the kingdom of God and all these things shall be added unto you. A person may ask how, with a practical view, in a scientific point of view, can we understand this? The answer is that all that is external is not in direct connection with you, and it is therefore unattainable in many cases. Therefore, sometimes you can attain, but many times you fail; but by seeking the kingdom of God you seek the center of all that is within and without. And all that is in heaven and earth is directly connected with the center, and therefore, from the

1. Lecture given at Collège de la Tour, Vevey, Switzerland, June 20, 1921.
2. Matthew 6:33.

center you are able to reach all that is on earth and in heaven. But by reaching what is not at the center, all may be snatched away from you.

In the Qur'an it is written, "God is the light of heavens and of the earth."[3] Besides the desire to obtain things of the earth, there is that innermost desire unconsciously working at every moment of life; and that desire is to come in touch with the infinite. When painters are painting, and when musicians are singing or playing, if they think that, "It is my painting, my playing, my music," perhaps they have a satisfaction, but it is like a drop in the ocean. But if they connect their painting, their art with the consciousness of God, if they think, "It is thy painting, thy music, not mine," then they connect themselves with the center and their life becomes the life of God. In life there is much that one can call good and there is much to be contented with and that one can admire, if one can only bring about that attitude. And it is that attitude that can make a person contented and make life happy. Another thing is that God is the painter of all this beautiful creation, and if you do not connect yourself with the painter, you cannot admire the divine painting.

When one goes to the house of a friend whom one likes and admires, every little thing is so pleasant; but if you go into the house of an enemy, everything is disagreeable. Your devotion, your love, your friendship to God can make this whole creation a source of happiness for you.

In the house of a dear friend, a loaf of bread or a glass of milk is most delicious; and in the house of the one whom we dislike, all the delicious dishes are no use. And as soon as one begins to realize there are many mansions in the house of the Creator in this world—with many religions, many races, and many nations—but it is the house of God, then however humble and difficult the situation of life, it must become, sooner or later, happier and better because you feel that you are in the house of

3. Qur'an 24:35.

the One you have loved, have admired. And all that you meet with, you take it with love and gratitude, because it comes from the One whom you love.

Friends, if we can think for a moment of the condition of the world just now, how the nations, the communities, the churches, the religions all divide human beings who are the children of one parent who loves them all and for whom there is no distinction. Humankind, with all its claims of civilization and of progress in life, seems to have fallen into the greatest error for centuries. The world is, just now, one nation hating another, looking with contempt at another. What can we call it? Is it progress? Is it a standstill? It has been worse than that for centuries.

Is this not then the time when thinking souls should open their eyes from sleep and devote themselves to the effort, in that work of doing what good they can to humanity to better the conditions of the world and, when each one is thinking only of their own interest, to think of the interest of all.

The Sufi message brings to the world the message of unity, uniting in the parenthood of God, beyond all differences and distinctions. The chief object of this movement of the Sufis is to bring about a friendly understanding between the people of different nations and of different races, to bring closer the people of different religions in one understanding, the understanding of truth.

Is not this the message of Christ? The message that brought the tidings of the love of God and the unity of humankind in the love of God? There cannot be two religions. There is always one religion, and there cannot be a new religion; there is always one only, as Solomon has said that there is nothing new under the sun.[4] Whenever the message of love and wisdom is given, it is not a new religion but it is the revivification of religion, to bring to humankind the realization of the truth of the religion each follows.

4. Ecclesiastes 1:9.

Therefore, the Sufi Movement does not bring a new religion. It brings the life and the light that are now necessary to revivify the religion that has always existed. Those who have taken an interest in the objects that the Sufi Movement has set before itself are in America, England, France, and now some in Switzerland. Their idea is to study the questions of the deeper side of life and also to receive the personal guidance from the teacher in the way of silence, in the way of meditation, in understanding the way of looking at life and of thinking of God. All are welcome to it, whatever be their faith, whatever their religion, since this is a strength to understand one's own religion and not an idea that could cause one to leave one's own religion

18

SHAIKH MUSLIH AD-DIN SA'DI 1

MY subject this afternoon is Sa'di, the great Sufi poet of Persia.[1] In point of fact, all the poets of Persia were Sufi poets, and their point of view is recognized as the Sufi point of view—and not only the poets of Persia, but also the poets of India. The works of Sa'di have been considered in the East simple, and at the same time educational, and at the same time uplifting.

The beauty of the works of Sa'di is that they begin with the education of children. His "Karima" is taught to children of nine, ten, or eleven. And at the same time, it is not just a legend or an amusing story: it is like a seed sown in the heart of the child of that age, that in time it may flourish and bring forth fruits of good thought and imagination. "Karima" is a thanksgiving poem. In it, the first lesson Sa'di gives is to learn how to be grateful, how to express gratitude, how to appreciate. And so he teaches the lesson of gratefulness and appreciation for all in the world—for the kindness and love of mother and father, and of friend and companion—by teaching first the gratefulness to God for all the blessings and benefits each receives. Sa'di begins in "Karima" by saying, "Oh Lord, most merciful, I ask Thy forgiveness for I am limited, and in this life of limitation I am always apt to err."

He teaches as the first lesson for humankind to recognize its limited condition, and that this limitation makes one subject to error. And at the same time, he suggests the innermost desire

1. Lecture given at Paul Elder Gallery, San Francisco, April 24, 1923.

of every soul to rise above the limitations and keep from error, to seek divine love and ask pardon, and to appreciate all the blessings received in life in order to rise toward that ideal stage of the humane person. And as we see life today, it seems this is the very thing that is lacking.

When children grow up without that tendency of appreciation, they often cannot understand what their mother has done for them, what their father has done for them, what their duty is to their kind friends, to elderly people, to their teacher. And when they grow without developing that gratefulness in their nature, the egoistic nature, which naturally develops, becomes terrible. A child who does not appreciate in childhood all that a parent has done for the child, cannot then learn to be tender and gentle to a spouse, for the first lesson the child has learned is from a parent. Everything that by nature springs up has to be refined, and, in its fulfillment, it has to become perfect.

In human nature there is a self-asserting tendency from childhood. Most pronounced in the nature of the child is "I," and for everything that it possesses it says "My." And if that is not changed, if the same attitude remains when that child grows older, it becomes hard to those around it, for its "I," and, for everything that it possesses, its "My," become difficult for all those around.

The whole religious, spiritual, and philosophical teaching leads us toward the development of the personality. There is something that is made by nature in a person, but there is something that people themselves have to make. A human being is born as a human being but develops to become humane. And if people remain only as they are born, and the other qualities with which they are born remain undeveloped, without being made refined, then they do not fulfill the object of life. All the great teachers and masters of this world who have come from time to time, and whom we recognize as saints and sages, masters, teachers, and inspired helpers—it is not always the philosophy they taught humankind, it is not always the dogmas or the form of religion they gave, but what has been of the greatest importance is their personality, is their person.

The teachings of Buddha are held by many millions, but more than his teachings are the life he lived and the wisdom he expressed in his life, for there is the fulfillment. A human being is born with a purpose, and that purpose is fulfilled in the refinement of the personality. This unrefined nature of the ego, when developed through life, has an effect like the sting of a thorn. Wherever, whoever, whatever it touches, it causes some harm or disturbance, some destruction. And so personalities in human beings, when they are not refined and they have before them all temptations—all things that attract them, things they like and admire and wish to have—then they go against the conflicting activities of life. They rub up against everything like a thorn, tearing it in pieces. And what happens? No doubt when thorns rub against thorns they crush one another, and they feel it less. But when thorns rub against flowers, they tear them to pieces.

If you will ask individuals in this world, in all walks of life, "Tell me, what is your difficulty in life," perhaps they will tell you that they lack wealth or power or position; but mostly the complaint will be that they are in some way or other hurt by others; by friend or parent or child, life-mate or neighbor or co-worker; they are disturbed or troubled and in difficulty from this thornlike influence from morning to evening, touching them and scratching them. And yet humankind does not seem to think deeply on this subject. Life is blinding, and it keeps humanity busy and engaged in finding fault with others. People do not find the thorn in themselves; they always see the thorn in others.

Sa'di, in simple language, has tried to give humanity a helping hand toward the development in the personality of that flowerlike quality, to train this personality that was made to be a flower and to help. His whole life's work has been to explain to humanity how life can turn into a flower. He has called his books *Gulistan*, which means a "flower bed" or a "rose garden," and *Bostan*, a "place of fragrance." In this he has tried to explain to humanity how the heart can be turned into a flower. In reality it is a flower, it is made to be a flower, it is made to spread its perfume. If only you trained it and tended it, it would show the delicacy and beauty and fragrance of a flower, and that is the purpose of your life.

There is no mystification in Sa'di's poetry. It is full of wit and intelligence and, at the same time, original. And the most wonderful thing that one sees in the poetry of Sa'di is his humorous trend of mind. He is ready to look at the funny side of things and to amuse himself and enjoy it. And how few of us in this world know what real, true mirth means. Humor that is not vulgarized, not abused, shows the rhythm and tune of the soul. Without humor life is dull and depressing. Humor is the reflection of that divine life and sun that makes life like the day. And those who reflect divine wisdom and divine joy add to the expression of their thought when they express their ideas with mirth.

One day Sa'di was sitting in a bookseller's shop where his books were sold. The bookseller was absent, and someone came in and asked for one of Sa'di's books, not knowing that he was speaking to Sa'di himself. Sa'di asked, "What do you like about Sa'di's books?" The man replied, "Oh, he is a funny fellow." Whereupon Sa'di made him a present of the book, and when the person wished to pay for it, said, "No, I am Sa'di, and when you called me a funny fellow, you gave me all the reward I wish."

He wanted life to be joyous. Spirituality is not in a long face and deep sigh. No doubt there are moments when you will sympathize with the troubles of others, there are moments that move you to tears, and there are times when you must just close your lips. But there are other moments when you can see the joyous side of life and enjoy its beauties. Humankind is not born into this world for depression and unhappiness. A person's very being is happiness. Depression is something unnatural. By this I do not mean to say that sorrow is a sin, or suffering is always avoidable. We all have to experience both in life to accomplish the purpose of life. We cannot always be smiling. There is no spiritual evolution in ignoring either side of life. Spirituality is in every side of life. As long as one is not bound, it is no sin to stand in the midst of life. Human beings need not go into the forest, away from all people, to show goodness and virtue. Of what use is our goodness and virtue if we bury ourselves in the forest? It is right in the midst of life that we have to develop and express all that is beautiful and perfect and divine in our souls.

19

SHAIKH MUSLIH AD-DIN SA'DI 2

SA'DI has expressed a wonderful thought in his work called the *Gulistan*, and in simple words.[1] He says that every soul was meant for a certain purpose, and the light of that purpose was kindled in the soul. It is one little verse, but it is a book in itself. What does this suggest to us? That this whole universe is like one symphony, and all souls are as different notes. Their activities are according to the rhythm of this symphony, and their life is purposed to perfect this symphony.

People are anxious to do something, and wait for years and years, unhappy and in despair, waiting for that moment to come. It shows that the soul knows in its subconscious that there is a note to strike. And the moment when it shall strike that note, the soul shall be satisfied and yet does not know what note it is nor when it shall be struck. What is life, and what keeps us living in this world of limitation, this world of continual changes, this world full of falsehood, and world full of suffering and trouble? If there is anything in this world that keeps us alive, it is hope; hope is the honey of life.

There is not one soul in this world who says, "Now I am satisfied. I have no further desire." In everyone, whatever be the position of life—one very rich or one very poor, one full of life and the other ill—in all conditions a person is continually yearning and waiting for something to come. One does not know what, but one is waiting. The real explanation of life is

1. Lecture given at Paul Elder Gallery, San Francisco, April 24, 1923.

waiting, waiting for something. And what is it that humanity awaits? It is the fulfillment of the purpose of life, which comes when the soul strikes the note, the note that is meant to be one's own note. And this a person seeks, whether in the outer plane or the inner plane. And one has not fulfilled one's life's purpose until striking the note that is one's own note.

And the greatest tragedy in life is the obscurity of purpose. When purpose is not clear, an individual suffers and cannot breathe. One knows not what is the purpose, what one must do. This life will present things that will interest for the moment, but the moment one possesses that thing, one will say, "No, this is not it. It is something else." So humankind goes on in an illusion, constantly seeking and yet not knowing what it seeks. Blessed are they who know their life's purpose, for that is the first step toward fulfillment.

And how are we to know life's purpose? Can anybody tell us? No. No one can tell us, for life in its very nature is self-revealing; and it is our own fault if we are not open to the revelation that life offers to us. It is not the fault of life, because the very nature of life is revealing. Humanity is the offspring of nature, therefore its purpose is nature. But the artificiality of life brings obscurity, which prevents humanity from arriving at the knowledge that may be called the revelation of one's own soul.

And if you ask me how one should proceed, I would advise you to study every object, whether false or true, which holds and attracts you, to which you are outwardly attracted and also inwardly attracted. And do not be doubting and suspicious. What Christ taught from morning until night was faith, but the interpretation of this word is not made clear. People have said it is faith in a priest, in a church, or in a sect. That is not the meaning. The true meaning of faith is trust in one's self. A person came to me and said, "I wish to follow your ideas. Will you receive me? Will you have me follow you?" I said, "Yes, but will you tell me if you have faith?" This person looked perplexed for a moment, then he said, "Well, I have faith in you."

I asked, "Have you faith in yourself?" He said, "Well, I am not sure." I said, "Your faith in me would be of no use to me. What I need is your faith in you."

Friends, what we must learn in life is first to trust ourselves. This wobbling tendency of mind—Shall I or shall I not? Is it good or is it bad?—this keeps us in confusion. And for years people may have the best intentions but will linger in the same place. They will not advance, for their own confusion will paralyze their legs. They will think they are going on but will be stepping in the same place where they are standing.

Humankind must have initiative. And this is the word from which comes *initiation*. Who is the initiate? The brave, the courageous. Who is brave and courageous? Those who trust themselves. Only their trust in themselves will be of any use to themselves or others. People say those of simple faith and trust suffer much and come to failure. I will say no, because what is gained is so much more than what is lost. In order to strengthen trust, one has to meet with some failures. I would rather trust and be badly treated, than to distrust. The strength that faith and trust gives is the divine strength. Those who trust their fellow creatures inspire trust in others. They can so develop that they will turn the untrustworthy into the trustworthy; with sufficient trust in their heart, they can develop the power to do this.

I always remember the blessing I received from my holy master, my teacher.[2] It was, "May your faith be strengthened." Being young, I wondered that he said nothing about happiness, long life, or prosperity. I have now learned to understand the meaning of that blessing and understand it better every day. All the blessings that people attain in life, all that is in heaven and earth, become their possession when their faith is strengthened. We read every day in the scriptures about faith, but how little we think of it, and how many people at the present moment are beginning to laugh at it. They give no attention to faith; it

2. Shaikh Muhammad Abu Hashim Madani.

is something that conveys nothing to them. It is so simple and yet so complex. It is a miracle. It is a wonder. All our weakness, all our failures, all our limitations, all our sufferings come from lack of the substance that is faith. In all success, happiness, and advance—in all that is achieved—the credit is due to faith.

The works of Sa'di, from the beginning, teach the first lesson of faith, of understanding: that we are not here in this world in vain, to waste our lives. We are here for a purpose, and each one of us for a particular purpose. And each one of us makes an atom of this universe and completes the symphony; and when we do not strike our note, it means that note is lacking in the symphony of the whole. And when we do not fulfill our life's purpose in this way, for which we are created, we are not living right, and therefore, we are not happy.

Our happiness depends on living right, and right living depends on striking that note; and the realization of that purpose is in the book of our heart. Open that book and look at it. All meditation, all concentration and contemplation is only to open this book, to focus our mind, and to see what purpose there is in our life. And no sooner do we see that our ultimate goal and our life's object and happiness, our true health and well-being, and our real wealth and welfare are in the fulfillment of our purpose, then the whole trend of life will change.

20

THE SOLUTION TO THE PROBLEM OF THE DAY

THE hustle and bustle of life leaves very little time for people to think of their general condition.[1] The only news they receive in life is from the newspapers, and so they depend upon the papers to have some idea; and the intoxication of life leaves them very little time to think about the real meaning of life. When one looks around one and considers the condition of nations today, one finds, in spite of all the progress, there is an ill feeling rising among nations. Friendship exists only for self-interest. One nation thinks about its own interest, whether it has to deal with friend or enemy. And if we consider the world as a body, we could say that a poison has been put in the heart owing to the feeling of hatred that arises from every person toward every other.

No period like this is to be traced in the history of the world.[2] This age has accomplished a much greater destruction than ever before. It reminds one of a spider that weaves its web in order to get comfort, but it cannot get out of the web it has made itself. And if we go to the root of the subject we see all these disasters, all this disorder has been caused by a spirit of materialism. Money seems to be the only gain and aim. It is undeniable that when one is continually thinking of such a subject, all one's thoughts and energy will go in that direction.

1. Lecture in autumn 1923, date and location unknown.
2. Post–World War I period.

And in the end perhaps one awakens and finds that all one's life, one has given one's thoughts to something which does not last, that does not even exist and is only an illusion.

No doubt this pessimism is the bridge from one optimism to another. This may be called disinterestedness: *vairagya*. It is not the one who leaves the world, but the one who lives in the world, understanding the difficulties and troubles that belong to humanity, who is great. It is that person who sees not the little self but the whole. Jesus Christ says to think of your fellow human beings, love your fellow human beings.[3] And what do we see today? Difficulties arising between employers and the workforce; peace conferences where nothing can be decided concerning peace. And all this because this point of view is not there, the point of view that "I will do for you, and you will do for me." "No," says everyone, "I will do for myself, and you will do for yourself." To serve one another, to love one another, to work for one another, that should be the aim of life that humankind has lost hold of altogether. Look at the central theme of the education of today. Only a short time is given to the child to prepare it for the kingliness of life and the freedom of the spirit. And every year children's intellectual burden is getting heavier; and the older the children grow, the more they see life before them as an ocean that they have to cross, as something dark awaiting them. And later on, the children, having become adults, give all their time to work, to the office, and there is even no time for love or friendship. And yet, after all, they cannot even take all these things with them. After sacrificing all their life to these things, what have they really gained? By their external life in the world the complications of life have increased.

The more laws are given, the more prisons are filled with criminals; the more contracts are signed, the less peace and kinship are to be found among humankind. Something more

3. See Matthew 22:39.

genuine in human life seems to be neglected, and yet no one is deprived of this human inheritance. There is a treasure in oneself that has to be found. There is religion that should have helped humanity on. The authorities of religion have very often failed to uphold the inner qualities of their religion. The question is not what religion one follows, but how to live one's religion. When religion has lost its hold on inner life and faith, there is nothing else. Many people, especially among the intellectual ones, have lost their religion; and among the younger ones there are a good many who even fear the name of God.

Now what is needed today? It is an education that will teach human beings to feel the essence of their religion in everyday life. A human being is not put on this earth to be an angel. One need not be praying in church all day long nor go into the wilderness. One has only to understand life better. One must learn to take a certain time in the day to think about one's own life and doings. One must ask oneself: Have I done an honest deed today? Have I proved myself worthy, in that place, in that capacity? In this way one can make one's everyday life a prayer. Among politicians, doctors, lawyers, and merchants it might be possible to have love as the battery behind every deed, every action, and a sense of harmony behind all these doings.

We need today the religion of tolerance. In daily life we all cannot meet on the same ground, being so different, being in different capacities and different states of evolution and with different tasks. In the homes we are not in the same state of evolution. So if we had no tolerance, no desire to forgive, we should never bring harmony into our soul. For to live in the world is not easy; every moment of the day demands a victory. If there is anything to learn it is this tolerance, and by teaching this simple religion of tolerance to one another we are helping the world. It is no use keeping the idea that the world is going from bad to worse; that germ of disease will spread and bring greater consequences. Every individual's being is good; in the depth of each heart there is something certainly good.

There are teachings about healings, but the best way is the way of character healing: healing one's own character. And instead of accomplishing miracles, in this way one's whole life becomes a miracle. The lack of religion today has created a strange belief in speaking with ghosts, fairies, etc., or about things one does not nor can understand. But this has very little to do with religion. The Bible is full of simple things; one would be happy if one could accomplish one of these things. There has been a great demand for getting knowledge of occult powers. But what has humankind reached with all its intellectuality but the destruction of sister and brother?

The need of the world today is not of learning, but how to become considerate to one another, to try to find out in what way happiness can be brought about, and so to realize the peace that is the longing of every soul, and to impart it to others, so attaining our life's goal: the sublimity of life.

21

POETRY 1

IN poetry it is the rhythm of the poet's soul that is expressed.[1] There are moments in the time of every soul, and at these moments the soul feels itself rhythmic. And the children, who are beyond the conventionalities of life, begin to dance at these moments or begin to speak by themselves words that rhyme, or repeat phrases that are alike, which harmonize together. It is a moment of the soul's awakening. One person's soul wakens oftener than another person's soul; but in the life of every soul there are times when such awakening comes. And the soul who is gifted with the expression of thought and ideas shows its gift in poetry.

Among all things in this world that are valuable, the word is most precious, for in the word you can find light that gems and jewels do not possess. In a word, you can find an intoxication that no wine can give; in a word, you can find a life that could heal the wounds of the heart. Therefore, poetry in which the soul is expressed is as living as a human being. If I were to say that if God bestows the greatest reward on humankind, it is eloquence and poetry, it would not be an exaggeration. For, as I have said, it is the gift of the poet which culminates in time to the gift of prophecy. There is a Hindu idea which explains this better, and that idea is that the vehicle of the goddess of learning is eloquence.

1. Lecture given in Paris, December 18, 1922.

Many live, and few think. Among the few who think, there are fewer still who can express. For those who think and cannot express, their soul's impulse is repressed; and it is in the expression of the soul that the divine purpose is fulfilled. And in poetry it is the divine impulse to express something that is fulfilled.

Yes, there is a true poetry and there is a false poetry, just as there is a true music and a false music. If a person, knowing many words and knowing syllables, fits them in together, that person mechanically will arrange something, but it is not poetry. Be it poetry, art, or music, it must suggest life; and it can only suggest life if it is the deepest impulse of the soul. But if it does not, then it is dead. There exist verses of great teachers, whatever period they have existed, whose verses have resisted the sweeping wind of destruction, every movement of all ages. And what is in their verse that has resisted against the ever-destroying influence of time? That resistive power in their words was the life that was put into it. The trees that live long have their roots deep set, and so are the living verses. We only read them as we see the trees; if we only saw where the root of these verses is, we shall find them in the soul, in the spirit.

Now, coming to the question of what awakens the soul to this rhythm that brings about poetry. It is something that touches in the poet the predisposition that is called love. For with love, harmony comes, beauty comes, rhythm comes, light comes, life comes. It seems all that is good and beautiful and worth attaining is centered in that one spark that is hidden in the heart of humankind. When the heart speaks of its joy, of its sorrow, it is all interesting, it is all appealing. The heart does not tell a lie, it always tells the truth; for by love it becomes sincere, and it is through the sincere heart that true love manifests. One may live in a company where there is always amusement, pastimes, merriment, and beauty. And one may live that life for twenty years, but the moment one realizes the movement in the depth of one's heart, one feels that the whole twenty years' life was nothing. One moment of living with a living heart is more worthwhile than a hundred years' long life with the heart dead. Many we see in this world with all their comfort and fortune and all that they need in life, yet leading an empty life. There is nothing; their life is more unhappy than perhaps the person who is starving through life for days. The person is to be more pitied whose soul is starving than the one whose body only is starving. For the one whose body is starving is yet alive, but the one whose soul is starving is dead.

Those who have shown great inspiration and who have given to the world precious words of wisdom were the farmers who were plowing the soil of their hearts. That is the reason why there are few poets in this world, for the path of the poet is contrary to the path of the worldly person. The real poets, although they exist on this earth, dream of a different world from where they get their ideas. The true poets are seers at the same time, or else they could not bring the subtle ideas that touch the heart of the listener. The true poets are lovers and admirers of beauty. If their souls were not impressed by beauty, they could not bring out beauty in their poetry.

22

Poetry 2

BUT now to tell you what stimulates the gift in the one who is born with the gift of poetry—is it pleasure or is it pain?[1] It is not at all pleasure; pleasure makes the gift frozen. It is the pain that the sensitive poet's soul has to go through in this life. One may ask if it would be a wise thing to seek pain if one wants to be good poet? It would be as if one thought crying was a virtue, and if one hurt oneself and cried a little. Who, with a living heart, can live in this world as it is and not suffer, and not experience pain? Who with any tendency to feel, to sympathize, to love would not go through pain? Who with any sincerity in their nature could go from morning till evening through insincerity and falsehood and crudity of human nature? In short, those with tender feelings and with open hearts cannot avoid suffering; at every step they take, suffering meets them.

Poets begin with the admiration of beauty, and their gift becomes mature in shedding tears over the disappointments that they meet with in life. When they have passed that phase, then comes another interesting phase when they begin to laugh at the world. They rise beyond tears after having shed enough. This does not mean that they become critical, that they sneer at life. No, they see the funny side of things and see the whole of life, which was once a tragedy, in the form of comedy. This stage is like a consolation for them from above, after their moments of great pain and suffering in life.

1. Lecture given in Paris, December 18, 1922.

And there comes another stage when they rise beyond that stage, when they see the divine element working in all forms and in all names, when they begin to see their Beloved in all forms and in all names. That comes in the life of poets as the joy in the life of a young lover; it brings in their lives another period. Whatever be their condition in life—rich or poor, in comfort or without—they are never without their Beloved. Their divine Beloved is always in their presence. When poets arrive at this period they pity that lover who has only a limited beloved to admire and to love, for they have now arrived to a stage that when alone, when in a crowd, when in the North or South or West or East, on earth or in heaven, always they are in the presence of their Beloved.

And if they reached one step further, then it becomes difficult for them to express their emotion, their impulse to poetry, for then they themselves become poetry. What they feel, what they think, what they say, what they do—all is poetry. At this stage they come to touch the ideal of unity that unites all things in one. But in order to enjoy this stage the soul must become so mature as to enjoy it. An infant soul would not be able to enjoy this particular consciousness of all-oneness.

From that time in the poetry of these poets, one will find glimpses of prophetic expressions. It is not only the beauty of words and meanings, but their words become illuminative, and their verses become life-giving. There are in this world souls who are pious, who are wise, who are spiritual; but among them the one who is capable of expressing the realization of life, of truth, is not only a poet but a prophet.

23

Music

THIS evening I would like to speak on music.[1] Many in the world take music as a source of amusement or pastime, and to many music is an art and a musician an entertainer. Yet no one has lived in this world who has thought and felt and has not considered music as the most sacred of all arts. For the fact is that what the art of painting cannot clearly suggest, poetry explains in words; but that which even a poet finds difficult to express in poetry, is expressed in music. But by this I do not only say that music is superior to art and poetry, but, in point of fact, music excels religion, for music raises the soul of humankind even higher than the so-called external form of religion.

But by this it must not be understood that music can take the place of religion. For every soul is not necessarily tuned to the pitch that can really benefit by music, nor is every music necessarily so high that it will exalt those who will hear it more than the effect that religion will make upon them. However, for those who follow the path of the inner school, music is most essential for their spiritual development. The reason is that the soul that is seeking for truth is in search of the formless God. Art, no doubt, is most elevating, but at the same time contains form; poetry has words and names suggestive of forms.

It is music only that has beauty, that has power and charm, and at the same time can raise the soul beyond form. It is therefore that in the ancient times the greatest of the prophets have been

1. Lecture given in rue de Séverin, Paris, December 6, 1922.

great musicians. For instance, in the life of the Hindu prophets one finds Narada, the great prophet of the Hindus and a great musician at the same time. And Shiva, a godlike prophet of the Hindus who was the inventor of their sacred vina. Krishna is always pictured with a flute. There is a well-known legend of the life of Moses, a legend that says how Moses heard a command, a divine command on Mount Sinai, in the words *Musa ke*: "Moses heard," or "Moses pondered,"[2] and in this the revelation that came to him was of tone and rhythm. And he called it by the same name of a man: *musake*, and the words such as *music* or *musake* have come from that word.

David, whose song and whose voice have been known for ages—his message was given to the world in the form of music. Orpheus of the Greek legends, was the knower of the mystery of tone and of rhythm, and had, by the knowledge of tone and rhythm, power over the hidden forces of nature. The goddess of learning, of knowledge among Hindus, whose name is Saraswati, is always pictured with the vina—and what does it suggest? It suggests that all learning has its essence in music. And besides the natural charm that music has, music has a magic power, a power that can be experienced even now. It seems that the human race has lost a great deal of the ancient science of magic, but if there exists any magic, it is in music. Music, besides power, is intoxication. When it intoxicates those who hear, how much more it must intoxicate those who play or sing themselves! And how much more it must intoxicate those who have touched the perfection in it, and those who have contemplated upon it for years and years! It gives them a greater joy and exaltation than even a king or queen feels when sitting on the throne.

According to the thinkers of the East there are four different intoxications: the intoxication of beauty and youth and of strength; then the intoxication of wealth; then the intoxication

2. See Qur'an 20:9–14.

of power, command of the power of ruling; and there is the fourth intoxication, which is the intoxication of learning, of knowledge. But all these four intoxications fade away just like stars before the sun in the presence of the intoxication of music. The reason is that it touches the deepest part of humanity's being. Music reaches further than any other impression one gets from the external world. And then the beauty of music is that music is the source of creation and the means of absorbing it. In other words, by music the world was created; and it is again music with which it is withdrawn into the source that has created it. In support of this argument you will read in the Bible that first was the Word and the Word was God.[3] That Word means "sound," and from sound you can grasp the idea of music. Then there is an Eastern legend that comes from centuries ago, the legend that when God made a human being out of clay and asked the soul to enter, the soul refused to enter into that prison house. And then God commanded the angels to sing, and as the angels sang the soul entered, being intoxicated by the song.

But now, in this scientific and material world, we also see an example of this kind. Before a machine, a mechanism must run, it must first make a noise. It first becomes audible and then shows its life. You can see that in a ship, in an airplane, in an automobile. Of course, I cannot explain this idea just now, because this idea belongs to the mysticism of sound. Just now I wish to deal with the subject of music. Before an infant is capable of admiring a color or form, it enjoys sound. If there is any art that can please the aged most, it is music. If there is any that can charge youths to life and to enthusiasm, to emotion and to passion, it is music. If there is any art in which a person can fully express feeling and emotion, it is music that is best suited for it. At the same time, it is something that gives humanity the force and the power of activity that makes the soldiers march with the beats of the drum and the sound of the trumpet.

3. John 1:1.

In the traditions of the past, it was said that on the Last Day there will be the sound of the trumpets before the end of the world.[4] This shows that music is connected with the beginning of creation, with its continuity, and with its end. The mystics of all ages have loved music most. In almost all the circles of the inner school in whatever part of the world they are, music seems to be the central part of their ritual. And with those who attain to the perfect peace that is called nirvana, or in the language of the Hindus is called samadhi, it is more easily done by music.

Therefore Sufis, especially those of the Chishtiyya school of the ancient times, have taken music as a source of their meditation; and by so meditating they derive much more benefit than those who meditate without the help of music. The effect that they experience is the unfoldment of the soul, the opening of the intuitive faculties. And their hearts, so to speak, open to all the beauty that is within and without, uplifting them and, at the same time, bringing them that perfection for which every soul yearns.

4. See 1 Corinthians 15:22 and Qur'an 39:68.

24

Harmony and Agitation

BELOVED ones of God, I would like to speak on the subject of kinship.[1] Kinship is not something that is learned or taught; kinship is a tendency, a tendency that arises from the heart that is tuned to a proper pitch. A tendency toward kinship, therefore, is the natural tendency in which is the real happiness, from which rises harmony, which culminates in peace. The message of kinship is a message of sympathy; a message of sympathy is a message of harmony. Those who are not in harmony with themselves cannot be harmonious to another. With all the teaching of kinship, and with all their learning, they will not be able to observe the law of kinship.

The whole system of the world's creation is a kind of blind impulse working in a kind of mechanism of the universe, and this impulse is more pronounced in living creatures. And the most pronounced form of this impulse is agitation. If you study the lives of the lower creation, you will find that it is not that they have a desire for food; their desire to move about with their mates. The first appetite is to sleep, but besides this there is one desire—an inclination, and that inclination manifests as agitation. And it is by this agitation the animals and the birds, fight together. Their whole life is filled with that agitation. Furthermore, the herbivorous animals are less agitated than carnivorous animals. In the carnivorous animals there is more desire for fighting. The lion and the tiger are more inclined to fight

1. Lecture given in Suresnes, France, September 6, 1924.

than horses and cows. That shows that the herbivorous animals are a step more advanced than the carnivorous animals. Therefore, a tendency to eat or drink or seek for pleasures or enjoy comfort or agitation, does not particularly belong to human beings as their special characteristic. It comes from the animal characteristic. The special human characteristic is sympathy and harmony, and this comes only when humanity rises above this agitation, which, so to speak, buries that spirit of sympathy that is considered to be the human characteristic. No doubt, people are educated, trained, have got some polish; they may be taught some manners, and therefore, they are not always able to show out their agitation. It is only at the time of weakness, when they cannot cover their agitation, that the agitation comes out and manifests to their own view as well as to the view of others, proving them not yet ready to be called human.

One might ask, is there any time in a person's life when one gets above this? Yes, one gets there sooner or later. But one gets above it if one tries to get above it. This spirit of agitation shows itself as intolerance, as rivalry, as jealousy, as a dominating spirit, irritability, patronizing: all such qualities show agitation of nature.

When we study the lives of those who have served humanity, that was the first thing that they had to conquer. When it is said in the life of Krishna that Krishna had a battle with Kansa, the monster, that monster was not outside of Krishna. That monster was inside of Krishna; the monster was that agitating spirit. Krishna had to fight it, and it is after conquering that spirit of agitation that Krishna became the messenger of love.

In the Bible we read that Jesus Christ went for forty days on the top of the mountain at the side of that spirit.[2] What is that spirit? The same spirit that is the greatest enemy of the human race: the spirit of agitation. And the Master had to fast for forty days. Then that spirit went among the creatures who were the

2. See Matthew 4:1–11.

receptacles of that spirit, to whom it belonged. You can study this in the Bible.

Halima[3] gives the description of the Prophet, symbolical, artistic, picturesque; but what is it after all? She says that the breast of the Prophet was cut open and some undesirable stuff was taken off from there. Behind this symbology there is only one thing: the spirit of agitation that was removed from there to make place for divine inspiration.

Does it not show that humanity inherits divine spirit? And yet this divine spirit is covered by earthly characteristics. Among all earthly characteristics, agitation is the principal characteristic. A child sometimes begins it against its parents. A child in the school begins it against its friends. A youth shows it with companions. A person shows it to a neighbor. And yet each one has a reason to give for one's own faults. For every right or wrong one does, there is a reason to justify oneself of that wrong. Agitation, therefore, is the sign of false ego. And when this false ego is broken, when this very agitation has crushed itself—just like fire burns itself—then purification arises.

Very little does humanity notice how far this spirit follows a person in the path of spiritual progress. A person may arrive at the gate of heaven; even to that length this spirit will travel with them. It may become weaker, but it is there. Only this spirit has no entrance into the shrine of God, and the soul that carries this spirit with it, therefore, has no entrance into that perfect goal. It may advance as far as the gate, the door of that inner temple, but it is not allowed in; it is held back by the power of the same spirit of agitation. For the shrine of God is called *dar-as-salam*; the corrupt word is "Jerusalem." And what does it mean? It means the "door to peace." Agitation, therefore, is not allowed to enter the door of peace; it must stay out. Therefore, as in the ancient times they used to say, you cannot follow two masters, God and Satan.[4] What is it? Satan is the spirit of agitation that is to be found within ourselves. God is

3. Halima Sadia was the foster-mother of Muhammad.

4. Matthew 6:24.

the spirit of peace in whom is our happiness, and we cannot follow two masters.

There are many movements and institutions for kinship, and all are doing what they can to promote this ideal, for this is an ideal that is the essence of religion and the soul of spirituality.

But how to attain to it? By creating in oneself, by trying to give to others, the idea of that natural inclination to sympathy. By strengthening ourselves, and thereby giving power to others also to fight against this spirit of agitation, which has always proved to be the worst enemy of humankind.

Now, one might ask where it comes from. From disorder, from the disorder of the body, from the disorder of the mind. If the body has not got its proper rhythm and proper tone, if the mind is not attuned to a proper rhythm and tone—these two things—if the mind and the body are not in tune with one another, if they are not in harmony, then this agitation comes. Sometimes it is the reflection of the mind upon the body, and sometimes it is the reflection of body upon mind. How true it is that humankind is its own enemy! But where is that enemy? That enemy is this spirit, this spirit that is never content, which does not appreciate, which does not respond, which does not sympathize, which does not agree, which does not endure, which does not tolerate, which does not harmonize—a spirit which stands against any influence of harmony, agreement, of sympathy, of kindness.

But, one might ask, what is it? Where does it come from? Is it a spirit? Is it a living being? Is it a Satan or devil? What is it? What is its explanation? What is its origin? The best explanation is that it is the same smooth silk thread that has at one end become entangled and turned into a knot. In the place where it is a knot and where it is very difficult to unravel it, it is the same silk thread just the same, only it is under a condition where it is difficult for itself because it is not free. It is difficult for others, for they cannot loosen it. And so a person becomes the same soul who has divine breath in it; the same soul who has come from heaven; the same soul who represents God on earth; but when it is turned into a knot, then it finds difficulty with itself and difficulty with others. Others find difficulty with it, and therefore, it becomes inharmony itself. It creates inharmony, it finds itself in a kind of inharmonious condition. It only means that it has lost its natural, original condition—that smoothness, that softness. And yet it remains silk, it has not turned into cotton; it is silk just the same. Call it Satan or devil or whatever you may, if you know the source, the origin, you cannot call it anything else but a condition. If there is anything most important to be done in the work of kinship, it is to develop that spirit in ourselves by going above all knots and difficulties, so that we may not have to follow the rules of kinship, so that all that naturally comes out of ourselves may express kinship.

25

Art and Religion

MY subject this evening is art and religion.[1] Very few in the world link religion with art or art with religion, but in point of fact, art is much more important than an average person realizes it to be, in spite of the saying that art is what humanity makes and nature is what God makes. But I would like to say that nature is what God makes as God, and art is what God makes as a person. The artists who have arrived at some perfection in their art, whatever be their art, will come to realize that it is not ever they who did it; it is someone else who came forward every time. And in the perfect things that the artists produce they hardly can imagine that it is produced by them, for they can do nothing but bow their heads in perfect humility before that unseen power and wisdom who takes their bodies, their hearts, their brains, and their eyes as its instrument. Whatever be that art—be it music or poetry or painting or writing or whatever manner—whenever beauty is produced it must not be thought that an individual produces it. It is through humanity that God finishes divine creation. Therefore, art is not only an imitation of nature, it is an improvement upon it. There is nothing that is done in this world and in heaven that is not a divine immanence, that is not the divine creation. It is the dividing of that divine work that makes the perplexity that separates human beings from their God. In the first place, all things that we see in this world, all our occupations that we engage ourselves in willingly or unwillingly—all this leads us to accomplish a cer-

1. Lecture given in rue Loxum, Brussels, December 18, 1923.

tain purpose. No doubt there are certain things in life in which we accomplish a greater purpose and that can be accomplished by an inspiration from within. Art is a domain through which the inspiration has a great faculty to manifest. In order to become spiritual, it is not necessary that humanity should be very religious or extra good. In order to attain to inspiration, what is necessary is love for beauty.

What is art? Art is a creation of beauty, in whatever form it be created. As long as artists think that whatever they create in the form of art is their own creation, and as long as artists become vain over their creation, they have not learned the true art. For the true art can only come by one condition, and that condition is that the artists forget themselves, forget themselves in the vision of beauty. And there is one condition when their art can be still more valuable, and that condition is when the artists begin to recognize the divine in their art. As long as artists have not realized this, they have not touched the perfection of art. The artist in the true sense of the word is the ruler of a certain kingdom that is even greater than the kingdom of the earth. There is a story known in the East, that Farabi was a great singer, a singer who was invited to the court of the sultan. The sultan received him very warmly in the court, and as the singer entered, the sultan went to the door to receive him. On coming in the drawing room, the sultan asked the singer to take his seat. "Where shall I sit?" said the singer. The sultan said, "Sit in any place that may be fitting to you." On hearing this he took the seat of the king. No doubt it astonished the sultan very much, but after hearing Farabi's art the sultan thought that even his own seat was not quite suitable. For the kingdom of the sultan had a certain limitation, but the kingdom of the artist is everywhere, wherever beauty prevails. As beauty is everywhere so the kingdom of the artist is everywhere.

But art is only a door, a door through which one can enter into still a wider area. Religions have, in different times, considered art as something outside, but this has been very often a kind of fanaticism on the part of religious authorities. And it is not only in the East, but it is in the West and East where one finds a kind of idea existing to separate art from religion. It does not mean that all religions do it, nor does it mean that any great teacher of religion has taught it. It has only come from people who have not yet realized the beauty of religion; in its form, they have forced its simplicity on it. No one who has touched the depth of religion can ever deny the fact that religion itself is an art, an art which accomplishes the greatest thing in a person's life; and to make that art be void of beauty—there cannot be a greater error than this.

In the first place, we can see in the ancient times, in all the Hindu and Buddhist churches and pagodas, there was music, there was poetry, there was sculpture, and there was painting. At the time when there were not printing presses, nor could books be brought out on philosophy and religion, if one can find any scriptures expressing the ancient religious and philosophical ideas, they can be found in the old, ancient art. For instance, in the mysticism and the religion of ancient Egypt, of which so much has been spoken and so little has been known, if there is any sign of it to be found, it is not in a manuscript; it is in art. Besides, the ideas of the ancient Sanskrit age are yet to be found in India in engravings on the carved stones, rocks, and temples. Very often the travelers of the Western world go to the East in order to see how far art had attained its perfection, but very few really know that it is not only the art that came to a certain perfection, but the art that has been given as something to communicate to those who can read. Besides that, the art of ancient Greece is the sign and proof of a great perfection in divine wisdom. Every movement that you see in the Greek pictures is not only a graceful movement but it has a meaning; and every little statue, in its action, denotes a great meaning if only a person can read it.

But from this we come to learn that in order to make a work of art, and in order to be able to understand a work of art, for both, intuition is necessary. And it is the very thing that today the human race seems to be losing more than in any time in the world's history. One might ask what is the reason that humanity has lost that intuitive faculty. It is because humanity has become so absorbed in material gains that it has, so to speak, become intoxicated by earthly life; and intuition, which is its birthright and its own property, it has lost to view. It does not mean that this has gone out from human beings; it only means that it has become buried in their own hearts.

Friends, we are vehicles, or instruments who respond. If we respond to goodness, goodness becomes our property; if to evil we respond, then evil becomes our property; if to love we respond, then love becomes our possession; if we respond to hatred, hatred becomes our life. And so, if we respond to the things of the earth so much that our whole life becomes absorbed in earthly things, then it is quite natural that we do not respond to the richness that is within us, and we are far removed from it. Intuition is not something that a person can read in books and learn, nor is intuition a thing that one can buy and sell. Intuition is something that is the very self and the deepest self of humankind, and it can be realized by the soberness that is desirable in life. Absence of intuition means absence of soberness. One might ask, why is every person intoxicated, and what is that soberness like? I would answer that it is just like a little pool of water: when the water of that little pool is troubled, you cannot see the reflection, but when it is not troubled, then it is quiet, and then you can see, when the water is clear. So is the heart of humanity. By the heart, I do not mean the piece of flesh; by heart, I only mean that inner being of humanity, which very often in the Bible is called spirit. It is the calmness and quietness of that spirit that quickens the tendency of inspiration. But when the mind is troubled by worries and anxieties and responsibility, then naturally that intuition is lost. But humanity asks often, "How can it be possible to leave the worries and troubles of life?" That is quite true; but at the same time, if one is thinking that one cannot leave out the troubles and anxieties, one is going further and further from the truth, the truth that is the safety of humankind. Many think that if we cannot be spiritual, then we shall be material. Of course, then we shall be more and more material, because we cannot be spiritual. But really speaking, the right thing would be to strike the happy medium; if life forces one to go into material things so much, so much the more it is necessary to go into spirituality. It matters very little what religion people claim and what faith they say they have, what way of prayers they adopt. What really matters is if they are really religious from their heart. The admission to that field of happiness is by tickets. For at the door of the station they do not ask you whose child you are, what class you belong to, what are your ancestors, how much money you have. What they ask is for the ticket, and the same thing is there, in that field of happiness. One has no entrance by saying, "I belong to a very high church," or "My prayers are better than others." No, there it is not so. It is only here that we hate one another by saying, "You are of a different religion. Your belief is bad, my belief is good." There is no distinction there. The question is if you are sincere, if you really are seeking after truth. Then they do not ask what channel you are coming from; they open the door, and you are allowed in.

But now, coming to the question of how can the art that is religion be attained. Even a religion is a kind of art. Of course, its elementary aspect makes it a religion of form. Of course, form is the outward art. Whether it is a ceremony, a ritual, a form of service, it is a form of art no doubt, but as one goes further, it is another art. Among the Sufis that art is called *akhlaq allah*, which means the "manner of God." And the first step in life is to know and understand how to become a human being; for as there are two words in the English language—*man* and *gentleman*—there is such a vast gulf between a man and a gentleman. No doubt if one bought a nice dress and put it on, one can become a gentleman very soon, but this is not what I mean. A true gentleman is the real sense of the word—what the word itself expresses. And what makes one gentle? A human being, by nature, is just like an uncut diamond; and that diamond wants cutting in order to reflect its light fully. A man becomes a gentleman not by becoming rich or in a high position. No, when the rough edges of one's character are cut, just like a diamond, then one becomes a gentleman. And if one judged oneself and did not judge the others, one will find how very difficult it is to become a gentleman. Of course, humanity keeps on in a kind of intoxication, not knowing its own faults. People are always busy finding fault with others, always they are complaining that the rough edges trouble them from others; and so the whole life goes, the life that is the greatest opportunity to rise and to become better. And for those who feel, after having been hurt from the rough edges of the other, that the rough edges of my part must also hurt others—when they begin to cut those rough edges, then they begin to learn the art, for other arts cannot be compared with the art of personality.

The character is not born with an individual's birth; the character is built after coming here. But even when one can call oneself a human being, still one has not yet known that greater art still, which may be rightfully called a true religion. For there is another grade to pursue, and that grade is the personality of God. As soon as one seeks for the personality of God, it is different from a human personality. For in the character of an individual, one has to make one's point of view a human point of view; but in the point of view of God, an individual has to make God's point of view. And it is such personalities who, whenever and at whatever time they came on the earth, have not only taught humanity but have given an example to humanity by their own lives. Some of them known, some of them unknown, came and went away. Each one of them was accepted by some and rejected by some: none of them was accepted by the whole religion nor rejected by it. But in spite of accepting and rejecting, the truth will prove to be by itself a victory, for to nothing else does victory belong. Victory only belongs to truth, and the victory that comes from falsehood is a false victory. The true victory only belongs to truth, and the person who more and more will probe the depths of life and its secret, will more and more realize it. Falsehood, whatever apparent success it has, has its limitation and its end. For at every step the false will feel falseness, and at every step people take to falsehood, they will feel their feet heavier and heavier. It is toward the truth that those who will walk will feel their feet lighter with every step they take. And it is by learning the art of life and by practicing it that one is led in the path of truth, to arrive at the goal that is the longing of every soul.

26

Khwaja Shams ad-Din Muhammad Hafiz 1

BELOVED ones of God, My address this afternoon is on the subject of Hafiz, whose name is well known to everyone interested in the poetry of Persia, because among the Persian poets, Hafiz stands unique in his expression, in his depth of thought, in the excellence of his symbolical expression of certain thoughts and philosophy.[1]

There was a time when a deep thinker and a free thinker had great difficulty in expressing their thoughts. And that time has not altogether ceased, but at the same time, in some ways, there seems to be much more freedom of expression in this age than in ancient times. At that time, anyone who expressed a thought freely about life and its hidden law, about soul, God, creation, and manifestation met with great difficulty. The difficulty was that the religious authorities of all kinds governed, and under the religious reign, the principles of the exoteric religion reigned. And therefore, those who attained in the esoteric side of philosophy always had difficulty in telling it to the people. Many were persecuted: they were stoned, they were flayed, they were put to death. All sorts of punishments were inflicted upon them, and in this way the progress of humanity was retarded. Today we do not see this. At the same time, the limited attitude of the human mind on religious and philosophical questions is to be found in all ages.

1. Lecture given at Paul Elder Gallery, San Francisco, May 1, 1923.

The Sufis who, by the help of meditation, found the source of knowledge in their own hearts—for them it was very difficult to give to the world in plain words what little they could explain of the truth. It is true that the truth cannot be spoken in words, but at the same time, those gifted with poetic and prophetic expression have always had that inclination and tendency to express what their souls experienced.

Hafiz found a way of expressing the experience of his soul and his philosophies in verse. For the soul enjoys expressing itself in verse because the soul itself is music, and when it is experiencing the realization of divine truth, the tendency of the soul is to express itself in poetry. Hafiz, therefore, expressed his soul in poetry. And what poetry! Poetry full of light and shade, line and color, and poetry full of feeling. No poetry in the world can be compared to that of Hafiz in its delicacy. Therefore, only the fine soul, who has the finest perception of light and shade expressed in words, can grasp the meaning of the illumination of the soul.

At the same time, the words of Hafiz have won all hearts that listen. Even if they do not wholly understand it, the phrase, rhythm, charm, and beauty of expression win them. It is the same style that Solomon adopted, but it was spoken in the language of the time. Hafiz spoke in the language that was most appropriate and most suitable to poetry. The Persian language is considered in the East the most delicious language, a language that stands supreme to all Eastern languages in poetry. It is soft, and its expression is tender. It is expressive. Every object has perhaps ten names for the poet to choose from; every little thought can be expressed in perhaps ten names for the poet to choose from; every little thought can be expressed in perhaps twenty different ways. And the poet has that freedom of choice, and therefore, the Persian language and Persian poetry both are rich in expression.

The mission of Hafiz was to express to a fanatically inclined, religious world, the presence of God, which is not to be found only in heaven but is also to be found here on earth. Very often religious belief in God and in the hereafter has kept human beings sleeping, waiting for that hour and that day to come when they will be face-to-face with their Lord. And they are certain that day will not come before they are dead. And therefore, they await their death in the hope that in the hereafter they will see God, for heaven alone is the place where God is to be found, and there is no other place where God will be found. And there is only a certain place that is a sacred place of worship; that is the church, and anywhere else God is not to be found. The mission of Hafiz was to take away this idea, and to make humankind conscious of the heaven by its side, and to tell humanity that all it expects in the hereafter as a reward could be had here, if one lived a fuller life.

The same ideal that one sees in all religions, that Jesus Christ taught, saying, God is love[2]—that was the main idea of Hafiz, the idea that has been expressed from morning to night in the *Diwan*. If there is anything divine in humanity, it is love. If God is to be found anywhere, it is in the heart of a human being, which is love. And if the love element is awakened in the heart, then God is made alive, so to speak, and is born in one's self. But at the same time, Hafiz has shown in his poetry the key to this; and that key is appreciation of beauty in all forms.

Beauty is not always in an object or in a person. Beauty depends upon one's attitude toward life, how one looks at it; and its effect depends upon our power of appreciation. The very same music or poetry or painting will touch some so that they feel its beauty to the very depth of their being; and perhaps there are others who look at it, but they do not see it. The whole manifestation has its beauty. Sometimes the beauty is manifest to you; sometimes you have to look for it. There comes a good person; we are always charmed by the beauty of goodness. There comes another person who looks bad, but at the same time, good is somewhere hidden in that person if we would

2. 1 John 4:8.

look for it, if we have the desire to draw it out. The bad is not always in objects and persons but in our looking. The whole trend of the poetry of Hafiz is to awaken the appreciation of beauty and love of beauty, which is the only condition through which to experience that bliss for which our life is purposed.

Someone asked a Sufi the reason for this whole creation. And the Sufi answered that God, whose being is love itself, had desired to experience the nature of God's own being, and in order to experience it, God had to manifest God's own self. God and God's manifestation, the soul and God—this dual aspect can be seen in all forms of nature: in the sun and the moon, in night and day, in male and female, in positive and negative, and in all things of opposite characters. In order that this love principle—itself the original and the only principle at the back of the whole manifestation—may have the scope of its full play, therefore, the fulfillment of the purpose of life was in the full expression of the love principle.

Very often people, by learning philosophy and by looking at this world with a pessimistic thought, have renounced the world and have called it material and false; and have left this world and have gone to the forest or desert or cave; and have taught the principles of self-denial and self-abnegation and renunciation. That was not the way of Hafiz. He said it is like journeying over the sea and coming to a new port. And before landing, one becomes frightened, saying, "But I shall perhaps be attacked by the people," or "The place will attract me so much that I will not be able to go back where I have come from." But one does not know why one has taken that journey; one has not taken the journey to go back without landing. The attitude of Hafiz is to land there, to risk it. If it is an attractive place, he is ready to be won. If it will crush him, he is ready to be crushed. This is a daring attitude: not running away from this false world, but in this false world to discover glimpses of the true, and in this maze to find God's purpose.

27

Khwaja Shams ad-Din Muhammad Hafiz 2

THERE is another great revelation that Hafiz has brought before humanity in a most beautiful form.[1] Now, there are many people in this world who have once believed in God, in God's mercy and compassion, in God's love and forgiveness but, after having suffered, after seeing catastrophes and injustices, have given up belief. Many people, after great sorrow and suffering, have given up religion. The reason is that the religion they have followed has taught them God as goodness, God as judge. Well then, they ask from a judge, justice—justice to satisfy their own ideas. They think their standard of justice is God's. They look for goodness as they understand it, and therefore, there comes a time of struggle in their hearts. They do not see justice, because they are looking from their own point of view. They are looking for goodness, kindness, and mercy from their own point of view; and there are many conditions that make them think that there is no justice, that there is no such thing as a forgiving element.

But the way of Hafiz is different. The name of God is hardly to be found in the *Diwan*. He does not give that belief of God as the just and good. His God is his Beloved, to whom he has surrendered in perfect love and devotion; and everything coming from the Beloved is taken by him, with love and devotion as the reward. He prefers poison coming from the hand of the Beloved to nectar from another. He prefers death to life, if it is the wish of the Beloved.

1. Lecture given at Paul Elder Gallery, San Francisco, May 1, 1923.

But, you may say, is it fair? There is no question of fairness where there is love. Love stands above law. Law is beneath love. Law is born of love. The mistake in this day is that we keep law higher than love. We do not see that the divine principle, which is love, stands above law. Humankind makes God a judge who is bound by law, who cannot do individual will but has to do according to what is written in their book. God is not justice. Justice is God's nature, but love is predominant. People give such importance to actions and their results. They do not know that above action and result is a law which can consume the fire of hell, and which can dominate if the whole world was being drowned in the flood of destruction, and that the love power is greater than any other.

Think of the hen when she takes care of her little ones. If they were threatened with danger, though it were a horse or an elephant, she would fight, because the love principle is predominant. A kind mother is ready to forgive when her child comes with head bowed and says, "Mother, I have been foolish, I have not listened to you, I have been insolent, I am sorry." She is ready to understand, she is ready to forgive. So we see mercy and compassion going out as love, a stream of love that can purify all the evil actions of years. Then, if a human being can actually forgive, cannot God forgive? Many of the dogmatic religions have taken away the love element that is predominant, that makes God sovereign. And they make a god who is limited, who is bound by the book, and who cannot show compassion. If God were so limited, God could not be just. An individual would be better, because an individual can forgive.

Hafiz gives a picture of human nature: hate, jealousy, love, kindness, vanity, the play of friendly impulse, the play of pride—all aspects of life. Hafiz is not a poet, he is a painter. He has made a picture of the different aspects of life. Every verse is a picture. And in every picture, whatever be its color—vanity, pride or conceit, love, mercy, or compassion—in all its garbs, he sees only one spirit: the spirit of the Beloved. And he shows his devotion, appreciation, and love to all the manifestations of that one and the same Beloved.

There are many religions and beliefs where it is said that there will come a day when humanity will be able to communicate with God. But when will that day come? Life is so short, and our hearts so hungry! And if it does not come today, perhaps it will not come at all. Therefore, the only thing that Hafiz has pointed out from beginning to end is this: Do not wait for that day to come tomorrow. Communicate with the Beloved just now. The Beloved is before you here in the form of your friend and in the form of your enemy, with a bowl of poison or with a rose. Recognize it and know it, for this is the purpose of life. Religions have made this like a journey of millions of miles. Hafiz has made it right at hand.

Humankind likes complexity. It does not want to take one step; it is more interesting to look forward to millions of steps. The individuals who are seeking the truth get into a puzzle, and that puzzle interests them. They want to go through that puzzle a thousand times more. Just like children, their whole interest is in running around. They do not want to see the door and go out until they are very tired. And so with the grown-up people: they all say they are seeking truth, but they like the puzzle. That is why the mystics made the greatest truths a mystery to be given to the few who were ready for it, and to let the others play because it is the time for them to play.

As the love principle is the first principle according to the idea of the Sufis and according to the idea of all the prophets and knowers who have ever come to this world, so it is the last principle. There are different yogas practiced by the people of India that are the intellectual, scientific, philosophical, and moral paths to God. But the most desirable path to God that the Hindus have ever found, and that makes the whole life beautiful, is bhakti yoga, the path of devotion, because it is the natural path. Humanity's inclination is love. If one is cold, it is because one is longing for love; if one is warm, it is because love is alive. If one is suffering from depression, is yearning or sorrowing, it is because the love principle is not alive. The only life, the very source of inspiration, salvation, and liberation is love.

And among those great souls who have brought the message of God to humanity from time to time—Buddha, Krishna, Jesus Christ, Moses, Abraham, Zarathushtra—they were well known as most learned. And what they learned, they learned from the love principle. What they knew was compassion, forgiveness, sympathy, and tolerance; that attitude of appreciation; that opening of the heart to humanity. What they taught was love, a simple truth. If religions seem complex, they have been added to. In every case what was brought by the prophet was simple, and it was expressed in the prophet's personality and life; and it is that influence that has remained for centuries after the prophet has passed away. It is not the literature the prophets have left; most of the literature is from their pupils. It is the simple truth shown in the prophets' personalities and their lives.

The error of this day and age is that we cannot understand the simple truth, the truth as manifested everywhere, instead of trying to find truth covered in a shell.

Hafiz, at the same time, teaches one to see the ultimate truth and the ultimate justice in one and the same thing, and that is God. That justice is not related to things; perfect justice is in totality. And he shows that the power behind manifestation is the love power, and it is by this power that this whole world was created. It is the love principle, whether it works through God or humankind. And if that principle is at the back of the whole creation, then it is the same principle which helps humankind to fulfill the purpose of life.

28

THE SUFI'S AIM IN LIFE

BELOVED ones of God, my subject this evening is the Sufi's aim in life. The aim of every individual, in the end, is the same.[1] In the beginning, the aim of every individual is different. In the end, people come to a stage when their object becomes the object of their soul; and as long as they have not arrived at this object, they have several objects before them. But the accomplishment of any motive is not satisfactory for long.

According to the philosophy of the Hindus, there are four motives in life. One motive is what they call dharma, which means "duty." There are some who consider virtue in performing their duty, and when that particular duty is before them they perform it and feel that is the accomplishment of their life. But if one duty is accomplished, another is waiting—life is full of duties. When the child is young it says, "My mother, my father is my duty." Then a time comes that the pleasure of a spouse is one's duty; and as time goes on there is a duty of the parent toward the children. But even there it does not end: there comes the duty of the grandparent. There is no phase in life that duty expires. It begins in one form, and it goes on in another. For those who consider duty a pleasure, duty is their pleasure; for those who consider it a virtue, it is a virtue; but for those who consider duty as a captivity or a pain, for them it is a pain. For one person it becomes a virtue, for another it becomes an ache. For one it is a privilege, for another a crime.

1. Lecture given in Morges, Switzerland, November, 1922.

In the Hindu language there exists the word *artha* which means the "acquirement or collecting of wealth." It begins with the need of daily bread, and it culminates in millions and is never finished. The more one has, the less one feels one has. The attainment of wealth is never fully satisfactory—there is always a lack.

And then there comes a third motive, which is pleasure. For this one neglects, one sacrifices that which is the main object in life; but at the same time, pleasure is such a thing that desire is never satisfied. The more one experiences the pleasures of this earth, the more there comes a desire to experience. Pleasure is not lasting and costs more than it is worth.

And there is the fourth desire, which is of a different character, and that is in a kind of reward in the hereafter. It is for the attainment of a paradise or reaching some bliss that one does not know. It is a desire for some kind of gain or happiness, bliss or exaltation, which one does not know but hopes to experience some day. But even that, if it were vouchsafed, would not be fully satisfactory. And from this the Sufi derives that from all these four different things that humanity is pursuing, there is no stage where one can say it is finished. It has no end. Therefore, their effort is to arrive above these four different desires that humanity has. And the moment they rise above these four desires, there comes only one desire, and that desire is the search for truth. Not only Sufis, but every person disappointed in this world, has only this desire.

Seekers after truth go out in the world and find so many sects, so many different religions; they do not know where to go. Then the desire is to find out what is beyond, hidden under these sects, these different religions. And therefore, they find the object that they wish to gain in time and to find from wisdom. Wisdom is a veil over truth, but even wisdom cannot be called the truth. God alone is truth, and it is truth that is God. And truth neither can be studied nor taught nor learned. It is to be touched, it is to be realized; and that can be realized by the unfoldment of the heart.

For a Sufi, belief in God is not sufficient. A belief that has no foundation underneath is just like a scrap of paper. When there is no air, it will fall on the ground. How many in this world, with all their belief, give in when there is a strong influence in their surroundings of one who does not believe? If belief is such a thing that can be erased, then what use can this belief be for? Really speaking, it is not only belief; the next step one takes after belief is the love of God. For the one who only believes in God, in that person God is not living. For the one who loves God, in that person God is living. But even that is not sufficient, for what is human love? The human being is limited; human love is limited.

The more one has seen the world, the more one knows of human nature, the more one knows the falsehood of human love. Even those who cannot be constant to a human being who is around them, how can they be true in love for the Beloved, whom they have never seen? Therefore, even what humankind calls the love of God is not sufficient. What is necessary is the knowledge of God. For it is the knowledge of God that gives the love for God, and it is the knowledge and love of God that give a perfect belief of God. No one can have the knowledge of God and have no love of God, but one can have a love for God and no knowledge of God. No one can have the knowledge of God, love in God, and no belief in God; but there can be someone who has a belief in God but no love in God.

Therefore, for Sufis, these three stages are necessary for the attainment of their aim in life. In the first place, they accomplish with their belief a respect for the beliefs of others. Complete believers are those who do not themselves believe but who respect the beliefs of others. For Sufis, in this world there is no one, heathen or pagan, who is to be despised. For they believe in that God who is not the God of one, a chosen sect, but the God of the whole world. They do not believe in the God of one nation, but of all nations. For to them, if different houses where people worship stand in the street, it makes no difference. It is the holy place where they worship; they leave sectarianism to the sect. They have respect for all. They are not prejudiced against any nor despising any; they feel sympathy for all.

Now, about the love of God. The idea of the Sufis is that the one who does not love one's fellow human being cannot love God. They think, as Christ has said, "Love your neighbor; love your enemy."[2] And what does it mean? It means not to love them because you consider them enemies, but to love them because in God you are related to that person, there is a human bond. If humanity had belief in this simple and worthy and most valuable teaching, these wars would not have taken place. Do they think that all this hatred that exists—one nation against the other, one party against the other, there seems to be a conflict everywhere—do they think if the world had believed, it would not have taken place? Is it the work of the political people to bring this home to humankind, or the work of commerce? No, it is the work of the church, of the religion. But when religious authorities will make for themselves a sect and divide it, and look upon each other with prejudice, then the truth brought by Christ is not practiced.

You must know that every change that takes place in the multitude, in time, comes among the individuals. For instance, if two nations are against one another, opposed to one another, working to hurt one another, what will be the consequence? The result will be that in those nations there will be parties that will oppose each other. And when this will come, the same opposition will come in the families. And you will find that in time, that spirit will be found in a family of two people—two people living in a house and both in conflict with each other. And where will it culminate? It will culminate in the individuals in conflict with themselves.

2. Matthew 5:44 and 22:39.

Where does the Sufi learn this? A Sufi learns it in the wisdom of God. Those who do not recognize God in divine creation never will recognize God in humanity, where this whole creation stands before them. It is all right for those simple believers in God and religion who went quietly about and did not meddle with the world, but now the conditions have changed. Now there is a great battle between truth and life. Illusion of matter is in the fullness of the role that it is performing in life. Therefore, there is a greater battle that life is fighting with truth than religion has ever had before. On one side science cries: matter, matter, matter! On the other side the politicians are crying: self, self, self-interest! The religions are crying: sect, sect, sect! And where must humankind stop thinking about the ultimate truth that is the only thing that the soul seeks?

The Sufi message, therefore, has its mission, not for a particular race, nor for a particular nation, nor for a particular church. It is a call to unite in wisdom, which is *sophia* in Greek, and which we call Sufi. The order of the Sufis, the movement of the Sufis, is a group of people belonging to different religions, who have not left their religion but have learned a better understanding of their religion. And their service is in life, in the service for God and humanity instead of for a particular section. The principal work that the Sufi Order has to accomplish is to bring about a better understanding between East and West, and between the nations and races of this world. And the note that the Sufi message is striking at the present is the note that sounds the divinity of human soul—to make human beings recognize the divinity in the human soul. If there is any principle that the Sufi Movement brings, it is that the whole humanity is as one body; and any organ of that body, hurt or troubled, can cause trouble to the whole body indirectly. And as the health of the body depends upon the health of the whole body, so the health of the whole world depends upon the cooperation of every nation. Besides that, to the souls who are being awakened and who feel now there is a moment that they feel like knowing the deeper side of life and of truth, to them the order extends its help without asking them to what religion, sect, or dogma they belong. The knowledge of the Sufi is helpful to everyone, not only in living life aright, but in each one's own religion. The Sufi Order does not call people away from their belief or church; it calls people to live it. In short, it is a movement intended by God to unite humanity in kinship and in wisdom.

Thank you all for your sympathetic response. May God bless you.

29

RENUNCIATION

RENUNCIATION, in point of fact, is a denial of the self and the denial of that which one will use. As all things in this world can be used and abused, so the principle of renunciation can be used and abused.[1] If renunciation, as a principle, was a good thing, then there seems to be no purpose at the back of the whole creation. The creation might as well have not been manifested if renunciation was the principle. Therefore, renunciation in itself is neither virtue nor sin; it becomes a virtue or a sin according to the use we make of it. When one considers this from the metaphysical point of view, one finds that this principle is used as a staircase to come above things. It is the nature of life in this world that all things we become attracted to, in time, not only become ties but burdens. When we consider life, it is an eternal journey. The more one is loaded with burdens on one's shoulders, the more the journey becomes heavy. Think how the soul, whose constant desire is to go forward, is daily retained by ties, daily more burdens. Two things one sees: as the soul goes on, it finds on its legs chains; it wants to go forward, and at every step the soul goes forward it is more attracted, but it becomes more difficult to go forward. Therefore, all the thinkers and the wise who have come to the realization of life have taken renunciation as a remedy. A picture that the sage makes is like the fable of a dog and a piece of bread. A dog carrying a loaf in its mouth came to a pool and saw the bread

1. Lecture given at The Hague, the Netherlands.

in the water. When it saw its own shadow, it thought that the shadow was another dog. The dog howled, barked, and lost its own bread. The more we see our errors of human life, our petty desires, the more we find we are not far from the fable of the dog. Think of the national catastrophes lately,[2] and how these material things of the world, ever changing and not everlasting, have been pulled at and fought for. This shows that humanity, blinded by material life, disregards the secret, hidden things behind life.

When we come to reason out what we must renounce and in what way we must practice renunciation, there is a lesson to be learned, because no virtue is a virtue if it is forced upon one incapable of it. A person forced by a virtue, forced to renounce, cannot do the right renunciation. No virtue is a virtue if it gives pain. If it gives a pain, how can it be a virtue? It is called virtue because it gives happiness. That which takes away happiness is never a virtue. Therefore, renunciation is rightly practiced by those who understand renunciation and are capable of practicing it. For instance, there is a person who has only one loaf of bread. Traveling in the train, that person finds somebody hungry, in need of bread. That person is hungry also and has only one piece of bread. If that person thinks it is dharma to give, and starves and is unhappy about it, it would have been better not to give, because it has no virtue. If one has done it once, surely next time one will not, because one has suffered by it. The virtue brought unhappiness. This virtue will never develop one's character. That person alone is capable of renunciation who finds a greater satisfaction in seeing another with the piece of bread. The person whose heart fills with joy, full of happiness for the action, that person alone must do renunciation.

This shows that renunciation is not a thing that can be learned or taught. It comes by itself as the soul develops, when the soul begins to see the true value of things. All that is valuable to others, a seer's soul begins to see otherwise. This shows that all things that we see are precious or not precious—their

2. World War I and its aftermath.

value is according to the way we look at them. For one person, the renunciation of a penny is too much; for others, all they have is nothing. It depends on how we look at things. All things one renounces in life, one rises above. People are slaves of the thing that they have not renounced; of things that they have renounced, they become the ruler. This whole world can become a kingdom in their hands if people have renounced, but renunciation depends upon the evolution of soul. One who has not evolved spiritually cannot well renounce. For the grown-ups, little toys so valuable for children are nothing. It is easy for them to renounce. So it is for those who develop spiritually: all things are easy to renounce.

Now, the question is, how can one progress in renunciation? One progresses in this path of renunciation by becoming able to discriminate between two things: Which is better? Those with the character of the dog in the fable cannot renounce; they lose both things. Life is such that when there are two things before our view, it is demanded of us to lose one of them. It depends upon the individuals themselves, the discrimination of what to renounce and for what; whether to renounce heaven for the world, or the world for heaven; wealth for honor, or honor for wealth. Whether to renounce things momentarily precious for everlasting things, or everlasting things for things momentarily precious. The nature of life is such that it always shows two things. Many times it is a great puzzle to really choose between two. Very often one thing is at hand and the other further from reach. It is a puzzle whether to renounce one or how to get the other. Very often a person lacks willpower to renounce. It does not require only discrimination between two things, but also willpower to do what we wish to do. It is not an easy thing for us to do in life what we wish to do. Think how difficult is life—when we cannot listen to ourselves, how difficult then for others to listen to us! Many a time one cannot renounce because one cannot listen to one's own self.

Renunciation can be learned naturally. One must first train one's sense of discrimination to discriminate between what is more valuable and what is less valuable. That one can learn by testing it as gold is tested by imitation gold: that which lasts for a little while and then turns black is imitation; that which always keeps its color is real. This shows that the value of things can be realized by their constancy. You might ask if we should not recognize the value of things by their beauty. Yes, true, we must recognize beauty; but we must recognize beauty by its lasting. Think of the difference of price of the flower and of the diamond. The flower with all its fineness, beauty of color, and fragrance, falls short in comparison to the diamond. The only reason is that the beauty of the flower will fade next day, and that of the diamond will last. This shows a natural tendency. We need not learn it, we are always seeking for beauty, also for that which is lasting. A friendship that does not last, however beautiful—what value has it? Position, honor that does not last—what value has it? Although humanity is like the child running after all that attracts and is always changing, still the soul seeks constancy.

Therefore, in learning the lesson of renunciation one can only study one's own nature, what the innermost being is yearning for, and to try and follow one's own inmost desire. Wisdom comes by this process of renunciation. Wisdom and renunciation—both—go together. By renunciation, a person becomes wiser; by being wise, a person becomes capable of renunciation. The whole trouble in the lives of people in their houses and in nations and everywhere is always the trouble of an incapability of renunciation. If civilization can be explained in other words, it is only a developed sense of renunciation that manifests itself in consideration for each other. Every act of courtesy and politeness shows renunciation. When people offer their seats to others or offer something that is good, it is renunciation. Civilization, in its real sense, is renunciation. The highest and greatest goal that every soul has to reach is God.

As everything wants renunciation, that highest goal wants the highest renunciation, although a forced renunciation, even for God, is not proper, not legitimate. Proper renunciation is that done by those who are capable of it. There is a story of Abraham having sacrificed his son in the Bible.[3] People today are likely to laugh at some of the ancient stories, reasoning according to their own point of view. But think how many fathers and mothers have given their children as sacrifice in this war for their nation, their people, or their honor. This shows that no sacrifice can be too great a sacrifice for one's ideal. There is only the difference of ideal: whether it is a material or spiritual ideal, whether for earthly gain or spiritual gain, whether for humanity or God.

As long as renunciation is practiced for spiritual progress, so long it is the right way. As soon as renunciation has become a principle, renunciation is abused. Human beings, in point of fact, must be the masters of life. One must use renunciation and not go under in renunciation. Humanity is not for renunciation; renunciation is for humanity. So it is with all virtues. When virtues control one's life, they become idols. It is not idols we must worship; it is the ideal we must worship in the idol.

3. See Genesis 22:1–29.

30

FARID AD-DIN 'ATTAR

BELOVED ones of God, I am to speak today on the subject of 'Attar, and of his work.[1] Farid ad-Din 'Attar is one of the most ancient poets of Persia, and it is no exaggeration to say that the work of 'Attar has been the inspiration of Rumi and of many spiritual souls and many poets of Persia. He has pointed out the way to the ultimate aim of life by making a sort of picture in a poetic form. And almost all the great teachers of the world, if ever they have been able to show the right way to seeking souls, always have had to adopt a symbolical form of expression in the form of the story or legend that might give the key to one who is to know, and might interest the one who is not yet ready. And therefore, both may rejoice: the sleeping one and the one awakened. And this example has been followed by the poets of Persia and India, and especially the Hindustani poets. And they have made their story in such form that it would be acceptable, not only to the seekers after truth, but also to those in all different stages of evolution.

'Attar's best known work is called *The Conference of the Birds*, from which we have taken the idea of the bluebird; and very few have understood the idea of the bluebird or the conference of the birds. It is a very ancient teaching, through the use of the Persian word for sky. This points out that every soul has a capacity that may be called the sky, and this capacity can accom-

1. Lecture given at Paul Elder Gallery, San Francisco, May 8, 1923.

modate the world or the heaven, whatever it would partake of and hold in itself.

When one walks in the crowd, what does one see? One sees numerous faces. I call them various attitudes. All that you see in individuals, all that stands before you, has expression, has atmosphere, has form. If you call it by one name, it is attitude, the attitude they have toward life. Right or wrong, good or bad, whatever attitude they have, they are themselves that attitude. Does it not show how appropriate is the sky—which means whatever you call it, whatever you may think it? Plainly speaking, whatever one makes of oneself, one becomes. A source of happiness or unhappiness, all is in individuals themselves. When one is unaware of this, then one is not able to arrange one's life. And as one becomes more acquainted with this secret, one gains a mastery; and it is the process with which this mastery is attained that is the only fulfillment of this life. It is the process that is explained by 'Attar in his work of the seven valleys through which this bird of the sky had passed.

The first valley is that of the quest. How true it is that all children are born with the tendency to search, to know. What we call inquisitiveness or curiosity is born in them, and it represents that inner feeling of quest. This shows us that humanity is born with this; and one cannot be satisfied unless one has arrived at satisfaction, which means searching for the knowledge that one wishes to have. No doubt, what prevents people from gaining the knowledge that their soul is really searching for, is themselves. It is their small self, always standing against them, keeping them from the search of the only thing that is the seeking of every soul. And therefore, it may be safe to say that there is no one in this world who is a worse enemy of humanity than humanity itself.

In this search one thinks that one must perhaps find out, from science or from art, something that is behind it. And whether through material quest or spiritual, in the end one will arrive, and one must arrive, at that goal which is the goal of everyone. The scientists and engineers—people who are absorbed in making a search of material things and never think of spiritual things—even they, after a great deal of searching, arrive very near to the same knowledge, which is the ultimate knowledge. And therefore, whatever a person may seem to us —materialist, atheist, or agnostic—we cannot call them so, because in the end their goal is the same, their attainment is the same. If they really reach the depth of knowledge, if they go far enough, whatever their search, they will come to the same goal.

And when one has searched enough and found something satisfactory, still one cannot enjoy that satisfaction unless there is one faculty open, and that is the faculty of love and devotion. Do we not see in our everyday life that people of great intellect and wide interests very often seem to miss something? When it happens to be a couple where one is very intellectual, the other may feel there is something lacking to make their lives complete and may feel that intellect alone is not enough. What is it? It is the heart that balances life, and the absence of which keeps life dry. It is just like the positive and negative forces: knowledge and heart. It is these two things that make life balanced. If the heart quality is very strong and the intellect lacking, then also life lacks balance; knowledge and the heart quality must be developed in balance.

And therefore, according to 'Attar, that faculty of devotion or quality of heart is the second valley. And the third valley is the knowledge that illuminates, which comes by the help of the love element and the intellect. It is the knowledge that is called spiritual knowledge. Without the love quality developed, is humanity incapable of having that knowledge? I will answer, yes. There are fine lights and shades in one's life that cannot be perceived and understood fully without having touched the deeper side of life, which is the devotional side. The person who has not in life been wholly grateful, cannot know what it is. One who has not experienced in life humbleness, does not know its beauty. The one who has not known gentleness or modesty, cannot appreciate its beauty or recognize it. No doubt those of fine qualities are often ridiculed if they happen to be in a place where it is not understood, where it is a foreign language. This shows there is a fineness in life for which intellect alone is not sufficient. The heart quality must become open.

A very intellectual man went to Jami[2] and asked Jami to take him as his pupil and give him initiation. Jami looked at the person and said, "Have you loved anybody?" This man said, "No, I have not loved." Then Jami said, "Go and love first, then come to me, and I will show you the way." Love has its time in every stage of life. As a child, as a youth, as a grown-up person, and whatever stage of life one has reached, love is always asked for. And love has always its part to perform, whatever situation you are placed in: among friends or foes; among those who understand you and those who do not; in ease and in difficulty, in all places, at all times, it has its part to perform. And when one thinks, "I must not let the principle of love have its way, I must close myself against it," one imprisons the soul.

There is only one thing in the world, and that is pure, unselfish love, which shows the sign of heaven, which shows the divine sign, which gives the proof of God. For all the noble qualities that are hidden in the soul will spring forth and come to bloom when love helps them and nurtures them. A person may have a great good within and may be very intelligent, but as long as the heart is closed, that person cannot show that nobleness, that goodness, which is hidden in the heart. And the psychology of the heart is such that, once one begins to know the heart, life is a continual phenomenon. Every moment of life becomes a miracle; it throws a searchlight upon human nature, and all things become so clear that one does not ask for any greater phenomenon or miracle—it is a miracle in itself. What they call telepathy, thought-reading, or clairvoyance—all these things come by themselves when the heart is open.

2. Nur ad-Din 'Abd ar-Rahman Jami, Persian Sufi poet (1414–1492).

If people are cold and stiff, they feel within themselves as if they were in a grave. They are not living, they cannot enjoy this life, for they cannot express themselves, they cannot see the light and life outside, they are in their grave. And what keeps people back from the development of the heart quality? Their exacting attitude. They want to make a business of love. They say, "If you will love me, I will love you." As soon as people exact and measure and weigh their favors, their services, and all that they do for one whom they love, they do not know love.

Love sees the Beloved and nothing else. As Rumi says, whether you love a human being or you love God, there will come a day when all lovers, either of humanity or of God, will be brought before the throne of love, and the presence of that one Beloved will reign there. What does this show? In loving our friend, in loving our neighbor, even in the love that we show to our enemy, we only love God. And the one who says, "I love God, but I cannot love humanity," does not love God and cannot love God. It is like saying: "I love you very much, but I do not like to look at your face."

And after this third valley, where the knowledge of human nature and of the fine feelings that are called virtues is attained, the next step is what is called in the English language, annihilation. But what we call destruction or annihilation is nothing but change. Neither substance nor form nor spirit—nothing is absolutely destroyed. It is only changed, but humankind does not like sometimes to change. People do not know that they cannot live without change. They do not like it, but they cannot live without it. There is not one single moment of our life that change does not come; whether we accept it or not, the change is there. Destruction or annihilation or death might seem a very different change, and yet there are a thousand deaths that we die. Every disappointment, the moment when our heart breaks, is worse than death. Often our experiences through life are worse than death, yet we go through them. At the moment they seem unbearable; we think we cannot stand it, and yet we live. If, after dying a thousand deaths, we still live, there is nothing in the world to be afraid of. It is humanity's delusion, one's own imagination; one makes it dreadful to oneself. Can anyone kill life? If there is any death, it is for death; life will not die. To a Sufi, someone went with a question and said, "I have been puzzling for many, many years and reading in books, and have not been able to find a definite answer. Tell me, what happens after death?" The Sufi said, "Please ask that question of someone who is going to die. I am going to live."

The principle is that there is one sky, which is your own being. It is like the sky; in other words, you call it an accommodation. And who has taken possession of this accommodation? A deluded ego which says "I." It is deluded by this body and mind, and has called itself an individual. When one has a ragged coat one says "I am poor." In reality one's coat is poor, not oneself. What this capacity contains becomes one's knowledge, one's realization; and that limits a person, forms that limitation which is the tragedy of every soul.

Now, this capacity either may be filled with self or it may be filled with God. There is only a place for one. Either we live with our limitation or let God reign there, in divine unlimited being. In other words, we take away the home that always belonged to someone else, and fill it with delusion and call it our own—and not only call it our own, but call it our self. That is humanity's delusion, and all religious and philosophical teachings are given to rid humankind of this delusion that deprives humanity of its spiritual wealth. Spiritual wealth is the greatest wealth. Spiritual happiness is the only happiness; there is no other happiness.

Once people are able to disillusion themselves, they arrive at the stage described in the fourth valley, the valley of non-attachment, and they are afraid. They think, "How can I give my home to someone else, even if it is God? This is my body, my mind, my home, my individuality. How can I give it away, even to God?" But in reality, it is not something one can rely upon. It is delusion from top to toe and subject to destruction. Does anything stand above destruction? Nothing. Then why fear to think for the moment that it is nothing? That natural fear of humanity comes because it is unaccustomed to face reality. People are so used to dreams that they are afraid of reality. There is a fear in the minds of people of losing themselves, but they do not know that it is not losing oneself. It is losing illusion, and in reality they will find themselves when they lose this illusion. In this illusion one has lost one's soul, and the process is to come out of it, to rise above it.

When the fifth valley, the valley of unity, is reached, by that time one has disillusioned oneself; and it is that act that is called in the Bible rebirth, when the soul has become disillusioned. It is the birth of the soul. There is the birth of the body and the birth of the soul. And how does this birth of soul express itself? What does one feel? It first expresses itself in a kind of bewilderment with great joy. One's interest in life is increased; all that one sees, one enjoys. One concerns oneself little but wonders at all things. The bewilderment is such that it is a wonderful amusement to look at life. The whole world becomes a kind of stage, full of players. One then begins to amuse oneself with the people of this world, as one might play with children and yet not be concerned with what they do, for one expects no better. If children do something different from the parents, the parents are not much concerned; they know it is the stage of the child's life and one cannot expect any better of it. So with this person, likes and dislikes, favor and disfavor, interest but do not concern.

And there is another stage. This bewilderment brings people to see the reflection of that someone who has taken possession of their heart, to see their Beloved in everyone, even in their enemy. The Beloved is seen in all things. The bowl of poison given by the Beloved is not so bitter. Those who have sacrificed themselves and suffered for humanity, such as Christ, have given to the world an example showing a soul that has reached the stage where even the enemy appears before the eyes of the God-conscious as a friend, as the Beloved. And it is not an unattainable stage, because the soul is made of love; it is going toward the perfection of love. All the virtues a person has learned, love has taught to them. Therefore, this world of good and bad, thorns and flowers, becomes nothing but a place of splendor.

The sixth valley, the valley of amazement, is the valley where one recognizes and understands what is behind things, the reason of all reasons, the cause of all causes; for all intuition and power develop in a person with this unfoldment.

And the seventh valley, the valley of realization of God, is that peace which every soul is looking for—whether the spiritual or the material—seeking from morning until night for something that will give peace. To some souls, that peace comes when asleep. But for the God-conscious, that peace becomes their home. No sooner have they closed their eyes, no sooner have they relaxed their bodies and stilled their minds, and lost from their consciousness the limited, than they begin to float in the unlimited spheres.

31

FATE AND FREE WILL

BELOVED ones of God, my subject this evening is fate and free will.[1] This is the subject that comes up in the mind of every intelligent person. Very few people ask themselves if it is fate that governs their life or if it is their free will. And there is one temperament that takes one point of view, and there is another temperament that takes the other point of view. And when the people of these two opposite points of view meet together and discuss, they have a thousand reasons to give in support of their own arguments. For instance, those who think that fate governs life can find a thousand reasons by examining their own lives or by looking at the life of another—when one thinks of the mystery behind what we call coincidence; when one finds the secret of what one calls accident; and when one finds the times in life when success comes continually and other times when failure follows failure.

Besides that, when a person has perhaps one pain, a thousand other pains are also attracted. Often it happens that in one week's time a person has heard bad news from several places; and there are times when, in one day's time perhaps, from many corners good news comes. If a person wishes to see the truth behind what one calls fate, there are a thousand reasons. For instance, is it always the qualified who is successful? Is it always the most learned whose name and fame rises high? Is it always the most capable who becomes rich? Not always; very

1. Lecture given at Salle de l'Athénée, Geneva, October 13, 1923.

often quite the contrary. Often you will find those in business knowing very little about their business, but in every move they make there is a success. And there are others, perhaps they are learned and experienced and understand business, and yet they try all their life and success is never there.

And when we come to think about the point of view of those who think that there is free will, that there is no such thing as fate, we can give a thousand arguments in support of their idea also. There are many in this life who are lazy and inactive, and they will always say, "It is because of my fate that things go wrong. There is no use in taking any step." They remain where they are. Besides, for a person who has the desire to attain either health or wealth or power or rank or position or learning or wisdom, it is all attained by effort, by hope. One finds in the lives of individuals, as well as of the people collectively, that for those who make the effort to advance, there is the advance. In support of the idea, of the belief of the fatalist, one may quote the saying in the English language that man proposes, God disposes. And in support of those who believe in free will, one may quote an English saying that where there is a will there is a way.

Now, a question arises in the mind of an intelligent person: which to believe, the point of view of a fatalist or the point of view of those who believe in free will? And we come to a realization from the point of view of metaphysics. From a mystical point of view, both are right, and yet both lack the complete idea. It is like the blind people, after having seen the elephant by touching. One day some blind people were allowed to see an elephant. As they could not see, they went near to the elephant and touched it; and coming together, they began to dispute and to fight. One had felt that the trunk was the elephant, the other had felt its leg to be the elephant. When the argument went still further there came a fight of fists; and only someone who had seen the elephant said, "My friends, both are right. You have seen only part of the elephant; I have seen the whole."

The mystical point of view comes from the study of life, from the observation of life. The nature of creation is such that not only every object is an object, but even every person is an object. A chair is made to sit upon, and a table is made to write upon. And so every object is made for a certain purpose, and so there is a purpose in the life of every individual. Of course, people will become offended if they are told that they are a thing, not a being. But one must know that a soul begins its life as a thing. As everything, every object is affected by the climate, and the weather has its influence upon every object, so with human beings. Then what appeals to human sense? What appeals to sense, and what deludes humanity? What makes humanity intoxicated? All these things show that humanity is, so to speak, an object that is used by conditions.

Where does sorrow come, where does joy come in life? And then depression and fear and doubt and confusion? In all this people show that they are the instruments that are handled by the whole of life, by all conditions. But that is one part of their life. But the next part of their life, or the advance of human life, is different. And that life is such, that when one begins to distinguish and when one has choice and when one can attract or repel by one's power, there is something—a new life—developed. And what does this life represent in humanity? It represents heaven. The sense of distinction and the sense of desire, the sense of attaining and the power together with it of attaining, all this shows the heritage humanity has from heaven. And this shows that humanity has an earthly heritage and a heritage from heaven. The heritage that humanity has from the earth makes humanity a thing; the heritage that humanity has from heaven makes a human being. Then what does fate belong to? Fate belongs to the heritage in a person, the heritage that a person has from the earth. And to what part of a person's being does free will belong? It belongs to heaven, for it is from God. It is not only that the weather and conditions affect one and have their influence upon one, but also a human being is a tool in the hands of planetary influence, in the hands of visible and invisible influences. And therefore, the more heritage from the earth one has and the more one holds to the heritage one has from the earth, the more helpless one is and the more influenced by fate. But the more heritage one has from above, from heaven, the more portion of free will one has to rise above the influences of effect and conditions, or of the planets or of the beings, visible or invisible.

Is it necessary for human beings, then, to hold the heritage of the earth? Why should they not give it away and just keep and cling to the heritage they have from heaven? Certainly it is necessary to hold on to the heritage humanity has from the earth, for it is the only condition of living on earth: to wear the coat that is given humanity from the earth. And therefore, there is no fault on the part of human beings that they hold the heritage of the earth, for it was meant and necessary for their existence on the earth that they should have the heritage of the earth. It is only their fault when they hold and cling to the heritage they have from the earth, and neglect and ignore that heritage they have from heaven and which is the secret of their safety.

Friends, life is a continual rising. It is climbing a mountain; it is going to the top of it from its bottom. And when people are standing at the bottom of this life's mountain, they are a thing, they are subject to fate. They are not only subject to the planetary influences and to the effects from the visible and an invisible world, but they are also under the influence of their own thought, speech, and action. And in this way there is no end to their limitation. But as they rise upward, so they feel a freedom from all influences that belong to the earth, all influences to which the earthly beings are subject. And experiencing this freedom as they go upward, they experience more; and in this experience they find that secret of free will. Do not be surprised, therefore, in this world where one person is not much different from the other person in size of tallness or thinness, if you find such a vast difference between two people. If you heard one saying, "Oh, life is hopeless, nothing can be done. On one side there is a river, on the other side there is a stone wall. There is no way to go, there is nothing to be done. I wish I was dead." And there is another person who is saying, "There is nothing that is impossible, there is nothing that cannot be attained." Think of the vast difference between two souls: one in captivity, the other flying in freedom. What does it show? It shows one is conscious of the heavenly heritage, and the other is buried in the earthly heritage. A success for the first one is not a difficult thing. Whatever be the situation, whatever be the difficulty, that person will make a way. The condition will be heartbreaking, but that person's heart is something that cannot break, and it breaks conditions that stand against it. A person of the latter kind is hopeless, is pessimistic. Such a person has no courage, nothing to look forward to in life, and life becomes worse than death. For what is life? Life is not even the experience you have just now; life is something you look forward to. Rich environments, comfortable surroundings do not give happiness; they give pleasure and comfort for the moment, but they do not give life. Life is hope, life is aspiration. That which raises the eyes looking at the horizon, the something that I expect will come, must come. That soul is living, and not only living but life-giving to those who have lost their lives. Therefore, friends, it is good for a pastime to dispute whether it is fate or whether it is not fate, whether it is free will. Both these contrary beliefs are true, and yet the truth is beyond it.

What is, then, the teaching of the Sufis in this respect? The teaching of the Sufis is to observe life keenly, to analyze oneself and one's being, and to find within oneself what heritage one has from the earth and what heritage one has from heaven. One knows how to make the best of these heritages when one knows how to expand in order to draw from heaven the divine, which is given to humanity. And by doing this one rises above life's difficulties and troubles and worries that make one helpless. And as one goes on in the study and practice of what we call Sufism, one begins to see, in every moment of the day, an expansion of the soul and unfoldment of the spirit. The development of each being will not be at the same speed, but it will be in accordance with every individual's response to that divine heritage. For the conception of the Sufi is that life lives and death dies. The faith of the Sufi is in God, the Creator, the Almighty; and as this faith in the Almighty develops, so the power and influence over all things develops. And there arrives a day in one's life, when one begins to see the truth of that prayer which has been repeated by Christians for thousands of years: "Thy will be done, on earth as in heaven."[2] Then one sees that divine will is done in life through one's limited human personality. And as God's will is done, the promise of the life of humanity is fulfilled.

---

2. Matthew 6:10.

32

THE HEART QUALITY

BELOVED ones of God, I would like to speak this evening on the subject of the heart quality.[1] There are people who look at life through the brain and call it the head. And there are others who look at life through their hearts. And the points of view of these two kinds of people have a vast difference, and so much difference that something that one can see on the earth, the other sees in heaven. Something that one sees as small, the other sees as great. Something that one sees as limited, the other sees the unlimitedness of. These two people become opposite poles. It is like one looking at the sky, the other looking at the earth. And no one will admit that: "I look at things with my head," for everyone will say: "I look at life with my heart." But if one knows what it is to look at life from the heart, the best person in the world will say: "I have not yet learned to look at life from the heart. I would like to know it; I would like to learn it." One might say that there are emotional and devotional people flying in the clouds, and there are others with reason and logic standing on the earth. Yes, it is true. But in the first place, angels ride on clouds. If the soul has an angelic quality, the clouds are its spheres, not the earth. But one asks where is the place for practicality in life. Yes, but what one calls in everyday life practical, and what one is very careful about—what is it? How long does it last, what is it worth? No doubt that it is true that humanity is born on earth to bear the weight of this physical

1. Lecture given in Suresnes, France, September 6, 1925.

body with all its needs—a roof overhead and a piece of bread to sustain it. And if that is all there is to think about, people are making a great mistake if they devote all their life to what they call practicality, a practical life, and never think of the heavenly treasure that is hidden in the heart of humanity.

The heart is likened to water. Either it is frozen, and then it is snow; or it is water, and then it is liquid. When it is frozen, it has turned into a crystal. When it is liquid, it will be in a running order, for it is natural for the water to be running. And then there are two principal kinds of water: there is salt water and there is sweet water. The sea, which is quite content in itself and indifferent to everything else, has salt water because it is independent of anything else. It gives health, happiness, and pleasure to those who go around it, because it represents perfection, and it asks nothing from anyone. It is rising and falling within itself; it is independent. It is immense, and in that way it shows perfection. But with that independent perfection, its water is not sweet.

The ascetics who have closed their hearts with the perfection of God and with the realization of truth are like the sea: independent, indifferent to all things. Their presence heals people. Their contact gives joy, gives peace, and yet their personality is uninteresting. The water of the sea is salt water; and when the sea is calm, it is a pleasure to travel in it. And when the sea is rough, there is no worse illness than seasickness. And there is a powerful mind, a mind of a soul that has touched perfection. It is with the tranquility and calmness and peace that the mind gives everyone a way into it, as the sea lays itself before those who journey into the sea with open hearts. Ships and boats pass through, and those who journey enjoy their traveling in the sea. But when the perfect mind is disturbed with the wind, by the storm, it is perfect in its annoyance. It can shake the boats and steamers, and so that mind of the sage can have an effect upon all things in nature. It can cause volcanic eruptions; it can cause disasters.

But the little stream expresses the nature of an innocent heart—the heart that is innocent, the heart that cannot be prevented from being sympathetic, from being loving by any experience of the world that makes the water turn bitter. The bitter experience has not touched it, and it is pure and clear. It inspires the poets, and it uplifts a composer. It quenches the thirst of the thirsty one. It is an ideal spot for a painter to paint. With its modesty, it has purity; and with its purity it has life.

And then there is a water in a little pool, a little pool of water. It is sometimes muddy, sometimes dirty. Why? Because of its narrowness, it is small. In this way the narrowness of heart always has mud in it, because it is narrow and because it is not deep enough. Therefore, all the elements of the earth come into it and take away its purity.

But then there is the water of a large pool where water lilies grow and where little fishes swim; where the sun is reflected and where the moonlight produces a beautiful vision; where one would like to sit and look at it, because it expresses to everyone that sees it the liquid nature of the heart, the heart that is not frozen, the heart that has water. It is still, and it is calm. It is something that can make one's heart tranquil, to sit by its side. You can see in it your reflection, for it is calm, it is tranquil.

The water of the spring is most healing and most inspiring, because it comes from above and falls onto the earth; that is the character of the inspirational mind. The heart that springs, like a spring, pours water in the form of inspiration, be it in poetry, be it in music, in whatever form—in revolutions and all manner of things when once its tranquility is disturbed. Knowing this nature of the heart, and knowing the great powers that a person who has touched divine perfection possesses, the people in the East regard closely the pleasure and the displeasure of the sage. They think to annoy a sage is like annoying the whole of nature. To disturb the sage's tranquility means to shake the whole universe, because a storm in the sea is a very small thing, but the heart that has touched perfection, if once upset, can upset the whole universe.

But the water of the river is all sweet. It is sweet because it is attracted to the sea. It is longing to reach the sea. The river represents a loving quality, a quality that is seeking for the object that it loves. For a heart that loves God and God's perfection is likened to the river that seeks the sea. It is therefore that the personality of the seeker is more pleasant than the personality of the one who is content with what one knows. There is little danger in traveling in the river. There is a great joy in swimming in the river, and there is fine scenery to look around the river. And so it is with the personality that is like a river. That running of the feeling of sympathy, that continual running sympathy, means a living sympathy. It helps the trees and plants and the earth that is around it. And so is the kind, sympathetic people whose feeling is liquid. Then everywhere they go they take with them the influence that nourishes, which helps souls to flourish and to progress.

And there is a little stream sometimes that runs, which is not a river. It is a small little stream running, and it is even more beautiful to look at, for it expresses modesty. It expresses fineness of character. It expresses purity, for always the water of a little stream is pure. It has beauty, and it has healing quality. It can take away all the worries and anxieties and difficulties and troubles of those who come to it; and as the water of the spring, it does not only inspire but it heals.

And then there is a fountain that rises and falls in so many drops; this is made by human beings, and so personality is made by human beings also. When a person has made a personality, then through that personality the feeling that rises from the heart is like the fountain. Each drop falling from it comes in the form of a virtue.

But the water that rises from the sea toward the sky in the form of vapor represents the aspiration of the heart, the heart that aspires upward, that heart that wishes to reach upward.

That heart shows the quality of the vapor. It is the heart of the devotee, it is the heart of the seeker. It is the heart of the one who is always conscientious of seeking the higher ideal, touching the higher principles in the form of clouds. That heart of aspiration forms itself and pours down, just like the rain, in bringing the celestial beauty in the form of art or poetry, in the form of music, and in the form of anything that is good and beautiful.

There are hearts which have been impregnated by the fire for a long, long time, and there comes a sulfur water from them—purifying and healing, for it has gone through fire. It has gone through a suffering, and for those who suffer, it heals them. There are hearts with many different qualities, like different waters with chemical substances. Those who have suffered, those who have gone through patience, those who have contemplated, they all represent one or the other kind of the water that heals. And so are the personalities of people who have had deep experiences of any kind of suffering, of agonies, of love, of hate, of solitude, of association, of success of failure. They all have a particular quality—a quality which has a particular use for others.

And when one knows this, one will come to this conclusion: that whatever has been my life's destiny, my heart has prepared a chemical substance through sorrow or pain, through joy or through pleasure—a chemical substance that is for some certain purpose for humanity. And I can only give that chemical substance for the use of humanity if I keep my heart awakened and open. Once it is closed, once it is frozen, once it has turned from hot to stone, a person is no longer living. It does not matter what a person has gone through, for even the worst poisons can be of some use. There is no person, therefore, however wicked, who is of no use; if only a person knows that the condition of being useful to humanity is only one, and that is to keep the heart open.

Apart from all other things, when we come to spiritual attainment, it is something that we can never absorb through the head. It is something that can only be received from the heart. Let two persons, one with heart and the other with head, listen to the teachings of a teacher. One will be thinking, is it so or is it not so? Or how is it, if it is so? How can it be? And if it is, why is it? And there is never an end to the why. And others will listen with the heart. And both things—logic and reason—are at their disposal, but at the same time, they are not troubling them. Their hearts are open. They listen to it, and the quality of heart is such that whatever falls upon it, upon an open heart, becomes revealed instantly. Remember, when one says, "I cannot understand you," it is just like saying, "I have my heart closed to you." There is no other reason for not understanding. That is the only reason. And when one says, "I have understood it all," that means the heart was open. That is why the person has understood it. Therefore, understanding does not depend upon the head, it depends upon the heart. By the help of the head, one can make it more clear, it becomes intelligible, one can express it better. But it must begin, it must come from the heart, not from the head. Besides, a person with head says, "Yes, it must be so because I think so." The person with the heart says, "It is so because I believe it so." That is the difference. In one person there is a doubt, in the other there is conviction.

There is one thing, a word that is very difficult to translate; that word is called *iman* in the Eastern language. It is not exactly faith or belief. The nearest word one can find for it is *conviction*: a conviction that cannot be changed by anything, a conviction that does not come from outside. One always seeks for conviction. Will anybody convince me, or will this thing convince me? Nothing convinces, nobody convinces. Conviction is something that comes from one's own heart. And it is something that stands above faith and belief, because belief is the beginning of the same thing, and faith is the development of it. Conviction is the culmination of belief.

What is spiritual attainment? Spiritual attainment is conviction. People may think perhaps it is so. They may think about the best doctrine or about the highest ideal that there is, and they will think it is so, perhaps; but there is "perhaps" attached to it. But then there are others who cannot use the word *perhaps*, because they do not think about it. They cannot say it may be so when they know that it is so. When a person arrives at the stage when the knowledge of reality becomes a conviction, then there is nothing in the world that will change it. And if there is anything to be attained to, it is the conviction that one can never find in the outside world; it must rise from the bottom of one's own heart.

God bless you.

33

The Difference between Will, Wish, and Desire

BELOVED Ones of God, I will speak on the subject of the difference between will, wish, and desire.[1] Will is the development of the wish. When one says that it was divine will, it means that it was a command, a wish developed into action. When the wish becomes action, it becomes will, it becomes a command. One might think it is only one's wish, but it is wish as long as it is still there. It is there, it has not sprung up. It is inactive just like a seed in the ground; it is a wish. But the moment the seed from the ground comes out as a seedling and is in the process of becoming a plant, then it is a will. Therefore, these two different names are the names of the same one thing—the same thing in its undeveloped state, and the same thing in its process of development.

And now, I would like to explain what I mean by desire. It is as a weaker or primitive stage of the wish. When an idea, a thought, is not yet made clear in the mind, the mind has not taken a decision that it must be so, that "I would like it to be so." Then it is a desire, it is a fancy. It comes and it goes, and a person does not care. But when that desire is a little more developed, then it is a wish. Then it stays there; then it does not go away like clouds. It is tangible, it is there, and yet it is not fulfilled, because for fulfillment it must develop.

Now, there are some in this world who say: "All my life I had bad luck. The bad luck was this: that never in my life was my

1. Lecture given in Suresnes, France, June 27, 1926.

wish granted." They can very easily imagine also that this was because there was a spirit against them or something that was keeping back their wish. But it is not always so.

In the first place, God wishes the same that we wish. If God wished differently from our wish, we could not worship that God who always was against us. It is not so. Besides, there is no benefit in opposing the wish of humanity; there is no advantage in doing so to God. No doubt there are planetary reasons, there are reasons of the universe working, there are reasons of the cosmos that oppose the wish. As they say in English: man proposes, God disposes. The name God is put in the place of the cosmic forces, but God, with divine mercy and compassion, never has a desire to oppose anyone's wish. God apart, good-hearted people would never like to oppose anybody's wish; they would do anything possible to make anybody's wish complete, for a person's wish to come true. A kindly person would do it, but what mostly happens is that humanity proves to be the worst enemy of its own desire, for many reasons. There is one reason that people are never sure of their desires. One out of one hundred persons you will find who knows what is desired. But ninety-nine say: "Do I desire, or do I not desire? I do not know. I think I desire, but I do not know if I desire." Ninety-nine percent among humankind are in this condition. They really do not know if they desire. One day they say: "Yes, I do." Another day they say: "No, I do not think I desire." Therefore, their desires are decomposed in the unclearness of their minds.

Then there are others who analyze their desire. And they analyze it till they have broken it to pieces. There are many analytical people who have all through their life destroyed their desires by analyzing. And there is a third kind who have adopted a kind of passive attitude. They say it is a sin to desire, and yet they cannot be without a desire. And in this passive attitude, they say: "Well, I will not desire." They have crossed the desire that was there. And there is a fourth kind who desire something, but by the lack of concentration they cannot turn their desire into a wish. And therefore, desire stays in its primitive stage all the time. And there is a fifth kind who develop desire into a wish, but they go so far and no further. But the wish must be developed into the will, so the desire is not put through, so to speak, and there never comes a culmination of the desire.

Now, this is a subject that is of the greatest importance in the life of every person in the world. No person in the world can exist in the world without wishing for anything. And if there are those who have no wish, they need not stay in the world. They must go out in the mountains, somewhere to oversee the world. They must not be in the crowd, they cannot exist there. And even there, they should turn into a tree or into a rock in order to exist, because to be a living being without a wish is not possible. The difference between those high and low is according to the wish they have. One wishes for the earth; the other wishes for heaven. The desire of some takes them to the height of spiritual progress, and the desire of the others takes them to the depths of the earth. Humanity is great or small, humanity is wise or foolish, humanity is on the right road or wrong road, according to the desire it has.

And now, we come to the question of the opposing forces. There is, according to the Sufis, *qaza'* and *qadr*. Qaza' is a universal will, universal power. Qadr is the individual will and the individual power. No doubt the individual power in comparison to the universal power is like a drop compared with the sea. It cannot stand against the sweeping waves of the sea, for this comes and destroys it. Nevertheless, the drop, being of the same source as the sea, has also a certain amount of strength and individual will. It also has a certain strength and individual will to hold it against opposing forces.

But if we will make it more clear—the individual will and the universal will—it is in small things we can make it clear. A person who is walking in the street and says: "I feel hungry, I should like to go in a restaurant and have a meal"—now that is individual will. And a person goes in the street and sees a poor man and says: "Ah, this man seems to be poor. He must have something—can I not do something for him? I want to see him happier looking." As soon as one thinks for the good of another person, at once one's will becomes the universal will. The reason is that the boundary that limits the will of an individual is the thought of self. As soon as one has forgotten every thought of self, as soon as one thinks of another, that boundary breaks and the will becomes stronger. Those teachers of humanity, those who have been able to do great things in the world—where did they get their will? It was their own will that was expanded by the breaking of the boundaries of the thought of self. By this, I do not mean that one must never think of oneself, never think of one's lunch and dinner. The self is there, one has to think about it. But at the same time, in order to expand, in order to let the will grow, the more one forgets oneself, the more one is helped. There are some who take the path of resignation, neither doing good for themselves nor doing good for another. They say it is a kind of attitude they take: it will come from somewhere, or somebody will do it. If I am hungry, somebody will come and feed me; or if another person is in need, somebody will come and help that person. Their wish is not active. They do not let their wish become a will, they remain there. They are passive. No doubt an intelligent passiveness and resignation also can bring about a wonderful result, but many of them do it unintelligently.

The quality of the saints is to be resigned to all that comes, but then they do not even make a wish. They take all that comes; flowers or thorns, everything that comes, they take it. They look into thorns and see that they are flowers. With praise and with blame they are content. They are content—rise and fall, they take all that comes. They take life as it is; that is the intelligent way of doing it. The unintelligent way of doing is that for anything that is difficult one says: "Somebody will come and do it." It is laziness, it is a kind of laziness. They might think it is passiveness, but it is laziness if one has to do something and if one thinks somebody will come and do it. In India there is a saying that someone was lying under the cherry tree, and some ripe cherries were falling near him, but the cherries were just lying there. There was another who came from a distance. The person said, "Please come here. Will you please put this cherry in my mouth?" There are many to be found like this.

It comes only by a feeling, a helplessness, laziness. They give up. They have no enthusiasm, they have no courage. And in that way willpower is broken down, and in the end they are helpless. There is no comparison between the saintly spirit and the spirit of helplessness. Although both become resigned, the one is not resigned. He would like the cherry to be in his mouth; the other must give it. The saints do not care if they eat it or if they do not eat it. It is just the same to them. In that case it is allowable.

Then there are others who are overly anxious for their wish to come true. They destroy the wish, because of the greater strength, the pressure they put upon their wish. It is just like guarding a plant against the sun and the water. The very thing that should help it to grow—if one guards it against it, then the plant cannot grow. It is the same thing with the wish. If people say: "This is my wish and must come true. No one must think about it, no one must look at it," they are always afraid that perhaps this will not come true. They are eager, but then they are always thinking with doubt, fear, and suspicion. Therefore, that will destroy their own wish.

And again, there are those who are willing to sacrifice anything or to persevere as much as it requires for even a small wish, which they do not value very much when it comes to value. And yet they give every thought, and they do everything in their power to get that wish to come true. They are taking the same path as the path of the teachers. They must have success, and it is success which brings a success. If once a person is successful, the success attracts success. Once a person fails, then failure attracts failure, for the same reason that if one is on the path of accomplishment, each accomplishment gives one a greater power to go forward. And when a person is going downward, then every step leads one downward.

And now, the question is which desire and wish one must give up and which one one must rear. One must have that discrimination. If there is no discrimination, then one will take a wrong way. It may be a success, but success will be in a wrong way. If one tunes every desire and wish and thought that must be accomplished, then sometimes it may be right and sometimes it is wrong, not right. The discrimination must be first developed to know what leads one to happiness, a lasting happiness, a greater peace, a higher attainment. But once one has discrimination and has chosen a wish, then do not analyze it too much. Many have formed a habit of analyzing everything every day. If people hold a wish for ten years, and after every day they analyze it in their mind, they are against it. They look at it from a new point of view, they try to find the wrong points of their own wish and try to crush it in every way possible. Then in ten years' time when their wish should come true, it is broken into pieces. Many intellectual people, many people with doubts, many analytical people are the greatest enemies of their wishes.

And now there comes a question: If a person expresses a wish in prayer, is it wrong? Because many say that since God knows everything, why must you tell God that such and such thing should be done? God knows the secret of every heart. Besides, is it not selfish, many ask, to bring our wishes before God? If it was a good wish, it must come true by itself. The answer is that prayer is a reminder to God, prayer is a song sung before God, who enjoys it, who hears it, and who is reminded about something. But one thinks: "How can our prayer, our little voice reach God?" It reaches God through our ears. God is within us. If our soul can hear our voice, God can hear it too. Prayer is the best way, because the wish is beautifully put, which harmonizes one with God, which brings about a greater relation between humanity and God. And then one asks: Is it good to think about the wish one has? I say one can never think too many times of the wish one has. Dream about it and think about it and imagine it and keep it in mind and retain it in mind and do everything possible toward its fulfillment, but with poise, with tranquility, with patience, with confidence, with ease, and not by thinking hard.

The one who thinks hard about a wish destroys it because it is just like too much heat or too much water to a plant; the very thing that will help it, destroys it. If one worries about a wish, one certainly either has no patience or has some fear or some doubt; all these things destroy the wish. A wish must be cherished easily, with comfort, with hope, with confidence, and with patience.

Doubt is like a rust to the wish: it eats it. And fear is still worse: it destroys it. And when one has no discrimination and one is not sure whether it is a right wish or a wrong, whether it should come or not, then one day: "I should so much like it to come," and another day: "I do not care if it comes." After a week, one says: "I wish it so much to come." And after a month, one says: "Oh, I do not care now." It is just like making a fire and then putting it out, and then making a fire and again putting it out and extinguishing it. And therefore, every time one extinguishes it, the fire is gone, and one will have to make it anew. And if for ten years one has cherished it, made that wish, each time it is broken one has to make it anew.

And now going to the question of what wish is the most desirable to make. It depends upon one's own stage of evolution. Those who are only so much evolved that they can make no greater wish than the need of their daily life, they may do it; they must not think: "Because it is the need of daily life it is nothing, I must wish for something higher." They must not think that. If they think that their heart is inclined to the need of daily life, they must think of it first. But if the heart thinks: "No, I cannot think about it, I can think of something much higher than this," then one must take the consequences for it. The consequence will be that one must go through a test and trial, and if one does not mind, so much the better.

There are many things in this world that I want and that we need, and yet we do not necessarily think about them. If they come, it is all right; and if they do not come we feel for the time uncomfortable, but that feeling goes away. We cannot put our mind upon them if we are evolved, because if we are evolved, we think of something else. We think of something higher. Our thought is involved in something much higher, and this slips from our grasp. And it is therefore that greater poets and thinkers and saints were very often hard up for things that one could get in everyday life. With all the power that they had, they could command all the gold to come to their house; they had only to command it. If they commanded the army to come, it would come—the army, everything. Anything they could command would come with that command, yet they could not put their minds to it. They could only wish something which was equal to their particular evolution. So each one can wish for something equal to one's evolution. One cannot wish properly for something that is beneath one's evolution, even if one was told.

Very often, in order to help a person in a present situation, I have told the person: "Now, think of this particular object." But the person, being much more evolved, has thought with the brain, but the heart was somewhere else, and so it never came true. One can give one's heart and mind and whole being to something that is equal to one's evolution. If not equal, one cannot give one's whole being to it. Maybe one gives one's thought to it, but what is thought without feeling? Thought without feeling is not power. If there is not the soul and the spirit at the back of it, there is no power. So it must be understood that our wish must be different from what we need in everyday life. Never mix it; always think that what we need in everyday life is one thing, it is something practical. If it be our wish, then it is all right to cherish it, to maintain our wish as something sacred–something given to us by God to cherish–and to bring it to fulfillment. It is in the fulfillment of one's highest and best and deepest wish that there lies the purpose of life.

God bless you

34

THE POWER OF THOUGHT

THERE are some who, by life's experience, have learned that thought has some power; and there are others who wonder sometimes if thought really has some power.[1] But there are many who listen to this subject with the preconceived idea that even if every thought has a power, it also has its limits. But if I were to give my candid opinion on the subject, I would say that it is no exaggeration that thought has a power which is unimaginable. And in order to find proof of this idea we do not have to go very far. All that we see in this world is but a phenomenon of thought. We live in it, and we see it morning till evening, and yet we doubt if it is so. This doubt gives us a pride and shows that we understand things better. The less one believes in the power of thought, the more positively one thinks one stands on the earth. Nevertheless, consciously or unconsciously, one feels one's limitation and is searching for something that will strengthen one's belief in thought.

Thought can be divided into five different aspects: imagination, thought, dream, vision, and materialization. Imagination is that action of mind which is automatic. From morning till evening, either a person is working or is resting; and if resting, that person's mind is working just the same through imagination. It is automatic thinking; what it produces is called imagination. And then we come to the word *thought*. Thought is thinking which has willpower behind it. And in this way we

1. Lecture given at the Sorbonne, Paris, March 24, 1925.

distinguish between the imaginative and the thoughtful. And therefore, these two kinds of people cannot be confused, for one is imaginative whose thinking is powerless, automatic; and the other is thoughtful whose thinking is powerful.

And when this automatic action takes place in the state of sleep, it is called a dream. No doubt, this is distinct and different from imagination, because while a person is imagining, the senses are open to the objective world, and therefore, the imagination does not take a concrete form. But the same automatic action of mind goes on in the dream, and there is no objective world to compare it with. Therefore, the dream brings more imagination than a wakeful state. Therefore, the mystic can always see the person's condition of mind by hearing the dream of the person, by knowing about how a person dreams; because in the dream the automatic working of the person's mind is much more concrete than in the imagination.

There are some who can perhaps read the character of a person, some who can read what they call the future by knowing what a person imagines. They always ask a person, "Give me a name of a flower, of a fruit, of something you love, you like," so that they can find the stream of imagination, where it goes. And from that stream of imagination they find out something about the character of that person and about that person's life. And it is not necessary for a person to be a character-reader or a fortune-teller in order to know what any wise and thoughtful person can understand by the way someone dresses or by someone's environment. A thoughtful person can understand what way someone's thoughts go, what someone's imaginations are. Since the state of dream gives the mind the possibility to express itself more concretely, the dream is the best way to understand in what state of mind a person is. And once that is understood, there is little reason left to doubt whether the dream has any effect upon a person's life and future. For I would repeat the same thing again that I have said at the commencement of my lecture: that a human being does not know, and cannot imagine, to what extent thought works upon life.

And now, coming to the question of what we call vision. In order to make it simple, I would explain vision as that state of dream which one experiences in the wakeful state. A person who is imaginative or a person who is capable of imagining is capable of making a thought. And when this thought which one has created becomes one's own, an object upon which one's mind is focused, then all else becomes hidden; there is only that particular imagination that stands before one as a picture. No doubt, the effect of this vision is greater than the effect of a dream. The reason is that this imagination, which can stand before one's mind in one's wakeful state, is naturally stronger than the imagination which was working in one's state of sleep.

But then the fifth aspect is materialization of thought, and it is in the study of this subject that we find the greatest secret of life. No doubt, a person if asked will accept that it is by the architect's imagination that the beautiful building is built, that it is by the gardener's imagination that a beautiful garden is made. But when it comes to nature and all things that spring from nature, then one begins to wonder how far imagination or thought has any power upon it. Nowadays, as psychology is beginning to spread throughout the Western world, people would at least patiently listen to what it is. But otherwise there are many who would take a medicine and have a great belief in it, but if they are told that a thought can cure you, they will smile at it. And this shows that, with all the progress that humanity seems to have made, it has gone backward in one direction; and that direction is in regard to the higher thought, the elevated thought. For a person today generally disbelieves in thought and still less believes in what one calls emotion. And in the point of fact, if there is a soul to be found in thought, that soul is the feeling which is at the back of it. The reason is that souls become confused when there are only words and there is no feeling behind them. What convinces in a thought is the power behind it, and that power consists of feeling. The general tendency is to wave off what is called imagination. "Those ones imagine" means that "those ones amuse themselves." When a person says, "Oh, you think it, but it does not exist in reality. You just think it." But in reality when one has imagined, that imagination is created, and what is once created exists. And what is thought exists, and that lives longer, because thought is more powerful than imagination. And what a person today calls sentimentality, which means nothing, in this way ignores that power which is the only power and the greatest power that exists. It is with this power that the heroes have conquered battles. And it is with this power that, if anyone has accomplished a great thing in the world, it is with the power of heart that one has accomplished it and not with the power of brain. The music of the most wonderful composers and the poetry of the great poets of the world—it has come from the bottom of their heart; it has not come from their brain. And if we close the door to sentimentality, to imagination, and to thought, that only means that we close the door to life.

And now, coming to fancies and fantasies. Perhaps some, if not all of you, have read the stories of fakirs and dervishes in the East. Perhaps you have read about them in a novel, and perhaps they have been exaggerated in some way in order to make the book more beautiful. Nevertheless, I ask you to study the matter a little more and to understand something of a race, a nation, that has for so many thousands of years devoted itself, at the sacrifice of the whole life, to thought.

There exists perhaps in every little district, in every little village, a person who is called the healer of the scorpion sting. And in the heat, as it is in India, scorpions can be found in the house, especially in summertime. And it is not seldom that a child or a grown-up person is stung by a scorpion, and the sting is very poisonous and very painful. But, in spite of all that, there are healers, and several of them. And sometimes there is a healer who says, "You are cured. It is gone." And immediately the person is well. And then we come to the sting of the snake-bites. The poison of the serpent is such that hardly a person lives after a serpent bite. There are some who by the passing of their hands have cured it. There are some who have cured it by saying, "It is cured."

And then I will tell you my own experience, that once there was a dervish to whom a person came and said, "There is a case going to be in the court next week." And he said, "I am so poor that I cannot even have a lawyer to speak for me. And the other person, being rich, he will use every influence, and I am without it." And that dervish said, "Tell me what is the condition." And after hearing it all he said, "As you are not found guilty in this, I dismiss this case." He told him simply to go, "All will be well." When the man went to the court, he was asked everything by the judge; at the end, the judge wrote exactly the same words that the dervish had said. If I were to give any explanation, words fail to explain it. Only this can be said, that the heart of the judge, for this dervish, was just like the receptive machine of wireless telegraphy.

The great seer and mystic of Persia, Jalal ad-Din Rumi, says that, "Fire, water, earth, and air are dead things to those who see in them no person. But before the Creator they are all live beings; they are the Creator's obedient servants." And the great thinker of the Hindus says in the Sanskrit language that this whole creation is the dream of Brahma, which means the Creator.

And now I come to Sufism and what the Sufi thinks of the idea of the Creator and the creation. The Sufi sees both, the Creator and the creation, in humanity. The limited part of the human being is the creation, and the innermost part of the human being is the Creator. And if that is true, then the human being is both limited and unlimited. If one wishes to be limited, one can be more and more limited. If one wishes to be unlimited, one can be more and more unlimited. If one cultivates in oneself the illusion of being a creation, one can be more and more that. But if one cultivates in oneself the knowledge of the Creator, one can also be more and more that.

With every kind of weakness, every kind of illness, every kind of misery, the more one gives in to it, the more it falls upon one's back. And one can even give into it to such an extent sometimes that the whole world falls on one's back and one is buried under it. And then there is another person who gets out of it. It may be difficult, but at the same time it is possible. Little by little, gradually, but with courage and patience, one can get out of it and stand upon the same world which would have otherwise crushed one under it.

The former thing is going down, the latter thing is coming up. Both things depend upon the attitude of our mind, and it is changing this attitude that is the principal thing in life, whether from a material point of view or from a spiritual point of view. All that is taught in the Sufi esoteric studies and practices is to gain that mastery in order to arrive little by little, gradually, at that fulfillment which is called mastery. But, you will say, it is a great struggle. But, I will answer, the struggle is in both ways; in coming down and in going up; in both ways there is a struggle. It is just as well to struggle and come up instead of struggling and going down. And whenever a person goes down, it only means that person is feeble in thought. And why that person is feeble in thought is because that person is weak in feeling. If feeling protects thought, and if thought stands firm, whatever be the difficulty in the life of a human being, it will be surmounted.

35

East and West

BELOVED Ones of God, it is my great happiness to speak to you this afternoon on the subject of East and West, being invited by Mr. Otlet,[1] the friend of East and West.[2] For it is the friendship for the East and for the West which gives him that scope of serving the world at large. I very much wish that at this time there were more souls like he, who are open with their hearts to all the wisdom coming from different sources, from different parts of the world; so as the Palais Mondial accommodates the world, so does the heart of our friend.

Now, coming to the question of East and West. In order to distinguish East from West, it is natural that I shall give the points where they differ. Now, the points that differ, if we thought about them more, we shall say the same thing as the great English poet has said, "East is East, and West is West, and they can never meet."[3] I should like to first give those points that prove his saying true. The idea is that the people in the East, in all ages, had one object in view, and that object was to get in touch with the deeper side of life. Some came sooner to that point, some later; some had to struggle along, and for

1. Paul Marie Ghislain Otlet (1868–1944) was a Belgian visionary and peace activist who co-created an international center called Palais Mondial.
2. Lecture given at Palais Mondial, Brussels, December 18, 1923.
3. "Oh, East is East, and West is West, and never the twain shall meet," from "The Ballad of East and West" by Rudyard Kipling.

some it was easy. But naturally, to the wise and foolish there was less contact with the outer world. By this I do not mean to say that there are not people who are after material gain and material things, and that there are not people who love wealth and all that belongs to the earth. There are earth worshipers in all places, and there are hell worshipers in all places. This is just talking about the generality. Now, for instance, if you go among the most learned people in the East, they will show their great learning and knowledge about things, about science and about art; but at the same time, you will find it is all to gain the knowledge of the deeper side of life. You can see artists there, and you can talk to them. You can find that in any work they are doing, you can see that their whole motive is to gain the deeper side of life.

In the same way, for the politicians and warriors of that time, their minds were always attached to the same idea. For instance, we have before us the history of the Prophet Muhammad, a prophet who was not only a mystic but a general of his army and a statesman who was the first in the history of the Orientals to make a constitutional government in Mecca, the first constitutional government in the world. Those who formed the first parliament in Medina, which was called Madina, gave every man and every woman in the city the right to vote in that parliament. Remember, it is now fifteen hundred years ago. Muhammad was born in Mecca and was three times exiled from his place because he was giving new ideas of religion that were not agreeable to his people. There were people who killed his disciples and made every kind of difficulty, and all sorts of sufferings were thrown upon him. There came a time that he had a large number of disciples, when he said, "Shall I again go to my motherland? I want to go again and give the message which I have tried to give." They said, "Prophet, we shall come with you, and we shall give our lives in the cause. And we shall see that your message is received in the same land where they have insulted you, and three times you have been thrown out."

Muhammad went with his army of disciples not for invasion, but to give the message. But hearing that, he came with an army. They prepared an army, and there was a battle. In the end, Muhammad was victorious and entered Mecca. When he entered, the whole arrangement there—all the leaders—surrendered, and all those people were brought before him. When they were brought before him, he asked, "What treatment do you expect from me?" "What treatment could we expect," they said, "except the fitting treatment that would come from the prophet of God." And the answer of the Prophet was, "Yes, the same treatment will be given to you; all you have done to me and to my people, I have forgiven." He turned to his army and said, "Have you come for territorial ambition" "Not in the least," said the warriors, "but for truth and for the ideal." "Do you then not wish any money from these men?" "No," said the warriors to the Prophet. "Then what do you want?" They said, "We have come, we have followed you to your country, but we want you." The Prophet said, "Yes, they will take my message, but I will go with you." After all that war and bloodshed, what did the Prophet do? He left the Qur'an and gave the principles, then left for Medina, and died.

The kinship between the people of Mecca and Medina that was founded then still exists now; and if today you saw the effect of that teaching in the most ordinary working people in the desert, they would not simply surprise. Arabs, as a rule, are ready to fight, and it takes them not a single moment to take their knives and grab each other's necks. But for such a furious and angry race as that, when two Arabs are fighting together, if a third person says to forgive one another or love one another in the name of the Prophet, they throw down their knives and shake hands together. Just on hearing that, no longer do they continue their grudge or complaint; they do not judge one another. As soon as forgiveness has come, it is finished.

I have very often seen domestic servants who have never had an education and who do not know how to write their names.

As soon as you begin to touch their sentiment and their hearts, the worthlessness of the material life is known to them as much perhaps, as to a great philosopher. They will talk to you on philosophy, perhaps for an hour, and from their deepest sentiment, with a full understanding of the worthlessness of this four days' life on the earth.[4] This does not mean that the East did not make a particular progress in material things, because if one takes, for instance, the science of medicine, the books of Avicenna[5] give us proof that he made a foundation for the whole world. Today I know one of my friends, a doctor in England,[6] who has studied Avicenna, and who has found out that the outline of medicine was made by him and was first introduced in Spain.

And in music, the music of the Vedas was not only a music but a psychological expression of sound and rhythm. And therefore, it was not only a music, but it was also a mystery for life and for health; a science so perfectly formed that it was useful not only for the worldly things but for a meditative purpose. Music became the most essential part in religious things. Now, today a man[7] comes and tells the world about the repetition of a word that cures people from illnesses. The scientific and unscientific world seems to be moving about and says, "What is this? It seems such a new thing." If the same man happens to go to the East, every person in the poorest house will say, "We have known that, we are doing that every day. We know what the power of the word means." They will not be able to give a definition; for that one must ask a learned person. In the form of Vedanta, religion was a science that has always existed, only it was not given to the world in an alphabetical manner; someone with an alphabetical science tells it, and it astonishes everyone.

4. Indian expression meaning a long period of time.
5. Abu 'Ali al-Husayn ibn Sina, (980–1037).
6. Dr. Oskar Cameron Gruner (1877–1972).
7. Émile Coué de la Châtaigneraie (1857–1926).

Now, coming to the Western world. In the first place, for a race which came from the ancient Aryan sources into a country where they had the difficulties of climate, where it was necessary that life had, owing to the climate, great responsibilities, it naturally made them more active; and being active, activity with the things of matter gave them communication with matter, the result of which is a phenomenon. All these inventions that we see today, are no less than a phenomenon—a miracle. But this miracle has come from communication with things of the earth and, as the product of things of the earth, is as visible and tangible as the earth. Now, for instance, if a parent has two children, and one day one child makes a rattle, another day a bicycle, a third day an airplane. The child has something to show its parent and says, "Look here, I have got something! Look here!" Another child is sitting, one hand upon another hand, and perhaps in its character, thoughts, and feelings is developing something but has nothing to show. It is something developing within, which the child itself cannot define very well; nor can others see it. Therefore, it is natural that progress made in the objective line is visible and tangible; for progress in the spiritual line it is difficult to say how far one has reached.

However, with all that difference human nature is the same. Those who have developed in their thought, in their feelings, are not only in the East; there are many of them to be found in the West also. Besides, those who have a material inclination and produce something from matter are not only in the West; they are in the East, also. But in the West there is scope to bring out what one has invented, what one has found out. But in the East, there is no scope to bring it out, and in this way, the difficulty arises. Nevertheless, the East and West both have their actions directed in two different poles. The material progress of the East has been hindered by one thing, which is the climate—a climate which makes the whole day useless. One would rather sit and dream than be active and work. That also makes a difference in inclinations. Besides that, very much of Western progress is due to the uniformity of the people, and the backwardness of the East in that line of progress is due to the lack of uniformity. Every person in the East has an individual progress. And whenever there is individualistic progress, it is a very free progress but, at the same time, a progress that is not recognized by the ones who do not understand individualistic progress.

I mean that if a scientist comes with a new invention that is not understood by other scientists, they will certainly oppose it. Therefore, all intelligent people in the East, whenever they progress in their own line, have a great opposition to meet with and find no one who can perfectly understand them. But in the West, it is the contrary. There are academies and associations and people who understand things; there are people to understand and encourage. No doubt uniformity pulls people back from the progress that comes from individualistic progress. Nevertheless, the idea is this: that now the time has come when, owing to the ships and trains and all these different communications, the East and West have been brought together. And that brings us to a great hope that East and West, which depend for their progress upon their mutual exchange and understanding, will soon come to unite. In industry, in politics, in all things, they can unite and benefit each other. But the greatest benefit that can come from the meeting of East and West together is by the interchange of thought and ideal. In order to meet in the light that is the light of intelligence and which is divine by nature, the Sufi Movement has directed all its efforts so that the East may be able to appreciate all that is good and worthwhile in the West, and so that the West may understand and sympathize with all that is worth understanding and sympathizing with in the East. Words cannot explain to what extent the world will become benefited if once this idea is realized, because just now, with the East working in its own way and the West working in its own way, it is like working with one eye open, the other eye closed.

It is in the unity of East and West that the vision will become complete, and in this completion, the great disasters and troubles which have kept the world in a kind of uneasiness will be rooted out. And, by the unity of East and West in wisdom, there is a real peace to be anticipated

36

THE AWAKENING OF THE SOUL

BELOVED Ones of God, my subject this evening is the awakening of the soul.[1] One sees that there is an awakening from childhood to youth, and from youth to a mature age. And in this development one's point of view is changing, one's outlook on life is changed. And then one sees that sometimes in one's life, one has gone through an illness or through a great suffering, and at the end of it the whole outlook on life has changed.

One also sees that a person has taken a long journey, and after having come from that journey the person is quite changed. Also one sees that after a friendship, after a pupilship, after a marriage, a sudden change comes in the outlook of a person. When we look at this we find that there are some cases where the change is so great that one can say that the person is entirely a new person. And then we see this, we can class such a change—which may be called a development—into three classes.

One class is pertaining to physical development. Another class is connected with the development of the mind, and the third class with the development of the soul. There are instances in the lives of many who will rarely say or admit it but, at the same time, they can recollect experiences in their childhood in which, after one moment's time, their whole outlook on life changed. As ripening is the desired result, it is the result of

1. Lecture given in Paris, December 1924.

every object in life to ripen and develop. Therefore, the fulfillment of life's purpose is to be expected in the awakening of the soul.

And now one might ask: What are the signs of the soul's awakening? The first sign of the soul's awakening is just like the birth of an infant. The infant, from the time of its birth, is interested to hear something—any sound that comes—and to see something, if it is a color or light, whatever it be attracted to. And therefore, those whose souls have awakened become awake to everything that they see and to everything that they hear. Compared to them, everyone else seems to be with open eyes and yet not seeing, seems to be with open ears and yet not hearing. And therefore, there are many with open ears, but one rarely who hears; and many with open eyes, but hardly one who sees. It is therefore that the natural seeing of the awakened soul is called clairvoyance, and that the natural hearing of the awakened soul is called clairaudience. Therefore, in English there is a simple word, and that word is *seer*; and that word explains that the seer has eyes, but together with the eyes, a sight. The moment the soul has awakened, to that soul music makes an appeal, poetry touches it, words move it, art has an influence upon it. It no longer is a sleeping soul; it is awakened, and it begins to enjoy life to a fuller extent.

It is this awakening of the soul that is mentioned in the Bible: that unless the soul is born again it will not enter the kingdom of heaven.[2] The soul being born again means that the soul is awakened after once having come on earth [*text missing*], and entering into the kingdom of heaven is in the same kingdom. This world in which we are just now standing, the same kingdom, turns into heaven as soon as the point of view has changed. Is it not interesting, and is it not most wonderful to think that the same earth that we walk on is earth to one person and heaven to another?

2. John 3:3.

And it still is more interesting to note that it is we who change it; we change it from earth to heaven, or we change it otherwise. And this change comes not by a study, not by anything else, but only by one thing, and that is the changing of our point of view.

I have seen people seeking after truth, people studying books about it, people having read hundreds of books on theology, and in the end they are in the same place where they have been standing before. This shows that all outward efforts are excuses. There is only one thing that brings one before reality, and that is the awakening of the soul.

All tragedy in life, all miseries, all inharmony and misunderstanding is caused by one thing, and that is the lack of understanding; and lack of understanding comes from lack of penetration. The person who does not see from that point of view that one ought to see from becomes disappointed, because that person cannot understand. It is not that the outward world must help us understand it better. It is we ourselves who should help ourselves to understand life better.

And then there is a further awakening, and this further awakening is a continuation of this same awakening that I have called the awakening of the soul. And the sign of that awakening is that, upon every person and upon every object, those who are awakened throw a light, a light of their soul, and see that object, that condition, in that light. It is their own soul that becomes a torch in their hands. It is their own light that illuminates their path. It is just like throwing a searchlight upon dark corners that one did not see before, and the corners become clear and illuminated again. It is like throwing light upon problems that one did not understand first; it is like seeing with an X-ray people who were a riddle before.

Since life becomes clear to the awakened soul, it shows another manifestation, and that manifestation is that every aspect of life becomes communicative with the soul. The idea is that life is communicating, the soul is communicating, but they do not communicate till a person is awakened. Once the soul is awakened, it becomes communicative with life. I had, as a young man, a great desire to visit the shrines of sages, of great teachers. And, with every desire of hearing from them something or asking them something, I always held my tongue back and sat quiet in their presence. And I had a greater satisfaction, and I felt a greater blessing by sitting quiet there than if I had discussed with them and argued and talked with them. Because I felt in the end that there was a communication, a communication that was much more satisfactory than these outer discussions and arguments of people who know not what they discuss. For it was enlightening, it was refreshing, and it was giving that power and inspiration with which one can see life in a better light.

Those who are awakened become lights—not only lights for themselves, but also lights for the others. And in their light, a person may not know it, but their presence itself helps to make problems which are most difficult, easy. This brings us to realize the fact that, as the scriptures have said, humankind is light, a light whose origin, whose source, is divine. And when this light is raised, then life becomes quite different. When the soul is awakened, furthermore, the condition is then as a person sitting in the midst of night among hundreds and thousands of people fast asleep. The picture is that the awakened person is sitting among them, standing among them, looking at them, hearing their sorrows and miseries and of their conditions, hundreds of them moving about in their sleep, in their own dreams, not awakened to the condition of the other one who is next to them. They may be friends or relations or acquaintances or enemies—whatever be their relation, little do they know about the awakened soul, all absorbed in their own troubles. This awakened soul, standing among them all, will listen to everyone, will see everyone, will recognize and realize all that they think and feel. But the awakened soul's language no one understands; the awakened soul's thought cannot be explained to everyone; the awakened soul's feeling cannot be expected to be felt by everyone. The awakened soul feels lonely, and nothing else can be felt. No doubt in that loneliness there is a sense of perfection, because perfection is loneliness.

When they say that the apostles knew all languages at the descent of the spirit,[3] this knowing of all languages is not like knowing the languages of all countries. They knew the language of the soul. For there are several languages that are spoken in different lands, but numberless languages that are spoken by each individual as that person's particular language. And that brings us to realize another idea of very great importance; and that idea is that the outer language can convey only outward things and feelings to one another, but there is an inner language, a language which can be understood by souls who are awakened. It is a universal language, a language of vibrations, a language of feeling, a language that touches the innermost sense. In order to support that argument, I shall say that heat and cold are different feelings that are called by different names in different countries, but at the same time, inwardly, they are the same feeling.

And then there are love and hate, kindness and unkindness, harmony and inharmony. All these words are spoken differently in different countries, but the feeling is the same experience to all people. When, in order to know the thought of another, we depend upon that person's outer word, then no doubt we fail to understand, because we perhaps do not know that person's language. But if we can communicate with another person soul to soul, we certainly can understand that person's meaning. For before people say a word, they have said it within themselves; and that word reaches inwardly before the word reaches outwardly. Before the word comes, the expression says it; before the thought has formed, the feeling speaks about it. And this shows that it is a feeling that forms a thought, a thought that

3. See Acts 2:4.

comes as a speech; that even before this, a feeling existed, and even there it can be caught when a person can communicate with the soul. It is this that is called communication: to communicate with the innermost being of a person. But who can communicate? Those who know how to communicate with themselves, those who are wakened, in other words.

And what becomes of the personality of an awakened soul? The personality of an awakened soul becomes different from every personality. It becomes more magnetic, because it is a living person who has magnetism; the dead corpse has no magnetism. It is the living who bring joy, and therefore it is the awakened soul who is joyous. And never for one moment think, as many imagine, that a spiritual person means a most sorrowful, dried up, long-faced person. Spirit is joy, spirit is life; and when this spirit has awakened, there is all the joy and pleasure that exists. As the sun takes away all darkness, so spiritual light takes away all worries and anxieties, sufferings and doubts.

If a spiritual awakening is not so precious, then what is the use of seeking it in life? A treasure nobody can take away from you, a light that will always keep and never will be extinguished, that is called spiritual awakening, and that is the fulfillment of life's purpose. Certainly, the things once a person had valued and considered more important become less important. Things lose their value, and things that are beautiful lose their color. It is just like seeing the stage in the light of the sun—all the big palaces and decoration on the stage mean nothing. No doubt this takes away that slavery to which everyone is put by the things of this world; a person becomes a master, but at the same time need not give them up. Optimism naturally develops, but an optimism with open eyes. A power becomes increased, a power of accomplishing things. And when a person has not accomplished something, that person will go after it till it is accomplished, however small it is.

It is very difficult, as they say in the Eastern language, to judge an awakened soul. For there is nothing outwardly that can prove to you that this person is an awakened soul. The best way of seeing an awakened soul is to awaken oneself. And no one in the world can pretend to be awakened when one is still asleep. For if a little child puts mustaches on its face, it will not prove to be a grown-up man. All other pretense will be taken, but not this one of the awakened soul, for it is a living light and no one can pretend to be it. For if there is any truth, the truth is in the waking of the soul, for truth is born in the awakening of the soul. The truth is not taught; the truth is discovered.

Very often people make an effort, but that effort is in vain, to try and awaken one's friend or one's near relation whom one loves. For in the first place, we know not if the person is more awakened than us; we may be trying in vain. And the other thing is this: that it is possible that a person is asleep and needs to sleep. Awakening, therefore, would be a sin instead of a virtue.

We are allowed only to give our hand to the one who is changing sides, who desires awakening. Only then a hand is given, and this giving of the hand is what we call initiation, an esoteric word. No doubt, outwardly, a teacher who is acquainted with this path may give a hand to the one who wishes to journey; but inwardly there is the teacher who gives a hand, who has always given, and always gives a hand to awakening souls—the same hand which has received the sages and masters of all times in a higher initiation. Verily, the seekers will find sooner or later, if only they kept steady on the path till they arrive at their destination.

Thank you all for your sympathetic listening. May God bless you.

37

THE POWER OF SILENCE

APART from meditative silence, even in our everyday life silence is the most essential thing.[1] There is an energy that gets accumulated, functioning in the innermost of our being, and it is in speech that one gives outlet to that energy. And that energy may best be called magnetism. It is inspiration and it is wisdom. It is therefore that you will always find in the less talkative person a greater wisdom than in the one who is talkative. Apart from wisdom, from a physical point of view, a talkative person is all the time giving out an energy which, if one conserved it, would make a great vital power in oneself. With some persons it becomes a passion to speak without purpose, without a reason to speak, because they like to speak. If one knew what the Bible says about the word, that first was the Word and the Word was God,[2] if one only knew what the tradition of humanity has been—it is the word. Those who have the esteem of the word, those who value the word, their word becomes precious. Their word is worth millions, and even millions are less than the price of their word.

The great teachers of humanity have come and passed away, and what they have left behind them, which the world prizes more than anything, is their word. If we keep anything as most sacred just now, whatever be our faith or religion, it is the word that has been given to us, it is the word which we keep as the

1. Lecture given in rue de Loxum, Brussels, December 8, 1924.
2. John 1:1.

most precious thing in the world. The moment that we begin to value our word, from that moment we begin to think about what we say. Those who have no value in their word are of little value themselves. The greater ones are those who stand for their word. However great some people may be, if they have no honor of their word, they cannot really be great. It is such a pity that, in this time of materialism, we are losing the idea of the most valuable thing we have; and we have got it from the heavens, for the word is heavenly and what is in the word is the soul, the spirit. And when that word is uselessly used, life is abused by it. Do we not see that there is a person who comes and speaks perhaps a thousand words to us, and not one word strikes us? There is another person who comes and speaks one word to us, but it penetrates, it makes an impression. That word is of value, for there is a living word and there is a dead word. A living word has a life, it acts chemically; the dead word has no life, it is only a corpse. The living word will go and float in space, it will go into the hearts of human beings and work. And the dead word will drop from the mouth on to the earth and will be buried in the dust.

And very often a person speaks because of weakness. That person is weak, cannot control the idea, the thought, and helplessly drops a word that should otherwise have been kept and not spoken. A gossiping person, a person who criticizes another, you will always find, is a person of weak character. It is not that they like to speak, it is because they cannot help speaking. It is just like a person who eats, but cannot digest. When one cannot keep one's own secret, when one cannot keep the secret of one's friend, one has no power of digestion, one's conscience will always feel guilty, and one's heart restless. There is another person who goes on like a machine, a machine which is hearing from the ears and speaking from the mouth, and it is going on all day, and it goes on like a machine. Is it not the experience of many of us that very often we think, "Oh, I wish I had not said that to that person"? Is it not the experience of many of us when we think that, "I should not have spoken so rudely with the other person"? Is it not the experience of many of us to think that, after having spoken, "Oh, what a terrible thing I have done. I have opened my heart to that person, I do not know what will become of it!" Sa'di, a great Persian poet, says in his poem that, "My intelligent friend, what use is your repentance after once you have dropped the word out of your lips?" To control the word is more difficult than controlling the most energetic horse. The one who controls one's word, controls one's mind.

There is another way of looking at this subject. When a person is talking to those not yet evolved to one's own grade of looking at things, one may say things of a greater wisdom which will prove to be as pebbles in the place of pearls. It is a loss of words of a higher ideal, of some greater truth, to a person who is not capable of understanding or appreciating. You have given something to the hand of another who will ridicule it, who will mock it, and to whom it is of no use. You would find it more thoughtful, more wise, that you did not speak the word at that time, but prepared the person to hear that word, even if it wouldn't be for ten years.

And then there are times when you meet with an evolved person to whom your words are of little importance; you are just like a child speaking to a grown person, which means very little. But the thing is this, that in doing so you will spoil that person's time as well as your own. Besides, many well know that many disagreements between relations, between friends, are brought about by useless talking. The talking had no importance whatever, but it has culminated perhaps in a great disharmony or separateness.

There is an amusing story that a woman went to the house of a healer, a magnetizer, and she asked him if he would tell her something, for she was in great distress. This distress was that every day she had a disagreement with her husband. The healer said, "It is very easy. I will give you some sweets, and you will put them in your mouth and keep your lips closed. Every time when your husband comes home, you put them in your mouth." The remedy proved successful. And the woman came after the sweets were finished to thank him and to ask for some more magnetized sweets. He said, "My dear lady, you do not need any more bonbons now. Just think that you have them and close your lips, and all will be all right." This example is for us all to learn, whether wise or foolish. For the wise it is the most beautiful thing; for the foolish it is the only dignified thing possible.

And now, coming to a still deeper side of silence. What is silence? Silence is something which we consciously or unconsciously are seeking every moment of our life. We are seeking for silence and running away from it, both at the same time. Where is the word of God heard? In silence. The seers, the saints, the sages, the prophets and masters, they have heard that voice which comes from within by making themselves silent. I do not mean by this that if one maintains a silence, one will be spoken to. I mean that one will hear the word which is constantly coming once one is silent. Once the mind has been made still, a person gets in communication with every person one meets. One does not need too many words; when the glances meet, one understands.

Two persons may talk and discuss their whole life and they will not understand one another. And two persons with still minds look at one another, and in one moment there is a communication. From where come the differences between people? It is by their activity. And when does agreement come? It comes by the stillness of mind. It is the noise which hinders a voice that we hear from a distance. And it is the troubled waters of a pool which hinder us seeing our own image reflected in the water. When the water is still it makes a clear reflection. And when our atmosphere is still, then we hear that voice which is constantly coming to the heart of every person. We are looking for guidance. We, all of us, search for truth, we search for the mystery. The mystery is in ourselves. The guidance is in our own soul. Besides this, very often one meets a person who makes one restless, nervous. The reason is that the person is not restful, not tranquil. This shows that being restless makes others restless, being calm makes others calm. And it is not easy to stand calm and to keep one's tranquility in the presence of a restless, agitated person.

The teaching of Christ is, "Resist not evil."[3] And that means: do not give in to that troubled condition, or do not respond to the troubled condition of a restless person. It is just like partaking of the fire that will burn oneself. And now how can one develop that power in oneself to stand, in everyday life, against all disturbing influences? For our life is exposed to this atmosphere every moment of the day. The answer is that one has to quiet oneself by the way of concentration. And now you may ask what I mean by concentration. Our mind is like a boat, a boat which is in the water, subject to being moved by the waves and subject to being influenced by the wind, both. And the waves for this boat are our own emotions and passions, our own thoughts and imaginations; and the wind is the outer influences which we have to meet with. And in order to stop the boat you ought to have the anchor to put in the water, and that anchor makes the boat still. And that anchor is the object which we concentrate upon. If this anchor be heavy and weighty, then it will stop the boat. But if this anchor is light, the boat will move and not be still, for it is in the water, it is in the air.

But now, coming to the question that by this we only control the boat, but utilizing the boat is another question again. The boat is not made to stand still, it is made for a purpose. To make it stand still is only to control the boat first. Although all of us may not know this, at the same time, at the end of the examination, this boat is made to go from one port to another port. Now, sailing the boat needs different conditions. And

3. Matthew 5:39.

those conditions are that the boat must not be more heavily laden than the weight that it is made to carry. And so our heart must not be heavily laden with the things that we attach ourselves to, because then the boat will not go. The boat must not be tied and chained to this one port, for then it is held back and will not go to that other port for which it is made. The boat may be tied to one port for a thousand years, but the boat is not doing its work then. In the first place it must have that responsiveness to the wind that will take it to that port. And that is the feeling that a soul gets from the spiritual side of life. That feeling of the wind helps one to go on, to go forward to that port to which we are all bound. The mind which is once concentrated fully must become a compass, as they have in the boat, which always points to the same side. A person who has a thousand different sides of interest, that person is not ready to travel in this boat. It is the one who has one thing in mind, all other things being secondary, who travels from this port to that port. It is this journey which is called mysticism. It is this journey which is called Sufism.

The efforts of the Sufi message is to give the opportunity to those serious seekers after truth that they may come in touch with the deeper side of life. No doubt, truth is never taught. Truth is discovered. It is not the wonderworking, it is not the love of phenomena that is the sign of the seeker. For it is in the search for truth that God is found, and it is in the finding of God that truth is realized. But where is God to be found? God is to be found in the human heart.

38

HUMANITY, THE SEED OF GOD

THERE are various ideas and beliefs as to the relation between God and humanity, and it is natural that there should be various beliefs, for the reason that everyone has one's own conception of God.[1] There is no comparison between God and humanity. The reason is that humanity, being limited, can be compared with another being; and God, being perfect, is beyond comparison. The prophets and masters in all ages have tried their best to give humanity some idea of God's being, but it has always been difficult, for it is impossible to define God in words. It is like trying to put the ocean in a bottle. However large a bottle, it can never accommodate the ocean. The words that we use in our everyday language are the names of limited forms, and we give God a name for our convenience, someone who is above name and form. And if there is any possibility of understanding God and Divine Being, it is only possible in finding the relation between humanity and God. The reason why the subject of this evening was called, "Humanity, the Seed of God" is because it is this picture that gives, to some extent, the idea of the relationship that exists between humanity and God.

There is a root, and there is a stem, and there are branches, and there are leaves. There comes a flower, but in the heart of the flower there is something that tells the history of the whole plant. One might say that it is for the sake of the flower that

1. Lecture at Salle de l'Athènèe, Geneva, October 15, 1923.

the plant was purposed, but, really speaking, it is the seed that comes in the heart of the flower that continues the race of the plant. It is the seed that is the secret of the plant, which is the source and goal of that plant. It is that seed that was the beginning. It is from out of that seed that the root came and the seedling came out; and so it became a plant. And then that seed disappeared, but after the coming of the leaves and branches and the flowers, it appeared again. It appeared again not as one seed, but as several seeds in multiplicity, and yet it is the same. And it is this seed that told us the story that first it was the seed and then the whole plant appeared. And toward what was the goal? What was the result? In order to come again as the result of a whole plant.

To the person of simple belief, to the one who believes only in one's own particular idea, for that person there is no relation between God and humanity. But the person who wishes to understand the relation between humanity and God, for that person the proof of this argument is to be found in everything. And it is this idea that is spoken of in the Bible, in the words where it is said that in our image We have created humanity.[2] If the seed, out of which the plant came and that came in the result, had said, "Out of my own image I have created the seed that will come forth from the heart of the flower," it would have been the same thing. Only that seed out of which the plant came could have said, "I shall appear in plurality, although in the beginning I am one grain." It is this idea again that tells us of the reason why it is said that "We have created humanity in our image," when the whole manifestation, the whole creation has come from God.

The leaf and the branch and the stem, all have come out of the seed, but that is not the image of the seed. The image of the seed is the seed itself, but not only this—the essence of the seed is in the seed. No doubt there is some energy, some power, some color, some fragrance in the flower, in the leaf, and in

2. Genesis 1:26.

the stem; but at the same time, all the property that is in the stem, flower, petal, and leaves is to be found in the grain. This shows to us the result that humankind is the culmination of the whole creation. And in humankind the whole universe is manifest. Either the mineral kingdom or the vegetable kingdom or the animal kingdom—these are all to be found in the being, in the spirit of humanity. It does not mean that the different properties, such as mineral and vegetable, are to be found in the physical body that is made for humanity, but also a person's mind and heart show all different qualities. The heart is just like a fertile soil or a barren desert: it shows love or lack of love, productive faculty or destructiveness.

There are different kinds of stones: there are precious stones, and there are pebbles and rocks. And so there are, among human hearts, a still larger variety. Think of those whose thoughts, whose feelings have proved to be more precious than anything that the world can offer: the poets, the artists, the inventors, the thinkers, the philosophers, and then the servants of humanity, the inspirers of humanity, the benefactors of humankind. No wealth, no precious stone, whether diamond or ruby, can be compared with it, and yet it is the same quality. And then there are rocklike hearts: one might knock against them and break oneself, and yet they will not move. Then there is the waxlike quality of the heart, and then there is the quality of the stone. There are melting hearts, and there are hearts that will never melt. Is there anything in nature that is not to be found in humankind? Has humanity not, in feeling, in thoughts, and in qualities, a picture of running water, a picture of fertile soil, and a picture of fruitful trees? Is there not in the heart of humankind the picture of the plants, of fragrant flowers? The flowers that come from the human heart live longer; their fragrance will spread throughout the whole world, and their color will be seen by all the people. The fruits that the human heart can bear—how delicious! They immortalize souls and lift them up. And then there are other mentalities where nothing springs up except the desire to hurt and harm their fellow being, producing thus the fruits and flowers of poison, hurting another person by thought, speech or action—and they can hurt more than thorns.

There are some whose feelings and whose thoughts are like gold and silver, and there are others whose thoughts are just like iron and steel. And the variety that one can see in human nature is so vast that all objects that one can get from this earth are too small in number. But does one only show in one's nature, in one's qualities, in one's body, in thought and feeling, the heritage of this earth? No, there is also the heritage of heaven. Humankind has the influence of the planets, has the influence of the sun, of the moon, of heat and cold, and air and water and fire—all different elements that make this whole cosmos system. All these elements are to be found in human thoughts, in a person's feelings, in a person's body. You can find a person with warmth representing heat, another person with cold representing water. There are human beings, in their thoughts, in their feelings, who represent the air element. Their quickness, their restlessness, it all shows the air element in them. Does humankind not represent the sun and moon in the positive and negative character, and does duality of sex not show this? Not only this, but in every man and in every woman there is the sun quality and there is the moon quality; and it is these two opposite qualities that give a balance in the character of humanity. When there is one quality most predominant and another not to be found, then somewhere there is balance lacking. And if one goes still further in the thought of mysticism, one will find that not only all the visible manifestation is to be found in humankind, but also all that is invisible.

The angels or fairies or ghosts or elementals or any imagination that humankind has made—if they can be found anywhere, they are to be found in human nature. The pictures of the angels, in all times, one finds in the image of humanity. If all that exists in the world and in heaven is to be found in humanity, then what remains? God has said in the scripture, "I have made humanity in my own image."[3] In other words, "If you wish to see me, I am found in humankind." How thoughtless on the part of human beings who, absorbed in high ideals, begin to condemn someone, to look down upon someone, however low and weak, wicked, and a sinner that person may be. Since in humanity there is the possibility of rising so high that nothing else in the whole manifestation can rise as high—either something on the earth or any being in heaven—none can reach the height that humankind is meant to reach.

What point of view, therefore, had the mystics, the thinkers of all ages? Their point of view you can see in their manner: a respectful attitude to all people. In Jesus Christ, the master of humankind—in his life's example one can see that compassion when a sinner was brought before him, someone who had done wrong. There was forgiveness, there was tolerance, there was the understanding that the master showed. One can be called a religious or a pious person, but one cannot be called a truly spiritual or wise person who has contempt toward one's fellow human beings, whatever be their condition. Those who have no respect for humankind have no worshipful attitude toward God. They may be the most religious people, but those who have not recognized the image of God in humanity have not seen the artist who has made this creation. They are deprived of that vision themselves, of that which is most sacred and most holy. Those who think that humankind is earthly do not know where their souls come from. The soul comes from above; it is in the soul of humanity that God is reflected.

Those who have hatred or contempt, whatever be their belief, faith, or religion, they have not understood the secret of all religions that is in the heart of humanity. And certainly, however good a person, however virtuous one may be, at the same time, if one has no tolerance or forgiveness, if one does not recognize God in humankind, one has not touched religion.

No doubt there is another side of the question. As people evolve, so they find the limitations, the errors, and the infir-

3. Genesis 1:26.

mities of human nature; and so it becomes difficult for them to live in the world and to withstand all that comes. Also it becomes very difficult for a person to be fine, to be good, to be kind, to be sensitive, and at the same time to be tolerant. And what comes as a tendency is to push away everything, and to find oneself away from everybody and every being. But the purpose of being born on earth is different. The purpose of being born on earth is to find the perfection that is within oneself. And however good and kind people may be, if they have not found for what purpose they are born on earth, they have not fulfilled the object of their lives. There are many different aspects of that purpose, as many people there are in the world; but behind all different aspects of that purpose there is one purpose. It is that purpose which may be called the purpose of the whole creation. And that purpose is when the inventors look at their inventions working; when the great architects build a house that they have designed and that was theirs, and when it is built, when they enter it and see how nicely it is accomplished. The purpose is accomplished when the producers of a play produce the play they have desired, and when the play is produced and they look at it—that is the purpose. Every individual seems to have a purpose, but the purpose is nothing but a step to the purpose that is one purpose and which is the purpose of God. Our small desires, if granted today, tomorrow there is another wish; and whatever be that desire, when it is granted, next day there is another desire. That shows that the whole humanity and every soul is directed toward one desire, and that is the object of God, which is the fuller experience of life within and without, a fuller knowledge of life, the life above and below.

It is in the widening of the outlook, that it may be so wide that the soul—which is vaster than the world—that in the soul all may be reflected, that the sight may become so keen that it may probe the depth of the earth and the highest of the heavens. It is in this that there is the fulfillment of the soul. And the soul who will not make every effort possible, with every sacrifice, for the attainment of this—that soul has not understood religion. What is the Sufi message? It is that esoteric training, working, and practicing through life toward the attainment that is the fulfillment of the object of God.

39

Our Activity Which Is Called the World Kinship

A few words I would like to say to explain to you a little more about this our activity that is called the world kinship.[1]

Today it is more than necessary that the activities in bringing about a feeling of kinship in humanity are of more value than any other activity in the line of culture. And although there are many societies and institutions that are established and working along this line of kinship, yet our contribution to this great service of God and humanity has its peculiarity, owing to its ideas being based on spiritual ideals. We believe that the kinship brought about by coming to an understanding of exchanging the good of one another in the interest of one another is not sufficient. The reason is that the nature of life is changeable. Where there is a day, there is a night, and there is light and darkness; and therefore, the interest in life is not always even. If two persons are friends with one another, and they make a condition that, "We shall be friends, and we shall love one another," if each wishes to regard justice, they will quarrel a thousand times a day. Because who is to be the judge? When two people quarrel, both are just, both think they are in the right, and a third person has no right to interfere. Therefore, kinship cannot be brought to satisfactory results only by teaching the law of reciprocity based upon self-interest. Because even if they said, "I will give you a pound in gold, and you will give me in return a pound," and the exchange is made, there is a dispute.

1. Lecture in Suresnes, France, July 22, 1923.

Because: "I gave you the pound in gold and you gave me the pound in notes!" A friendship that is based upon selfishness is not secure, it is not dependable; because seemingly they may be friends, but in reality each one is wanting for oneself. They are not the friend of the other, they are the friends of themselves. However greatly they show friendship to one another, in reality they are showing friendship to themselves. No, the kinship, from the spiritual point of view that may be learned, is the kinship of rivalry in kindness, in goodness. It is not weighing what good have they done to me, but it is trying to do more for another and not thinking what the other will do for me.

The ideas of the Sufis in all times have been different from the individual in the world, and yet not too difficult for someone to practice. The Sufi ideas are that when one does an act of kindness for another, it is because one wishes to do it, because the action itself is one's satisfaction, not a return, even in the form of appreciation. Any form of appreciation or any return they think consumes, takes away that act of goodness or kindness that one has done. And when one thinks that one does some good, expecting that another must return it, then it is a business. And a person who thinks that: "Perhaps I shall do twice more good to another from whom I received half the good I do for them," is in a very bad situation; for sooner or later there will be disappointment, because that person shares goodness that cannot be shared in this way.

As soon as one begins to think, "Has another person treated me like family? Why should I treat that person as family?" one does not know what kinship is, one will never be able to act as family. The Sufi point of view is that one must be concerned with oneself. If one does right, that is what one is concerned with and not whether another takes it right.

The trouble of kinship at this time, when humanity is so vastly divided, seems so very difficult to bring in practice. And yet I do not think, if we saw the idea of kinship in this light, that it would seem very difficult. For no sooner do people say, "If another person will do as I wish," than they create their displeasure. But for the one who says, "I will do what I think right and good, and I am not concerned with the others and whether they take it rightly. I have determined to do what I can," that is quite sufficient.

40

Art

MY subject this evening will be art.[1] Many think that art is something different from nature, but I would say that art is the finishing of nature. And one may ask, can humanity improve upon nature, which is made by God? But the fact is that God, through humanity, finishes divine creation in art. As all different elements are God's vehicles, as all the trees and plants are the divine instruments to create through, so art is the medium of God through which God creates and finishes divine creation. No doubt every so-called art is not necessarily art. By looking at the real art, one is able to say that Thy will is done on earth as in heaven.[2] In this whole creation, from one thing to another, through evolution, the Creator has worked. In humankind the Creator has finished, so to speak, nature. But at the same time, the creative faculty is still working through humankind, and therefore, art is the next step toward creation. In reality, all creation—scientific or artistic—is art; but mainly the object that is produced with the sense of beauty, and that appeals to the sense of beauty in people, is principally art.

Besides being the creative power of God, art is the expression of the soul of the artist. An artist cannot give what the artist has not collected, although humanity ignores the way the artist's soul conceives, only recognizing what the soul of the artist has produced. Once the artist is understood, then the artist

1. Lecture given in rue de Séverin, Paris, December 16, 1922.
2. Matthew 6:10.

conceives also and not only produces. And then it is not so difficult for one with an awakened heart to see into the soul of an artist, for art in color, in line, is nothing but the reecho of the artist's soul. If the soul of the artist is going through torture, the picture gives one the feeling of awe. If the soul of the artist is enjoying harmony, you will see harmony in the colors, in the lines. What does it show? It shows that the soul works automatically through the brush of the artist. The deeper the artist is touched by the beauty that the artist's soul conceives from outside, the greater appeal it makes to those who see their production.

Now, coming to the question: What is it in line and color that has such an influence on a person's faculty? It is the vibrations that the color produces which thrill the centers that are hidden in the body, and which are the centers of intuitive faculties. Sometimes a person looks at a color and immediately feels thrilled by it. The degrees of vibration that different colors produce are different, and therefore, the influence is different. At the same time, one person is more open to the effect and influence, and another person is so blocked that upon that person colors make little impression; and that very reason may be said to be the cause that makes woman more respondent to color and to line than man. For woman by nature is responsive, man by nature is expressive; therefore, while woman receives the impression of the color, man expels them. But at the same time, the difference between a man with fine feelings, with intuitive faculty awake, and a man whose faculties are not yet open is only this: that the former responds to the color, and the latter does not.

Now, coming to the question of strong colors and of mild colors. Strong colors make more distinct vibrations. Their effect is more distinct than that of mild colors, and therefore it is natural that strong colors can make impressions upon every soul. But at the same time, to distinguish the impression made by mild colors wants a delicacy of sense. For instance, the simple words of language of everyday life are understood by everyone, but the fine shades that follow the words are not understood by everybody. Therefore, sometimes the color that is only a color to everybody, to a person with a fine sense, it has its value, its degree of influence. The harmony of the color is based on the same foundation as the harmony of music. The reason is that music is audible vibrations, and color is a visible form of vibrations. But from the metaphysical point of view, color has a great significance in one's life. The first important thing that is to be understood in connection with color is that all different colors come from the essence of light. All different colors are the different degrees of light. No doubt there are three aspects of light, and it is this that produces confusion in the mind of those who have not thought upon the subject of whether color can be called light. And these three aspects of light are in this way: One aspect of light that manifests through the color is the radiance of the color itself; the other aspect is the light of the sun or of something else that throws its light upon the color, and the light of the color responds to that light. The third light is the light of the eyes that see. Therefore, the same color is not the same, nor is its influence the same for everybody, not only for the reason that the degree of sight of every person is different, and the difference of the light that falls on the subject is different, or that the degree of the color is different, but also the element which that particular color represents has a certain degree of response in a certain individual.

According to the mystical idea, there are four principal elements that can be distinguished and one which is indistinct. The distinct elements are earth, water, fire, and air—not according to the meaning that a scientist would take from it, but according to the meaning it has for the mystic. It will take perhaps time if I tried to explain the difference between the mystical conception and that of the scientist. The indistinct element is the ether. Now all these elements are in the body of an individual, in the mind and in the deeper self. The whole building of an individual existence is built by these five distinct elements, and it is not necessary that on every plane of existence a certain element is predominant and continues to be predominant in every plane. I mean that it is not a certain predominant element in one plane that continues to be predominant in all planes. It is possible that there can be harmony in the elements that are predominant in the inner plane with those that are predominant in the outer plane. In short, according to the working of the different elements in one's being, one is responsive to the different colors that represent the different elements.

From the point of view of a mystic, yellow is the color of the earth, green or white the color of the water element, red that of the fire element, and blue of the air element. If the color of the ether element was asked, the mystic says gray, and by *gray* you may think what you like. It is most interesting for a student of color to see that all colors are, so to speak, different shades of light. And what does it show? It shows that light itself has manifested in variety in the form of many colors.

Now, coming to the question of line. Many of those lovers or students of art feel a great influence, a great effect that a line makes. A straight line, a horizontal line, a line with curve, a circle, makes such a difference in the form. And the more one studies to what extent line makes a difference, the more one will find that the secret of the whole of beauty is in the line. And it is difficult to say what form, what line is the right line; and one has to accept that what one cannot learn by study, intuition teaches. The only reason from the mystical point of view that one can give about the secret of line, is that the effect of a certain line arranges the inner and outer planes of the human being in such a condition that, for the moment that one looks at the line, one is, so to speak, in a kind of spell of that line. The secret of this can be found in the secret of concentration: that every object one thinks upon, be it for a moment, has an effect upon one's whole being. And there is a harmony between lines. The harmony of lines is more difficult and more complex to understand than even the harmony of color, and the harmony of line touches deeper than the harmony of color. If a room is beautifully furnished with costly furniture, but if the things are not kept in harmony according to the science of lines, you will find a kind of confusion in the room. The same thing in dress. The dress may be costly, beautiful in color, and if it lacks line, it lacks a great deal in beauty. Therefore, in art, line is the principle thing. It is the secret of art, and it is the secret of its charm; and that artist who has conceived the beauty of line can only express it in art.

Art has three aspects. One aspect is that the artist tries to copy exactly that which the artist sees. That artist is contemplative, and it is not a small thing to be able to copy exactly as the object is. The success of this artist is sure. With everyone's craving for something new, what one really wants is something one has seen. Is it not something wonderful, is it not great to be able to copy nature as it is, and to produce the same in the soul of humankind, as it is in nature?

Another aspect of art is the improvement on nature that the artist makes by exaggeration. And the benefit of this art is more attraction than impression. No doubt, in this form of art artists can fulfill their soul's purpose. But at the same time, artists may go far away from nature, and the further they go, the more they destroy the beauty of art. For nature and art, both, must go hand in hand.

Now, coming to the third aspect of art, and that aspect is symbolical art. Symbology has not come from the human intellect, for it is born of the intuition. The finer the soul, the more it is equipped in some way or the other in the symbolical idea. A fine soul always dreams symbolical dreams, and when the soul becomes finer still, it interprets the dream to itself, understanding the meaning of that symbology. The artists who produce in their art a symbolical idea have learned it from what they have seen in nature and have interpreted that in their art.

Certainly it is inspiration. The finer is the artist, the finer the symbolical way of producing.

In every piece of art one can observe three things: its surface, its length and width, and its depth. I do not say this in the sense of ordinary words. The surface means what the picture is; the length and width is the story that it tells; and the depth is the meaning that it reveals. Therefore, in the best way of appreciating and studying the works of an artist, these three faculties must be developed. Art is a very vast subject. One lecture is not sufficient for this subject; therefore, I will leave it for this evening at this point.

41

The Divine Blood Circulation through the Veins of the Universe

OFTEN people have vague ideas as to the meaning of the word *divine*.[1] The word *divine* has become their ideal, but this ideal is to be made first into a reality. An ideal can only serve its proper purpose when it is made into a reality; if the ideal is not made into reality, the purpose is not accomplished.

In the first place we must inquire what it is that reminds us of the divine, what brings us to a feeling of the existence of the Divine Being. It is what may be called beauty: the beauty, the delicacy, the color in the flower; and the brilliancy and the light of the precious stone. For in all this, what is beautiful is intelligence, even manifested through material objects. The definition of the secret of fragrance, the secret of the brilliancy of the diamond, the beauty of the pearl, the secret behind all that appeals and attracts people, is intelligence. But true intelligence in all things is, so to speak, imprisoned and covered; and in living beings this intelligence begins to manifest, and in humankind there is the great possibility of the manifestation of this intelligence. Therefore, in things or beings, if anywhere there is a trace of the divine to be found, it is in the intelligence. And as many different degrees may be found in the beautiful flowers, one better than the others; and as many different degrees may be found between the pebble and the diamond, a million more different degrees may be found between one individual and another.

1. Lecture given at Musée Guimet, Paris, December 9, 1923.

At this present time, when humanity has disregarded this beauty and the value that is hidden in human personality, by this, humanity has disregarded the divine substance that is hidden in humankind. Today there is no place, there is no recognition of human culture, whereas every other object is classified and a value has been fixed to it. There are different studies and different practices and different degrees in the university and colleges; there are ranks and divisions in all other parts of life, but there is no distinct place for the understanding, for the intelligence of humanity in its true aspect. There is no loss to the person who possesses this wealth, only by this: that before the world, there is nothing distinguished and there is no chance for every person to find out what is behind the veil. If one could explain the real meaning of education and a true education, it would be, from the beginning to the end of a person's life, the realization of the circulation of the divine blood through the veins of the universe. There is no limitation of time for the study and practice of this, for it is endless.

The secret behind magnetism, which has its different aspects, is one and the same. No doubt magnetism, personal magnetism, is divided into several different parts. There is a physical magnetism that comes with youth, with energy, with the healthiness of the body. The more healthy the person is, especially at the time of youth, the more the person begins to show a certain energy in every action and in every movement; and by this a person expresses magnetism. Then there is a greater magnetism than that, and that is the magnetism of the mind. A person with a living mind is like a light, and as light attracts and its warmth comforts, so a comfort comes out of that person as a radiance. Besides, there is a magnetism of culture. For a person who is well trained and has a certain culture, that person's action, word, and thought all become rhythmic. And the fourth magnetism is the magnetism of the soul, the soul which is living. By living I mean that which is not closed or covered by a grave, but which is manifest outwardly as well as inwardly.

It is that soul which has another magnetism, a magnetism that is greater still and the greatest of all other aspects of magnetism.

Now, the question is, in order to attain to that highest magnetism that alone is the endurable magnetism—how can one attain it? It is by watching the divine essence, by noticing the divine essence in all things. You will always find the difference between two people of different temperaments. There is one who is appreciative of music, poetry, and art, respondent and ready to admire all that is good and beautiful; and there is another one who closes the self, is not open to appreciate anything, not ready to respond to anything or willing to admire anything. And when the door is closed from the divine manifestation that is in all things, then that continual source of attracting new life and magnetism is closed. Then the soul dies of poverty. For the physical body, since it is limited, its sustenance is also limited; but for the soul, as the soul is not limited, so its sustenance is not limited. The soul is not satisfied with one moment's meditation only, nor is the soul satisfied with one good action in the week, nor is the soul satisfied by attending one prayer perhaps in a week's time. The soul's hunger is greater than the hunger of body or mind. Its hunger is satisfied by beauty: beauty in all aspects, beauty of color, beauty of thought and imagination. Therefore, naturally the soul of the artist, of the poet, of the musician, of a thinker is always living. But at the same time, the difference is this: that the one who is fond of beauty and derives the nourishment that comes from beauty, also has only a limited food. For perfect satisfaction can only come when one knows all beauty to be one beauty, and that one beauty to be the divine beauty.

Very often humankind questions the idea of communication, of divine communication. But it is not an impossible thing; it is the most desirable thing there is. Only the person who thinks that divine communication can be made by going to heaven and leaving this earth may well wait for some time. As for the example, we have no lack of examples in the world, if only we can see. For instance, to true musicians, real musicians, music is not only an art, a symphony. It is something that speaks to them; it is something with which they communicate. A musician who arrives at this stage may be perhaps striking one chord, and the continual striking of that one chord will bring the musician to an ecstasy. For another person it is only striking a chord, but for the musician it is speaking with the piano: the musician is conversing with it. Besides all the great musicians I have seen in my country, I have heard the great pianist of the Western world, Paderewski,[2] and I valued my privilege of hearing him at his house when there were not many people, when he was himself. When he began to play, in his play it seemed as if there was a question of his soul and an answer of the piano; the whole time it was a question of his soul and an answer of music. In the end it seemed as if, at the close of the whole thing, the soul of the player and the music became one and perfect.

Now, this is one example, but there can be many other examples such as this. In order to attain to this perfection one need not be a musician. The whole life from morning to evening before us can speak to us, if we are able to speak to it, if we establish the communication with life. When one is not open, one is not even open to oneself; one cannot communicate with life, and then one is lonely. But those who are in communication with themselves may be in the forest, in the wilderness, yet they are in the world, and the whole universe is around. How many souls are among one's friends who live in this world of the crowd and yet are lonely, when it is so natural and possible that a person outside the world may keep in connection with the whole being.

The scientist today has discovered that by touching or attaching oneself to an electrical current, if one can get it in a certain part where the energy is less, more can be attained by it. If this material aspect of electricity can give a new life, a new vigor to

2. Ignace Paderewski (1860–1941).

the body, then this continual battery—if one came in contact with this, could one not attain from that all one desires? An energy that is everywhere, and everywhere one can get in touch with it if one only knew how to communicate with it; an energy that is not without an intelligence, but that is the perfection of intelligence; and the mind and soul, which become more and more intelligent by coming into contact with it. But now one might ask how one can attain to it. As it is necessary that in order to sing well one must cultivate one's voice, and as it is necessary that in order to get muscularly strong one has to make physical exercises, so it is most necessary to get in touch with the divine life that is all around and above us, that is within and without us, to practice to get in touch with it and to keep in touch with it. We see that in all different occupations of life, whether it is in scientific inventions or in industry or in business, one must be so absorbed in it in order to do something worthwhile in life.

The same law can be applicable to spiritual work as it is to material work. Concentration is the main thing, and when the concentration is not attained, then whatever a person will do, it will not bring about worthwhile results. You can find in all different occupations the cause of failures. In ninety-nine among a hundred cases it is the lack of concentration. When a student fails in passing the examination, when a business person fails in making real success, when an industrial person fails to bring about a certain result, in all this it is lack of concentration that causes the failure.

A spiritual or religious attitude apart, even from a material and selfish point of view one cannot deny the greatest value of concentration in life. But when we come to realize that there is one great energy, an energy that is not only an energy but intelligence itself, and which is divine, and which is all over, then one has come face-to-face with the object one is searching for. Only then what remains for people is that intellectual knowledge does not satisfy their purpose. For them it remains to try and find out how they can communicate, how they can come into touch with that all-pervading energy. And the answer is that one has to mold oneself, one has to prepare oneself in order to become a fitting instrument, in order to fit in with this all-pervading energy. And the question is, how has one to prepare? The answer is that every soul has been made to answer, in this symphony of the whole universe, as a certain note. And when one will not give that note, one will not be fulfilling one's life's purpose and thereby will always feel dissatisfied with oneself and others. And how will one arrive to attain or tune oneself to that note? By the ear training, in symbolical expression, and, plainly speaking, by studying the law, the nature, and the secret of harmony in life.

But how will one fit in with the rhythm? All distress, all misunderstanding, all the tragedy that one experiences through life is also the lack of keeping in life a certain rhythm that is asked of one by life. Does it not teach us that there are two important things to remember? One is to develop the sense of harmony in one's everyday life and to develop the sense of rhythm in everything one does. If one has developed the sense of harmony and yet has not known the secret of rhythm, one still will have difficulties. And if one knows the rhythm and how to fit in with the rhythm of the universe, and yet has no sense of the nature and secret of harmony, then also will one meet with failures. It teaches us that the whole of life is as music, and to study it we must study it as music. It is not only study, but it is also practice that makes humankind perfect. If anyone told me that a person is a miserable or a wretched person or a distressed person, the answer will be that person is out of tune. A distress or disappointment or failure is caused by falling short of answering one's own duty in playing the part in the symphony. Very often people will ask, "There is a good person. Why must that person suffer? There is a very nice person, a religious person. Why has that person such distress?" And there are others who will answer a thousand different reasons. They will say that perhaps in the life before, that person has done something wrong and, therefore, has to pay debts; or some will say goodness must always suffer. But when we come to the practical side of the question, the answer is simple: that human-made goodness is not nature's goodness. Nature demands, life demands, a certain standard of understanding, of thinking, of living. And this can be learned by learning the tune and the rhythm—and not only by learning, but by putting oneself to that tune and setting oneself to that particular rhythm that makes the music of life. It is by this, in this manner that the happiness is attained, the happiness that is the seeking of every soul. And it is in this manner that one will progress continually until one will touch the divine spirit, the spirit that pervades all and that is everywhere.

42

THE POWER OF THE WORD

THE word is, in itself, a profound mystery in every sense; and every scripture has considered the mystery of the word as the most profound mystery compared to all other secrets of life.[1] In the scripture that is most known to the Western world we read that first was the Word, and the Word was God.[2] And then again one reads that it was the word that was first and then came light.[3] These two sentences convey to us two things. The first conveys to us that if there existed anything, and if we can express what existed, we can only express it by the name *word*. And when we come to the second sentence, it explains another phase of the mystery, and that is, that in order for the soul that was surrounded by the darkness of this world of illusion to come to the light, the word was first necessary; which means that the original spirit was in the mystery of the word, and by the mystery of the word the mystery of the spirit was to be found.

And when we come to the Vedantic scriptures, which existed many thousand years ago, there also we realize the same thing. For instance there is a phrase in the Sanskrit language that says, *Nada Brahma*, which means, "the mystery of creation was in Nada," which means, "in the word." In the Qur'an one reads in Arabic the words *Kun fayakun*: that first was the exclamation

1. Lecture given in Rome, November 13, 1923.
2. John 1:1.
3. Genesis 1:3.

"'Be,' and it became."[4] The One who said, "Be," and it became, was not a mortal being. The One was and is and will be all the life there is. And if that is so, then the word was not the mystery of the past, but the word is a continual and everlasting mystery. And at this time, when humanity has engaged itself in the material phenomena and has progressed very far compared with the past in industry and in commercial activities, at this time this one aspect of discovering the might that lies under the word is still unexplored.

In the first place, the mystics who know the value of the word find that word in themselves first, for the secret of all knowledge that one acquires in the world, whether worldly knowledge or spiritual knowledge, is the knowledge of the self. For instance, music is played outside, but where is it realized? It is realized within. A good word or a bad word is spoken outside, but where is it realized? It is realized within. Then where is the realization of this whole manifestation, all this creation that stands before us in all its aspects? Its realization is within. And at the same time human error always continues: instead of finding it within, one always wants to find it without. It is just like those who want to see the moon and look for it on the ground. And if they sought for thousands of years for the moon, by looking on the earth they will never see it. They will have to lift up their heads and look at the sky. And so with those who are in search of the mystery of life outside: they will never find it, for the mystery of life is to be found within. There is the source and goal, and it is there that if one seeks, one will find.

What is sound? Is sound outside, or is it something within? The outside sound also becomes audible because the sound within is continued, and the day when the sound within is closed, this body is not capable of hearing the outside sound.

People today, living in the life of externality, have become so accustomed to the outside life that they hardly think of sitting alone. When they are alone they engage themselves with

4. Qur'an 2:117.

a newspaper or with something. Always working with the life that is outside, always occupied with the life outside, in this way they lose their attachment with the life within. One's life, therefore, becomes superficial. And the result is nothing but disappointment, for there is nothing in this world that is so attractive in the form of sound that is visible or audible, as the sound within, for all that the senses touch and all that is intelligible to the human mind has its limitation. It has its limitation of time and of effect; it does not have an effect further than it does.

The mystery lies in the breath. It is the breath and the pulsation that goes on, that keeps the mechanism of the body going. And it seems that the people of ancient times had a greater knowledge of this mystery than people today, for what is meant by the lute of Orpheus? It means the human body: it is a lute, it is meant to be played upon. When this lute is not realized, when it is not understood, when it is not used for its proper purpose, then that lute remains without the use for which it was created, because then it has not fulfilled the purpose for which it was made.

The breath is not alone as far as the person of material science knows it, one who only knows the vibrations of the air going out and coming in, and sees no further. Besides this pulsation, the beating of the heart and head, the pulse, all these things that keep a rhythm, one very rarely thinks what depends upon this rhythm. The whole life depends upon this. Besides, this breath that one breathes is certainly a secret in itself. It is not only a secret but the expression of all mystery, something upon which the psychology of life depends.

The science of medicine, for thousands of years has, to some extent, depended upon finding out the physical condition by the rhythm and by the breath. The ancient medicine knew that health depends upon vibration, and now again a time is coming when, in the Western world, physicians are striving to find out the law of vibrations upon which health depends. But humanity, absorbed in the material life, goes so far and no further.

The mystery of vibrations does not concern only the material plane, but it goes still further. If the human body is a lute, then every word one speaks, every word one hears has an effect upon the body. It has not only an effect upon the body, but also upon the mind. For instance, if people repeat or hear themselves called by the name "foolish," even if they were wise, in time they will turn foolish. And it is true also that for those who are simple. Call them wise and, in time, they will become wise. The effect of the name that a person has, has a great deal to do with that person's life. And very often one sees that the name has an effect upon one's life and career. The reason is only that often in the day one is called by that name. And is it not true that someone saying a humorous thing bursts out laughing, and someone saying a sad thing breaks into tears? If that is true, then every word that one speaks in one's everyday life—what an effect it has upon oneself and upon one's surroundings!

And the superstition that has existed in all times about not saying an unlucky word, an undesirable word—one can see that superstition has a meaning. In the East there has always been a training given to a child that the child must think before uttering a word, for it has a psychological meaning and effect. Very often people reading a poem or singing a song with great love, a song of sorrow or tragedy, are affected by it; and very often their life takes a turn and is affected by it. Those who speak of their illness nourish their illness by their speech. Very often I have heard people say that if there exists a pain, it is a reality, and how can one deny it? It is so amusing to hear them say this, because reality is so far away, and our everyday life is such that, from morning to evening, we do nothing but deny it. If one only knew where lies the truth, if one only knew what is the truth, if one only were to know it and see it, one would think that all else is nonexistent in reality. And if one studied the depth of this idea, then one must admit the power of the word; but then it is a science, a metaphysics that must be studied.

And yet the depth of the word of each person is very different. If a person has spoken a hundred words in one day, do you think that every word has the same power? No, the power and effect of a particular word depends upon the state in which that person was. It depends upon from what depth the word rises, and upon that depends the power and light of that word. For instance, with a person who has a habit of telling a lie, who is insincere, you will always find that person's word dropping down, having no force. And the one who speaks with conviction, who is sincere, who tells the truth, that person's word has a strength, the word has a light, the word penetrates. And besides this, sometimes from a person full of sadness, heartbroken, a voice comes, a word comes, which is full of sincerity; and it has all the power to penetrate, it has such an effect upon the listener! Then there is another person who is lighthearted, who is not deep, not serious enough in life. Everything that person says and does is always on the surface, and no one is inspired with confidence, for that person has no confidence.

But besides that, there is a power of the word according to the illumination of the soul, because then that word does not come from the human mind. That word comes from the depth, from behind; that word comes from some mysterious part that is hidden from the human mind. And it is in connection with such words that one reads in the scriptures of words such as "swords of flame,"[5] or "tongues of flames."[6] Whether it is a poet or whether it were a prophet, when that word came from the burning heart, then the word rose as a flame. In accordance with the divine spirit that is in the word, in accordance to it, that word has power, life, and inspiration. Think of the living words of ancient times, think of the living words that one reads in the scriptures, the living words of the holy ones, of the illuminated ones! They live, and will live forever. It is a music that

5. Genesis 3:24.
6. Acts 2:3.

may be called a magic, a magic for all times. Whenever such words are repeated they have that magic, that power.

What the sages of all ages have said, their words have been kept by the people, by their pupils. In whatever part of the world they have been born or have lived, what they have let fall as words has been taken as real pearls, has been kept as scriptures. And therefore, wherever one goes in the East one finds that the followers of different religions, whenever they pray, have the words of the illuminated ones, and they do not need to put them in their own language. And one finds in this way that the words said by the great ones have been preserved for ages, to be used for meditation.

Besides this, there is a still more scientific and a greater mystery of the word. It is not only what the word means, it is not only who has said the word, but the word in itself has also a dynamic power. The mystics and sages and seekers of all ages, knowing the mystery of the sacred word, have been always in its pursuit. The whole meditative life of the Sufis is built upon the mystery of the word. For the word *sufi,* according to the explanation of the initiates, is from *sophia*, which means "wisdom"—but wisdom not in the outer sense of the word, because worldly cleverness cannot be wisdom. The intellect, which very often is confused with wisdom, is only an illusion of wisdom. Wisdom is that which is learned from within, and intellect is that which is acquired from without. The source of wisdom is above, the source of intellect is below. And therefore it is not the same method, it is not the same process that one adopts in order to acquire wisdom as to acquire intellect. In short, the attainment of that wisdom is made in various ways by various people, but at the same time, the great mystery of attaining the divine wisdom is in the mystery of the word.

43

CONCENTRATION

BELOVED Ones of God, my subject this afternoon will be concentration.[1] Concentration is a simple word; in practice it is most difficult. Everyone knows the word *concentration*, but if one knows how to do it, one knows everything. Sometimes, to sit with closed eyes means concentration; but whether you close your eyes or whether you open your eyes, concentration has nothing to do with it. If you concentrate, you concentrate with open eyes or with closed eyes, in the middle of the crowd or in the solitude; and if you do not, you do not. But concentration is one state, a state that leads to contemplation. And so one goes through the meditation process to achieve that in which is the fulfillment of every soul's purpose in life.

Therefore it is that the ancient people called it *alchemy*, from which the words *chemical* or *chemistry* or *chimie*[2] come. Only now there are simple persons (even in the East we find many) who, by the meaning of alchemy, understand the turning of iron into gold. But when we consider it symbolically, the meaning that we find in alchemy is to turn this very personality, which is a human personality, from the baser metal into gold. But by alchemy it is not the gold that is made in order to possess it. The gold of the soul is made. One becomes gold oneself, and it is that gold which is of incomparably greater value than the gold of this mortal world. Then there are people

1. Lecture given in Geneva, January 17, 1925.
2. French word for chemistry.

who still remember the stories of the ancient times, the stories of the alchemists; and it is even now most interesting to get the meaning out of these symbolical stories, for they are always instructive.

There is a story of a king who was very fond of finding out the ways of alchemy, of turning baser metal into gold. And everyone who professed knowing alchemy had a welcome at the palace, but at the end of examination he found their profession futile. And then they found someone, and they said to the king, "Here is a real alchemist." And to the king's great sadness, when this alchemist came before the throne, he said, "No, King, I am not the man who knows the alchemy which you are looking for." The king said, "No, you know it. I feel confident in my heart that you are the person who knows it, and you must teach the study to me." The man continued refusing; the king continued persisting. And then he said, "Do you know that I am a king? And here I command you to do so, and if you still refuse, you know what I can do. I give you forty days' limit. If during this time you did not tell me, then do you know what is waiting for you? You will be beheaded." The man was taken to a prison. And the king visited him every morning, telling him, "Man, change your mind. Remember life is greater than gold. You can still teach me and save your life." And at night the same king came in the form of a working man, in the form of a servant. And he swept the floor, and he made the bed for him, and he cleaned the table for him, and he served his dinner, and he did every little thing possible to make this prisoner feel comfortable. And so every day this went on. In the evening the king visited as a servant, and in the morning he went as a king and gave him a warning again and again. And there came that last day, the day after which was waiting the death of this man, and the king gave him the last warning and said, "Now, tomorrow is the day. Be ready, for a king's command is his command." And in the evening the servant shed tears at the thought of this poor prisoner being taken to be beheaded. "Don't shed tears," he said, "life is such. But remember that which I refused to the king, to you I most willingly give, if you will keep it in confidence. And now you will see how great a trust it is, how sacred the thing is to me that I have guarded more than my life, that I have sacrificed my life in order to guard this, so that you will keep it in the same way." This servant said, "Well, I appreciate most what you give me, although I do not know its value. But at the same time, for you to be killed tomorrow, this I cannot bear, it tears my heart to pieces." "Be not sad, man," he said, "life is such. I give you this secret: gold that will make you gold." And he whispered in the servant's ears and enlightened him with his secret. And the morning came, and the king came for his last warning. There, soldiers were waiting to take him to be beheaded, and there he was awaiting his death. And the king is there to ask him for the last time if he will obey the command. "No," said this prisoner, "find someone else, King; I am not the person you are looking for." But the king said, "But you have given me that; don't you remember?" "Did I?" said the prisoner, "If I have given it, it is to the servant, not to the king."

To the hungry, food is given; and to the seeker, truth is given. But those who are not hungry, even if food is given, they cannot eat; and those who do not seek the truth, even the most ultimate truth given to them, they will not appreciate it. Those great ones who came to illuminate souls and who lived on this earth, they have touched millions; but did millions get that illumination? No. What remained afterward and was modified lost its fragrance, perhaps after thousands of years. Then, when it was dust, people began to talk; but at the time when it was given, people did not appreciate. It will always prove true: one is the worst enemy of one's best friend. Whom one strikes first are one's best friends. One has crucified them, has imprisoned them, has killed them, has beheaded them, has flayed them, and yet without meaning, without intending, with goodwill and with reason—what one calls reason in one's head.

I am coming now to the actual subject of this alchemy: what it is and how it is made. What they say in legends is that alchemists used to take mercury, and by putting some chemicals they used to still it; and in stilling that mercury, it turned into silver. And then, by putting it into a fire, the very silver turned in the flame and took on that flame color which we call gold. I am now coming to the question: What is this mercury symbolically? The mercury is a condition of the heart, the condition of the mind. It is never still. Automatically, one's mind takes up any impression and thought and, without intention, may hold it as a despair, as a depression. But as soon as one intentionally takes up a thought, the mind goes on in its active way and loses it. As soon as a person wishes the mind to take up a thought, the mind fails; and that is the nature of mercury: mercury is never still, and the mind is never still. The more you wish the mind to become still, the more active the mind becomes. And therefore, that precise object—that this mind can become still—is the process that is called concentration; and it is by this process that this mercury can be turned into silver.

The Sufis have different ways of posture, different ways of standing or sitting. All these different things are in order to still that mercury, not only in the mind but also in the body which keeps the mind always active, moving, restless. One hardly thinks how little power one has upon one's body. As soon as you tell people to sit still, the moment they know that they must control the body, the body will begin to move and be restless. And since mind and body are connected, one with the other, the stilling of the mind needs the stilling of the body at the same time. There are just now many movements, schools where they will teach how to move gracefully; but this is not the stilling of the mercury. The stilling of the mercury is how to sit restfully. That is another subject in life to learn and much more important, too.

Essential as it is to keep awake, so essential it is to sleep; and important as it is to move, so important it is to take repose. But when one's mind is controlled, one's body is made still, it has made one valuable, it has made that personality precious. And yet it is not gold, for the gold is gold because it has light in it. This tranquility that one has learned is in order to make one a vessel, a pitcher that can hold. But that pitcher must hold divine light in it, and when the pitcher has that divine light, then there is a value of that pitcher.

This shows that it is not only an intellectual conception of God or of life that is sufficient for humankind; the first thing is that one must develop that tranquility in one's body and mind so that this vessel may contain in itself the life and the light of God.

Sometimes it amuses me very much when I meet people who say to me, "Well, what is your conception of God? Please tell me." Here, for years and years, people have to train their bodies and their minds in order to get in tune, in order to find a glimpse of that truth of which people, with their intellect, come and ask, "Please tell me how do you believe, in what way do you consider God?" But this thought, as in other theories and different things that they read and learn in books—everything—they think that even God is a conception, an idea that can be explained in a sentence. Sometimes a person comes and asks me, "Well, do you believe in a personal God, or do you believe in an abstract God?" and before the answer they tell themselves, "I do not believe in a personal God. I only believe in an abstract. I can only believe in that idea." They come with their preconceived ideas of which they are not sure. They are asking only to be sure whether that fits in with their ideas, and if it does not fit in, then they go away. Others come, and they ask, "What do you think of the hereafter? What is your idea?" They want in one sentence what will come after death, whereas, in order to die that death, here in life people spent days and years in studying, in practice, in meditation, in order to experience themselves what is after death. And they have experienced it by dying a death here on earth. It is not impossible to know it, but it is not so easy to know as a person thinks. In order to keep people quiet, the wise had to tell them a thousand things in order to fit in with their particular conceptions. Well, that cannot be the truth. And if they say the truth, they cannot say it; truth cannot be said in words. Where is truth? Truth is life itself, and it is the realizing of the life that is the discovering of the truth. If truth is such a small thing that it can be spoken in words, then truth is no truth. And what are words? Words are something that covers truth. When one comprehends beyond words, it is then that one realizes truth. To become gold is to become light, and the light in this precise sense is truth itself. Light and life are two words, but in point of fact it is one, in the essence it is one. Call it light because it is knowing, call it life because it is living.

To a dervish, a person went and said, "Please tell me what happens after death." The dervish said, "Go to someone who is going to die, who is mortal. They will tell you what happens after death. Neither do I die, nor do I know what happens after death." And that explains the central thought of Sufism, and that thought is that life lives—it is death that dies. In spite of all the great masters, Jesus Christ had to teach the people to satisfy their fancies, to help them in their lives. But the central theme of the master's teaching is one, and that is to distinguish the immortality of the soul. The Sufis, therefore, are the pupils of wisdom; and since Sufis are the pupils of wisdom, they are the pupils of the all-wise. They see the source of wisdom in all its forms: in religious form, in philosophical form or in mystical form, and in scientific or artistic form. In all its forms, it has one source, and it is that source which is the master. And therefore, they are not in any disagreement with any religion, with any sect, or with any community. Those teachers that have adored their own teachers and their own scriptures that they worship and respect—for the Sufi they are all the same. The

Sufis' church, therefore, is in every place where they stand. The dome of that church is the sky, and the floor of that church is their thoughts. The whole scripture of the Sufis is all this life that teaches lessons from morning till evening. Therefore, the literature of all those great prophets and teachers, for them, is the interpretation that they have taken from this life, interpreted in the language of the people of that time. And yet that wisdom, for the Sufis, is not limited to a certain period. That wisdom has always been and, therefore, is and will always be, for they find the source of that wisdom, which they consider most sacred, is to be found in the heart of humanity.

Thank you for your sympathetic response, may God bless you.

44

THE INNER LIFE

THERE is one aspect of life that is known to us, which we call our everyday life.[1] The consciousness of doing all that we do in our everyday life is called the outer life. And there is a part of our life of which we are very often unconscious, and it is that part of our life which may be called the inner life. To be without inner life means to be without one arm or one leg or one eye or one ear; but even this simile does not sufficiently illustrate the idea of the inner life. The reason is that the inner life is much greater and nobler and much more powerful than the outer life. Humankind gives a great importance to the outer life, being absorbed in it from morning till evening, and not being conscious of another aspect of life that may be called the inner life. It is therefore that all that matters to people is what happens to them in their outer life; and the occupation of the outer life keeps them so absorbed that they hardly have a moment to think of the inner life. The disadvantage of not being conscious of the inner life is incomparably greater than all the advantage that one can derive by being conscious of the outer life, in which one always is.

The reason for this is that the inner life makes one richer, and the outer life, poorer. With all its riches and treasures that the earth can offer, humankind is poor. And very often the richer one is, the poorer one is; for the greater the riches, the more the limitation one finds in one's life. The inner life makes one

1. Lecture given in September 1922 in Katwijk, the Netherlands.

powerful, whereas the outer life and its consciousness makes one weak. It makes one weak because it is the consciousness of limitation. The consciousness of the inner life makes one powerful, because it is the consciousness of perfection. The outer life keeps one confused. However intellectual or learned people may be, they are never clear. Their knowledge is based upon reasons that are founded upon outer things, things that are liable to change and destruction. That is why, however wise those people may seem to be, their wisdom has limitations. What today one thinks right, after four days one thinks perhaps wrong. The inner life makes the mind clear. The reason is that it is the part of one's being that may be called divine, the essence of life, the pure intelligence. The phenomenon of it is that wherever the light of pure intelligence is thrown, things become clear. The absorption in the outer life, without what the inner life gives, makes one blind. All one says, thinks, or does is based upon outer experiences; and no one can realize to what extent the power gained by the inner life enables humankind to see through life. There exists the belief in the third eye. In reality, the third eye is the inner eye, the eye that is opened by one's wakening to the inner life.

Therefore, inner life, in other words, may be called the spiritual life. One can see it in the forest, that it is the rain from above that makes the forest beautiful, which means that what the forest needs is not all that it has, but it needs something that comes from above: the light, the rain. It is the sun and rain that make the forest complete. And in the desert there is no rain, and therefore, it is only one aspect; there is the earth, but there is no water, water from above. The water that gives life to the forest, that water is not to be found in the desert. The desert is unhappy as a person in the desert is unhappy, looking for a shade from the hot sun, because the desert is longing. And the person in the desert is longing too, for something that person cannot find. Whereas in the thick forest there is a joy, there is an inspiration, the heart is lifted up, because the forest is the picture of the inner life. It is not only the earth, not only the trees and plants, but it is that something it needs has been sent upon it. And so it is with humanity. Those who are solely occupied with the things of the world are in the outer life; in the midst of the world they may be, but they are in the desert. But it is the inner life that produces in them, not artificial virtues and not human-made qualities, but such virtues that only can rise from inner life besides the insight that makes the eyes see more than the mortal eyes can see.

And now the question is, how are we to be sure that this is an inner life? What proof is there? And the answer is there is not one moment in our life when we do not see the proof of inner life, only we do not look for it. All different communications, such as telegraphy and the telephone and new communications that are coming—radio and X-rays and all new inventions that make a person wonder how much humanity has accomplished—if one saw that all these machines and all these inventions are nothing but a little imitation, a poor imitation of what is this human body, of the human being—if only one knew what the human being is! Humankind is the center of joy, of happiness, of peace, of power, of life, and light. The phenomenon that can be vouchsafed to humanity is much greater than any other machine, if only one had the patience and perseverance to explore one's self. Only what we do is explore the others. When it comes to analysis, one thinks it is a great study to analyze things; and when one analyzes human nature, one calls it psychology. People analyze all others except themselves, and therefore, true psychology is never reached, because the real psychology is to analyze oneself first; and when one's self is analyzed, then one is able to analyze others.

If one only knew that besides what one says or does or thinks, and the effect of what one says, does, or thinks that is manifest to one, there is another action of the same that creates something in one's life that makes one's world. And perhaps in a week or in a month, or perhaps in a year or ten years, that which one has created one day comes before one as a world, as a world created by oneself. Such is the phenomenon of life. How insignificant a human being appears to be, just like a drop in the water; and at the same time, what effect one creates by every thought, by every feeling, by every act! And what influence it spreads, and what influence it has on the lives of the others! If one only knew, one would find that the outer life and the results of all one thinks, says, or does in the outer life are much smaller, incomparably smaller than the results produced by everything one thinks, says, or does in the inner life. It is therefore the inner life that makes humankind more responsible than the consciousness of the outer life. The responsibilities of the outer life, compared with the responsibilities of the inner life, are much smaller. For the moment they might appear to be heavy burdens, but they are nothing compared with the responsibilities one has with one's inner life. If one sees what one creates, the responsibility is much greater. As they say, in the Eastern language, of the chukar,[2] the donkey seems to be much happier than the chukar, which is the most intelligent bird. Those in the outer life seem quite pleased, because their responsibilities are less, their outlook small, their horizon narrow, and what they see of the world very little. But when the horizon is opened, when the heart has penetrated through the barrier that divides the here and hereafter, when one begins to see behind the veil, and all that appears on the surface becomes a screen behind which something else is hidden, then one experiences life quite differently. The view of the one who stands on the top of the mountain is quite different from the view of the one who stands at the bottom of the mountain. Both are human beings, both have the same eyes, but the horizon of one is different from the horizon of the other. Inner life, therefore, means the widening of the horizon and the change of direction of seeing.

2. A Eurasian partridge.

In the English language they call a mystic a seer; *seer* means the "one who sees." In the East there is a quotation of a great Yogi, who says, "In order to see what is before you, you must see within yourself." And this means that within yourself there is a mirror, and it is that mirror which may be called the inner world, the inner life. It is in this mirror that all that is before you is reflected. But when the eyes are looking outside, then one has turned one's back to the mirror that is inside. But when the eyes are turned inside, then one sees in this mirror all that is outside reflected. Therefore, all seeing by this process is so clear and manifests to such fullness that, in comparison, the vision that one has before one's eyes is a blurred or confused vision. Two people may live together for twenty-five years, for forty, fifty years, and may not be able to understand one another for the lack of the inner life; and the inner life would enable them to understand one another in one moment. When they said that the twelve apostles began to understand the language of all nations,[3] did they learn the grammar of all nations at that moment? No, they learned the language of the heart. The language of the heart speaks louder than words can speak. If the ears of the heart were open to hear that language, the outer words would not be necessary.

With all the progress that humanity is making, it still is most limited; and the more you see the limitations of this process, the more you find that it is limited because of the absence of the inner life. When you see, in the traditions and histories of the past, how many thieves there used to be, and robbers and murderers, and how many murders there were committed, one thinks what a horrid time it was. And yet when one thinks more about it, one sees that the time at present is much worse, and the time of robbers and murderers was much milder. One or two persons in a village were murdered; now towns and countries are swept away. One war has swept away such a large

3. Acts 2:1–11.

number of humanity.[4] Imagine if another war comes—what will be the result? They say people have progressed, they are more thoughtful. But, with all thoughtfulness, we have progressed to cause all the destruction and disasters that we find in a much greater degree. Does it mean that humanity is not progressing? It is progressing, but in which direction? Downward.

The condition of going in the path of the inner life is to be free first, in order to walk in that path. If the feet are pinned and the hands are nailed by beliefs, by preconceived ideas, by thoughts that one has, then people stand; they have every desire to go, but they are not going because they are holding on to something. Certain beliefs that they have—what they believed or what they thought—they are holding on to them; they are not going on, they are not going forward. And therefore, many with many good qualities and high ideals, and with religious tendencies, with devotional temperament, with all the spiritual qualities that one may have, can still stand in the same place. Either their ideas are holding them as pins or nails in the feet, or the hands are somewhere leaning on the railings and holding it, and they are not going further.

What the inner life requires first is the freedom in proceeding. The old meaning of freedom is very little understood, although everyone is seeking freedom. They say so much about freedom that one can be free of all things except of one thing, and that is the self. That is the last thing one thinks about. The conception of freedom is quite different at this time. Therefore, while seeking freedom people become anything but free, because they are caught in the trap of their own selves. That is the greatest captivity there is, and there they remain, as a jinn in the bottle. Besides that, the inner life requires sacrifice. As people consider their learning, their qualification, everything in their life is in order to be better qualified to gain all that they can in the world: power or possession or wealth or anything. And sacrifice is quite a contrary way to gain; therefore, one

4. World War I.

develops in oneself the nature of gaining instead of sacrificing. Besides, sacrifice requires a large mind, sacrifice requires deep sympathies, sacrifice requires great love; sacrifice is the most difficult thing. The inner life is something that is within oneself. It has been called a chamber of divine light in one's own heart. And the door remains closed until an effort is made to open it, and that effort is a sacrifice. In biblical terms there is a word—*self-denial*—but it is always misinterpreted by people. Self-denial, as people think generally, is to deny all that is good and beautiful, all that is worth attaining. Really, self-denial is not to deny all that is good and beautiful to the self, but to deny the self—and that is the last thing one wishes to deny. And the automatic action of this denial opens this door to the inner life.

And now, coming to the path of sages. The sages who have realized the inner life have realized it by the contemplative method. Humanity, from its infancy, is unaware of something within that is more than a faculty. By experiencing life through the outer senses, this faculty, which is the faculty of inner life—I use the word *faculty* because it expresses it a little better—this faculty, by not using it, becomes closed, just as if a door of a chamber of joy and light and of life is closed. And as from infancy one has not experienced the joy and the life and the light of this chamber, which may be called a celestial chamber in the human heart, one remains unaware of it, except for the feeling that one sometimes has and that one remains unconscious of. And sometimes when one is deeply touched, or sometimes when one has deeply suffered, sometimes when life has showed its hideous face, at such times or after an illness or by the help of meditation this feeling, which is unconsciously working there as a longing to unfold itself, this feeling becomes manifest. In what way? In love for solitude, in sympathy for the others, in a tendency to sincerity, in the form of inspiration of all that is good and beautiful.

It may manifest in the form of emotion, love, affection; in the form of inspiration; in the form of a revelation, vision, art, or poetry or music. In whatever form one allows it to express itself or one happens to be busy with, in that form it begins to manifest. And therefore, it is all spiritual when this door of the chamber of the heart is once open. If one is a musician, then one's music is celestial; if one is a poet, then one's poetry is spiritual; if one is an artist, then one's art is a spiritual work. Whatever one may do in life, that divine spirit manifests. One need not be a religious person, one need not be a philosopher, one need not be a mystic. Only that which was hidden within and which was keeping one incomplete in life, begins to manifest to view. That makes life perfect; that enables a person to express life to its fullness. Every attempt made today to better the condition of humanity by politics, by education, by social reconstruction, and by many other ways—all these, with excellent plans, can only be fulfilled if this something that was missing was added to them. But in the absence of this, all efforts of many, many years will prove to be fatal. For this something that is missing is the most essential of all things. The world cannot remain a world without rainfall. The world cannot progress without a spiritual stimulus, a spiritual awakening. If that is not the first thing—it is natural that it is not the first thing—still it can be the last thing; and if it is not even the last thing, then it is a pity.

Now, I should like to explain what reason I will give for the awakening of the meditative souls, how are they awakened, how would they experience the inner life. In the first place, the adept values the object of attaining the inner life more than anything else in life. As long as one does not value it, so long one remains unable to attain to it. That is the first condition: that one values the inner life more than anything else in the world—wealth or power, position, rank, or anything. It does not mean that one must not be in pursuit in this world of things one needs; it means one must give the greatest value to something that is really worthwhile. The next thing is that when one begins to give value to something, one thinks it is worthwhile to give time. Because today in the modern world, they say time is money; and money means the most valuable thing. If that which is money, if that which is precious, one gives to something one considers most worthwhile—more than anything else in the world—then no doubt that is the next step toward the inner life. And the third thing is that the condition of the mind is relieved of the pressure that always is in a person's heart while thinking that, "I have not done what I ought to have done toward my fellow human being"—be it one's father or mother, child, husband, wife, brother, friend, whoever it is—or "What I was expected to do toward the persons with whom I am put, or in the condition I am in, I have not done it." If that pressure is troubling the mind, then that mind is not yet fit. A person will give time to contemplation and spiritual life; but at the same time, if the mind is disturbed, the heart is not at rest, feeling, "I have not done my duty. I have a debt to pay to someone." It is a most essential point that the adept considers that any debt to be paid in life does not remain unpaid. When we look at life, is it not a marketplace? The give-and-take is to be seen in everything, and for what one has not paid just now, the bill will be presented afterward. People think: "I have gained without paying." They must wait till they realize that they will have to pay it with interest added to it. In what form one takes, in what form one gives, one is seldom aware of it. In giving service, kindness, sympathy it may be that one gives service, sympathy, kindness, money, all that one has, to the north; and from the south it comes, it comes back. When once one takes from the west, to the east one has to pay. Only people do not know in what form they have to pay, in what form they take. Very often they do not know when they take, what they give; but in give-and-take, every moment of their life is occupied. And with all the injustice of the word, it all adjusts itself in the end. It is the clear idea of this condition that shows that it all balances. If there was no balance of this, the world would not exist. This ever-moving world, turning round and round—what holds it? What makes it stand? It is the balance. It is not only the world that is going on, but everything is going on, the whole of life in its own way. What keeps it existing? It is the balance that holds it. We do not know that balance, being occupied by our worldly life. But when the inner eye is opened and one sees life keenly, one will find that it is a continual balancing process going on, and we are as particles of one mechanism that is constantly busy keeping this balance. When once the heart is at rest by the thought that one has paid, or one is paying one's debts, then one has come to a balanced condition. That balanced condition brings about a balance in one's life. That balance creates a condition in which the heart, which is likened to the sea, becomes then not a restless sea, as it is in the storm, but a calm sea, undisturbed water; and it is that condition which enables one to experience the inner life even better.

Do we not see in our everyday life the presence of persons who have not that tranquility, that peace, that calmness, and what influence it has—a terrible influence upon themselves and a disastrous influence upon others. One realizes it in one's everyday life if one sees it. One may be sitting in the office with someone, one may be standing in a place, one may be staying in the house where other people are standing or sitting, and one can realize by a person's atmosphere whether that person has reached a state of balance, tranquility, calm, and peace, or whether that person is in a state that is not rhythmic, not balanced. This again gives us an idea that what we call happiness and unhappiness is one's state: a balanced state or unbalanced state. When people are in a normal state in which their minds and hearts ought to be, in that state they are in a normal state; they need not seek for happiness, they are happiness itself, they radiate happiness. When that state is disturbed, they are unhappy. It is not that unhappiness comes to them, but they themselves are unhappiness. In Hindu terms, a Hindu idea is that *self* means "happiness," the depth of the self is happiness, which means all this structure which is outside—the physical body, the breath, the senses of perception, all these that make a person—all these stand outside; but their inner being can only be called by one name, and that is happiness. It is natural, therefore, that all are seeking after happiness, not knowing where to get it, always seeking for it outside of themselves. Therefore, instead of finding that happiness that is their own, they want to take away the happiness of another. And what happens? That neither can they get the happiness of another, nor can they give it. By trying to get it from another, they cause sorrow to the other, and the sorrow comes to them. There are very few robbers who go in the houses of others and steal; but there are so many robbers of happiness, and they seldom know they rob others of happiness. But the robbers of happiness are more foolish than the robbers who are after wealth, because when the robbers of wealth are successful they get something; but the robbers of happiness never get something, they only give sorrow to others.

Inner life, therefore, must not be considered, as many have thought it to be: a life that is in the forest or in the cave of the mountain or a retired life. Yes, there is a need for certain people who seek for solitude. They prefer to be away from the midst of the world, those whose inspiration is stimulated by being alone, who feel themselves when they are by themselves. But this is not a necessity of attaining to that happiness. One can be in the midst of the world, and one can stand above the world. Life has many woes, and the only way of getting rid of it is to stand above them all. And it is this that can be attained by one and only one thing, and that is the discovering of the inner life.

45

THE MATURITY OF THE SOUL

THE maturity of the soul may be pictured in the same way as that of a little child coming toward its youth, who does not give that importance and that attention to its dolls.[1] The child's sentiment, its desire is changed from that idea. It does not mean that the child did not have love before; the child had it. It does not mean that the child did not have sentiment before; the child had it. But here, with maturity, a consciousness has developed. The development of that consciousness has made all the toys and dolls, and all different things the child used to pay such attention to not matter. Is this maturity dependent upon a certain age? No. Does it depend upon certain environments? Yes. It is just that as a fruit put in the warmth ripens, so environments help the maturity of the soul. Nevertheless, the ripening of the fruit on the tree is ideal, for that is the place for the fruit to ripen. And all different attempts made in order to make the soul ripen, they all help. But they are like a fruit being put in some warmth; it is no longer on the tree.

There are people who think that by renouncing the world they will arrive at the maturity of the soul. There are others who think that by suffering all kinds of torture, by inflicting torments and suffering on oneself, one will arrive at the maturity of the soul. Often to me, friends have come and asked me that if they would have some kind of suffering, some kind of torture, would they arrive at the maturity of the soul? I told

1. Lecture given in Rome, November 27, 1923.

them that if they wanted to torture themselves, I would tell them a thousand things, or they might themselves find out a thousand things, but, as far as I know, there is no necessity. If one wants to torture oneself for the sake of torture, one may do so, but not for spiritual perfection. As the ripening of the fruit is in the course of nature, so it is in the course of nature that the soul should mature. And there is no use in being disappointed, being disheartened, about ourselves and those dear and near to us, worrying over the question why my husband, my wife, my father, my mother, does not look at life in the way I do—I am worrying about it. In the first place, no one, however great or pious, has the right to judge another soul. Who knows behind what action, what appearance, what speech, what manner, what is hidden. No one knows it. And when one begins to know what is hidden behind the human soul, in spite of all deluding appearances, one will have a respect, a respect for humankind, thinking that in the depth of a person's soul there is the divine whom one worships.

There is a story told in the East, that a wife was very much troubled, thinking that her husband was not religious enough. And the reason was that, besides all the goodness that the man had shown, she had never heard him say the name of the deity. She continually prayed and prayed for a long, long time, and after many years it happened that she heard her husband utter the name of the deity while asleep, when changing sides. The simple wife was full of joy. In the morning, as the husband awoke, she began to prepare all sorts of ceremonies and everything in the house celebrating that day, the day that her desire had arrived. After the whole celebration the husband asked, "My good wife, will you tell me what it is all about?" But she said, "It is too sacred and secret to be said." He said, "No, you must tell me." She said, "I have been in a kind of illusion, and now I was disillusioned. For I was most unhappy knowing you, my husband, to be a good man and yet as though godless. But last night I happened to hear you utter the name of the deity while changing sides, and this has made me most happy." "Did I?" said the husband. "Ah!" And he was finished. That was the last breath he took on the earth. He had no desire for it to be known that he loved that Beloved whom he had concealed in the depth of his heart. Who knows what is a person's inner religion, a person's inner conception? No one knows it. And many true souls one will find whose hearts are in a kind of shell, a hard shell, closed. No one knows that the very essence of God is in their hearts. The outer shell of the heart is so hard that no one can understand it. Therefore, a Sufi from Persia says, "I went among the pious and the godly, and was so often deceived; and I went among those looked down upon by others, and I found among them real souls." It is easy to blame, it is easy to look down upon someone; but it is difficult to really know how deep is the soul of a person.

No doubt there are signs of maturity, but who knows them, and how to know them? The signs of maturity are as the subtlety between youthful lovers. When the soul is matured, a passion has wakened in it—a passion for what? A passion for that incomprehensible, for that which is the longing of every soul. And what is that passion like? That passion is like *Gulliver's Travels*. The life on the earth is just like Gulliver's traveling: all souls, all persons, all seem to be of a different world; all seem to be of a different size; all seem to be different from what they claim to be. Before one there are many little children; before one there are numberless little children; before one there appear many drunken people, drunken souls. There is a saying of the Prophet that there will appear in the hereafter, on the Day of Judgment, a being in the form of a witch, and humanity will be frightened at the sight of this witch and will cry out, "Oh Lord, what a horrible sight is this! Who is this?" And they will receive the answer from the angels: "This is the same world, the world that all your life attracted you, which you have worshiped, which you have adored and have esteemed most valuable and all that you desired. This is the same world that is before you." All things of people's desire, whether wealth, rank, possession, position or honor, whether fame or pleasure, all these fade away when the maturity of the soul comes. All claims of love—of I am your brother or your sister or your son or your daughter—all these claims mean very little to the mature soul. A mature soul does not need to wait for the day in the hereafter in the form of a witch. It sees it now. No sooner has the soul matured than it sees the unreality of the world, which humanity has always considered real. And all such words that one uses every day, all these words become meaningless; they have no meaning as soon as the soul has matured. All distinctions and differences such as sect and creed and community and all different sections—all that means but little to the soul that has matured. And the experience of the mature soul is like the experience of the person who has looked at a play performed on the stage at night, and in the morning sees the same stage in the sun and sees that all the palaces and gardens and all the actors are unreal.

When a person has arrived at this stage, this maturity, what happens? It happens in the same way as a mature person, a grown-up person, either takes the right way or the wrong way. There are three aspects of the reaction that this realization of life produces on a person. One reaction it produces in a person is that one says, in answer to every claim of love and attention and respect, "Oh, no, no. I don't believe you, I have had enough. I understand what your claims are, but I don't belong to you. I don't listen." Of all that attracts them, they think, "Oh, you are a temptation. Go away, away from me. I want to be alone. I know what you are." And in this way a person becomes more and more indifferent to the world and isolated in the crowd. One feels solitary. Either one goes to the caves of the mountains or to the forest; one lives the life of an ascetic: at war with the world, at peace with God.

There is another aspect of the reaction. This aspect is that a person who understands the unreality of all things, becomes more sympathetic to fellow human beings. It is that person who, out of sympathy, sacrifices a love of solitude, a love of being exclusive, and goes in the crowd and stands amidst those who do not understand the person. But that person continually tries to understand them, from morning till evening. And the more one goes on in this path, the more one develops love. This one mourns over the unreality, over the falsity of life; but at the same time one is there, one is in the midst of it. Only this person's work is to help those who may be disappointed at the result of every little expectation they had in their love and devotion, as for every soul, every disappointment and every heartbreak is a surprise, is a shock, something that suddenly comes before them. And for this person it is continual; it is not new, it is the nature of life. A person stands by the side of the disappointed ones, comforts them, strengthens them. For instance, in the realm of religion, if one happens to be among those who have a form, a certain belief, a dogma, one may be above it, yet one will stand with them in that particular form, that dogma. One does not consider that one is different or above them. No, one stands with them. If one happens to be in a business, in an industry, in a worldly affair, although one has not in view any monetary affair, any profit, from it, yet at the same time, in order to keep harmony, one stands with them. One will sacrifice one's life in this way, and enjoy doing all things and caring nothing for it. There is a manner of this. It is the manner of an actor, an actor who acts on the stage. If he is made a king, he is not very proud of his kingship; if he is made a servant, he is not impressed by that, for he knows and understands, in his robe of a king or a servant, that "Neither am I a king nor am I a servant. I am myself." And it is such souls really who come to save the world. They are as the elder brothers and sisters of humanity who help the younger brothers and sisters. On them there is no impression of that position, that title, that spiritual grade. They are one with all, and they take part in the pain and joy of all.

But then there is a third reaction in souls, and these souls react by thinking, "If all that I touch, all that I see, and all that I perceive is unreal, I must find out, in whatever way I can, what is real." These ones are warriors, for they have a battle before them to fight. And what is this battle? This battle is that they are going to seek the truth, just like people swimming in the water, making their way; but at every step they advance, the waves of the sea come in their face, pushing them back. And at every effort they make to go forward, the billows come to push them back. And this is a continual struggle for the seekers after truth. Imagine, the industrial and business and domestic life apart, even in things that might seem to be covering the truth, even in such things the seekers may be deluded. For there is a very important thing that the seekers have to consider. As Christ has said, "I am the truth, and I am the way."[2] This shows that there are two things: there is the truth, and there is the way. The way may lead a person, and the way may become a puzzle for a person. It shows how careful one has to be, for even through the way that seems to lead to the truth, even in that way one may be puzzled. For in reality, life is a puzzle, a continual puzzle. And humankind seems to have the love of a puzzle and, therefore, goes into this puzzle. Even seekers after truth have it in their nature to go into the puzzle first. For instance, if a person of truth calls the seeker who has a love of the puzzle and tells the seeker, "Here is the truth," "Oh," the seeker says, "This is something unheard of, truth at the first step! How is it possible? It must be a thousand years before I can arrive at it. One life is not sufficient, a thousand lives I must live before I can realize the truth." But verily, for the lover of the puzzle, for that one, even a thousand lives are not enough. Besides, every person is not ready to accept the bare truth, is not accustomed to it. On hearing the truth, people say, "It is too simple. I want something which I cannot understand." In point of fact, if it is

2. John 14:6.

too simple, certainly it is simple. It is humankind who makes it difficult, because all other aspects of knowledge one has to get from outside, but the truth is something that is within oneself. It is something that is nearest to us, but that we imagine to be farthest from us. It is something that is within, but we imagine it to be without. It is something that is knowledge itself, but we want to acquire it. The seekers, therefore, have a continual struggle—a struggle with themselves, a struggle with others, and a struggle with life. And always the end and the result is that the one who has journeyed finds in the end, "I have journeyed because it was my destiny to journey; but in the end I found out that it was the starting point that was my final goal."

46

Physical Control

BELOVED Ones of God, I will speak this evening on the subject of physical control.[1] Life may be recognized in two aspects: the known aspect of life and the unknown aspect. What is called life is the known aspect of life. And the unknown aspect of life is unknown to many. The unknown aspect of life is that which may be called the immortal life, the eternal life. And it is the known aspect of life that may be called the mortal life. Therefore, what we know of life generally is the mortal part of life.

Our experience of life that we make through our physical being gives us evidence of life. It is therefore that the life known to us is the mortal life. The immortal life exists, but we do not know it. This is the absence of our knowledge and not the absence of immortal life.

Now today, I especially wish to speak on the subject of the life known to us, what we call life. Everything we have in this life, whether an object or a living being or a thought or a condition or a deed or an experience, all break and die away. Every one of the abovesaid things has birth and death. That which is composed must be decomposed sooner or later, that which is made must break, that which is built must be destroyed, and that which is visible now will disappear. This shows that there is a struggle between what we call life and between the life that is behind. In Sufi terms we call these two aspects of life *qaza'* and *qadr*: qaza' is the unlimited aspect of life, and qadr is the

1. Lecture given in San Francisco, April 5, 1926.

limited aspect of life. Qadr draws upon the life of qaza' for its existence, and qaza' waits with its mouth open to swallow what comes into it. Therefore, the thinkers and the wise, those who are called mystics or Sufis, have discovered the science of how to withhold the experience of life—which alone gives us the evidence of life—from the mouth of qaza', the ever-assimilating aspect of life. If we do not know how to withhold it, it will fall into the mouth of qaza', for it is always waiting with open mouth, as an illness awaits the moment when a person is lacking energy. So in all different forms, qaza' is waiting to assimilate all that comes into it, and then it is submerged in it.

And now the question comes: How can we withhold, how can we keep it from falling into the mouth of qaza'? And the answer is: by controlling the body and the mind. There is much known about physical culture, but what is known about it is what can be obtained by action, by gymnastics, by movements. But very little is known about what can be obtained by repose, by pause, and posture. I have seen in the East a person lifting a heavy stone on one finger. One might think, "How can the little finger that person has, these fine bones, stand such a heavy weight?" But it is only the power of will which sustains the heavy stone; the finger is an excuse. I have seen myself those who experiment in the field of spirit and matter, jumping into the raging fire and coming out safely, cutting the muscles of their body and healing them instantly. It is not a story that mystics knew how to levitate. The demonstration of this has been seen by thousands of people in India. By this I do not mean to say that it is something that is worth learning or following. I only wish to tell you what can be accomplished by the power of will. And in order to get the reign of will over the physical body, the first thing that is necessary is physical control.

In the cultures of different kinds known to the modern world, there is nothing that teaches the method or the way, the secret of sustaining every action. For instance, to be able to sit in the same posture without moving; or to be able to look at the same spot without moving the eyes; or to be able to hear something without being disturbed by something else; or to be able to experience the hardness, the softness, the heat, the cold, while keeping even vibrations; or to be able to retain the taste of salt and sweet and sour. Since all these experiences come and go, no one has control over the means of one's pleasure or joy. People cannot enjoy through any senses, any experiences that they make, as long as they wish to enjoy them. Therefore, one depends upon all outer things, and one has no control in sustaining the experience one makes. And if there is any way of sustaining every experience that one makes, it is the way of control.

There is another side of it. Unconsciously being aware of the fact that every experience that is pleasing and joyous will soon pass away, people are overly anxious; and instead of trying to retain it, they hurry it and lose it. For instance, with the habit of eating hastily, the habit of laughing before the mirthful sentence is finished, the reason is that if a person is overly anxious, the joy will go away. Therefore, even before the mirthful sentence is finished, one's joy is finished before it. In everything, one loses the power of sustaining the experience because of one's anxiety of losing its pleasure. It is the same thing with tragedy. The great joy of tragedy, the experience of tragedy, is to experience it to its fullness. But one is so thrilled, even in the beginning of the tragedy, that one has shed tears and nothing is left afterward. Once the zenith is reached, there is no more experience to be had; and so, instead of keeping from the mouth of eternal life every experience one makes, one throws it into the life behind without knowing the secret of it.

The mystics have, therefore, by sitting in different postures and by standing in different poses, gained control over their muscles and nervous system. And this makes an effect on their minds. A person who lacks control over the nervous system and muscular system, has no control over the mind; one eventually loses it. But having a control over one's muscular and nervous system, one gets control over the mind also. The means by which the life draws its power is through the breath. With every breath one draws in, with it one draws the life and power and intelligence from the unseen and unknown life. And when one knows the secret of the posture and draws from the unseen world the energy and power and inspiration, one gets the power of sustaining one's thought, one's word, one's experience, one's pleasure, one's joy.

Someone asked a wise person what was the cause of every tragedy in life. The wise person answered, "limitation." All miseries come from this one thing: limitation. Therefore, the mystics have tried by exercises, by practices, by studies to overcome limitation as much as possible. There is no worse enemy of humanity than helplessness. When a person feels, "I am helpless, I cannot help it," that is the end to that person's joy and happiness. Besides that, there is a thought power necessary with both posture and breath in order to gain physical control.

One must get above one's likes and dislikes, for they cause much weakness in life. When one says, "I cannot stand this; I cannot eat this; I cannot drink this; I cannot bear this; I cannot tolerate; I cannot endure," all these things show one's weakness. The greater the willpower, the greater the individual is able to stand all that comes along. It does not mean that one has no choice. One can have one's choice, but when one gives in to that choice, then life becomes difficult.

There is a false ego in humanity which is called *nafs* by the Sufis, and this ego feeds on weakness. This ego feels vain when one says, "I cannot bear it, I do not like it, I do not look at it." It all feeds this ego, its vanity. It thinks, "I am better than others," and thereby this ego becomes strong, and so one's weakness becomes strong. But one who has discrimination, distinction, choice, and at the same time they are all in one's control, the one who enjoys sweet but can drink a bowl of something bitter, is that person who has reached mastery.

Impulse also weakens when people give in to the impulse helplessly. For instance, there is an impulse: "I must go to the park"; and instead of waiting till there is the time to go to the park, they quickly put on their hats and go along. They follow their impulses immediately; they lose power over themselves. But one who subordinates the impulse—controlling it, utilizing it toward the best purpose—attains to mastery.

Besides, indulgence—to indulge in every comfort, to seek convenience, always to look for the path of least resistance, all these things bring weakness. However small the work may be, if one takes it seriously and finishes it with patience, one gains much power over oneself. Patience is the principal thing in life, although sometimes patience is as bitter, as hard, as unbearable as death. Sometimes one prefers death to patience.

It is a great difficulty that the people in this land of America are losing this quality every day, more and more, because providence has blessed them so well. They have conveniences, they have comforts, they are the spoiled children of providence; and when it comes to having patience, it becomes very hard to them. Therefore, individual people have to practice this spirit, for we do not know what may follow. We live in this world of uncertainty, and we do not know in what condition we may be put tomorrow. And if we have not the strength of resistance, we easily can break down. And therefore, for the human race, it is the most necessary thing to develop patience in all conditions of life, in all walks of life, in all positions of life, in all conditions. Whether we are rich or poor, high or low, this is the one quality that must be developed.

Besides, it is patience that gives endurance, it is patience that is all-powerful; and by the lack of patience one loses so much. Very often the answer of one's prayer is within one's reach, the hand of providence not very far, and one has lost one's patience and lost the opportunity. All these things are acquired by physical control, physical culture. Physical control can build a foundation for the character and for the personality, a foundation to be built in order to bring about spiritual attainment.

47

Seeing

BELOVED Ones of God, I would like to speak this evening on the subject of seeing.[1] You can see, you can look, and you can observe. These three words denote the same action, but at the same time, each word suggests something different. By observing, you understand something about it, about that which you see. By seeing, you take a full notice of it. By looking, you look at it. Whether you understand it or whether you do not understand it, whether you take notice of it or whether you do not, you have at least cast your glance on something. And so there are three conditions: looking at a thing on its surface, and seeing a thing properly, and seeing a thing with complete observation to observe it, to understand it while looking at it. All people take notice of things in these three ways. That which interests them most, they observe it keenly; that which attracts their thought, they see it, take notice of it; and that upon which their glance falls, they look at it. And there are, therefore, three different effects made upon a person of all that person sees: a deeper effect of that which one has observed fully; a clear effect of that which one has seen; and a passing effect of that which one has glanced through. Naturally, therefore, among all those who live under the sun, there are thinkers, there are seers, and there are those who have two eyes.

And there is another side of the question: that someone who is walking has a certain experience of the way this person has

1. Lecture given in Summer School, Suresnes, France, August 30, 1925.

gone through; and a person who goes the same way in an automobile has a different experience; and for one who flies on an airplane, the experience is different still. Perhaps those who have walked have not been able to reach the same speed as the one in the automobile and the one in the airplane. But the observations that they have made, the sights that they have seen, and the experiences that they have are not to be compared with the one going in the automobile or the one flying in the air. And in this way our minds work. There is one whose mind is working at the rate of the airplane, the speed of the airplane. And there is another person whose mind is working at the speed of the auto.

And the speed of those walking, whose minds are working at that speed, perhaps will not imagine so greatly as the other person. But what they will think, they will think thoroughly; what they will see, they will see thoroughly. It is they who will have insight into things. It is they who will understand the hidden law behind things, because the activity of their minds is normal. Of course, quick thinking does not always depend upon the quick activity of mind, but sometimes it is the quality of mind. An intelligent person is quick thinking also, but that is another thing. The difference of it can be seen between the two stones: the pebble and the diamond. They are both stones. One is precious, the other dull. So these are two different qualities of mind. One thinks quickly and intelligently. The other thinks quickly and is always mistaken. One is mistaken because one thinks quickly. For the other one, it is the quality of mind that, even in quick thinking, that person thinks rightly. Nevertheless, the rhythm of thinking has a great deal to do with one's life. Those who have traveled on foot, in the automobile, and the airplane all go the same way; and when the three meet together, and when the three speak of their experiences, you will find a greater difference in their experience. And it is in this way that different people who have gone through the same life, who have lived under the same sun, born on the same earth, yet are so different in their mentality. The reason is that the mind has traveled in a different speed. Their experiences are quite different, though they have gone through the same way. What they call seers are the ones who have not looked, but who have listened. And how have they seen? By controlling the impulses of walking quickly, by resisting the temptation of going to the right or to the left, by going steadily to the object that they have to reach—all these things make one a seer.

There are long interpretations of the word *seer*. Sometimes people say, "This person is a clairvoyant or spiritist, or sees fairies, ghosts, or spirits." But that person is a different person; that person is not a seer. A seer need not see the world unseen. There is much to be seen here in the world that is seen. For there is so much that is hidden from the eyes of all people that they could see in this objective world that, if all through life they were contemplating upon seeing in this objective world what they can see, they will find sufficient things to see and to think about.

It is a childish curiosity on the part of some when they want to see something that no one has seen. It is for their vanity to tell you they see something that others do not see. It is to satisfy their curiosity that they have seen something that is not to be seen in this world of objects. The world seen and the world unseen, both, are one and the same, and they are here. What we cannot see is the world unseen. What we can see is the world seen. And what we cannot see, it is not because it hides itself from our eyes. It is because we close our eyes to it.

And then there is a long sight and short sight and medium sight. There are some who can see far beyond, far back, or long before the happenings; that is a sight also. And there is another sight in which people only see what is immediately before them, what is next to them, and see nothing that is behind them. And their influence is as far as everything that stands next to them; it is that which influences them. They cannot see far behind or they cannot see far before. And there are others who have reasoned what they see; then they reason it, and that is a medium sight. They reason it as far as their reason allows them to reason. They cannot see beyond their reasoning. They go so far and no further. Naturally, when these three persons will meet, and when these three persons will hear, each will have their own language. It is not surprising if one does not understand the point of view of another, because one has one's own sight. And according to that sight, one looks at things; and no one can give one's own sight to another person to see it differently.

If spiritual people have in all ages taught faith, it is not because they had a wish that none should think for themselves but keep everything in faith that is taught to them. If they had that intention, they would not have been spiritual people. Nevertheless, however much clever a person is, however greatly devoted a person is, however much enthusiastic, without a faith the spiritual ones could not impart their knowledge to this person, because there is no such a thing as spiritual knowledge in the sense of learning. If there is anything spiritual that can be imparted to the pupil, it is the point of view, it is the outlook on life.

If some people already have that outlook on life, they do not need a spiritual guidance; they have it. But if they have not, then words or explanation will not explain it to them, because it is a point of view. It cannot be explained in words. However much explanation people would give about the sight that they had seen when they were on the top of the mountain, to the one who never climbs the mountain, that person will hear it and perhaps will refuse to believe in all that they say. Or if a person had a trust in those who are explaining what they saw from the top of the mountain, then perhaps that person will begin to listen to their guidance. One will not see it but will listen and will benefit by the experience of those who have seen it from the top of the mountain. But those who go on the top of the mount will see for themselves the same experience.

And now there is another side to the question, and that is from which height one looks at life. There is a quite different sight when a person looks at life standing on the ground; and it is quite different again when a person has climbed on the mountain; and it is again a different outlook if a person has climbed to the top of the mountain. And what are these grades? These grades are a consciousness. When a person is looking at life as "I" and "all else," that is a point of view. And when a person sees only "all else" and forgets "I," that is another point of view. And when a person sees all and identifies it with "I," that is another point of view. And the difference this point of view makes in a person's outlook is so vast that words can never explain it. What they call nirvana, or cosmic consciousness, is the idea that one gets by reaching the top of the mountain. And the idea of communicating with God is that when a person has reached the top of the mountain, the ideas of "I" and "you," and "he" and "she" and "it" are more when a person is standing on the ground.

Spiritual progress is an expansion of the soul. It is not always desirable to live on the top of the mountain, because the ground is made for humankind also. What is desirable is to have one's feet on the ground and head as high as the top of the mountain. A person who can observe from all sides, from all angles, will find and experience a different experience. Seeing from every angle, looking at every side will convey a new knowledge, a different knowledge than that person had known.

And then there is a question of the seeing and not seeing. This is understood by mystics: to be able to see at will and to be able to overlook. It is not easy for a person to overlook. It is something also to learn how to overlook. There is much that one can see, that one must see; and there is much that one may not see and that it is better that one did not see. If one cannot see, that is a disadvantage. But there is no disadvantage in not seeing something that one may not see, because there are so many things, things that could be seen, one may just as well avoid seeing them. They lack mastery who are held by that which is seen by them. They cannot help but see it; although they do not want to see it, they cannot help to see it. But those who have their sight in their hand, what they want to see, they see. What they do not want to see, they do not see; that is mastery.

And as it is true with the eyes that what is before you, you see, and what is behind you, you do not see, so it is true with the mind: what is before it, it sees; and what is behind it, it does not see. And therefore, a person who sees may see one side, and always the other side is hidden. Naturally, therefore, if this objective world is before one's eyes, the other world is hidden from one's sight; because what is before one, one sees, and what is behind one, one does not see. And as it is true also that what is behind one, one can only see by turning one's head back, so it is true also that what the mind does not see, can be seen by the mind when it is turned to the other side. What is learned in esotericism, in mysticism, is the turning of mind from the outer vision to the inner vision. And you might ask, what benefit does one derive from it? If it is profitable to rest at night after the whole day's work, so it is profitable to turn one's mind from this world of variety, in order to rest it and to give it another experience that belongs to it, which is its own, which it needs. It is that experience which is attained by meditative process.

A person who is able to think and not able to forget, a person who is able to speak but not able to keep silent, a person who is able to move and not able to keep still, a person who is able to cry and not able to laugh, that person does not know mastery. It is like having one hand. It is like standing on one foot. To have complete experience of life one must be able to act and take repose. One must be able to think, and one must be able to keep silent. There are many precious things in nature and in art, things that are beyond value; and yet there is nothing in this world that is more precious than sight, and that which is most precious is insight.

To be able to see, to be able to understand, to be able to learn, and to be able to know, that is the greatest gift that God can give; and all other things in life compared to it are small. In order to enrich one's knowledge, in order to raise one's soul to higher spheres, in order to allow one's consciousness to expand to perfection, if there is anything that one can do, it is to help in every way oneself, that the sight, which is the sign of God in humanity, may be open. It is the opening of the sight which is called the soul's unfoldment.

God bless you.

48

Sufi Mysticism

FRIENDS, I would like to speak on the subject of Sufi mysticism.[1] Mysticism is neither a faith nor a belief, neither is it a principle nor a dogma. A mystic is born; mystic is a temperament, and mystic is a certain outlook on life. It is therefore that many are confused by the word *mystic*, because mysticism cannot be explained in plain words.

Impulse, for a mystic, has divine significance. In every impulse, therefore, a mystic sees divine direction. What people call free will is something that does not exist for mystics. They see one plan working and making its way toward a desired result, and every person, whether willingly or unwillingly, contributes toward the accomplishment of that plan. And that which one contributes to this plan is considered by one free will, and by another, an accident. Those who feel that: "This is my impulse, this is my idea, this I must bring to action," only know of that idea from the moment the idea has manifested to their view. They therefore call it free will. But from where did that idea come to them? Where does an impulse come from? It comes directly or indirectly from within. Sometimes it may seem to be coming from without, but its beginning is from within. Therefore, every impulse, for a mystic, is a divine impulse. But you might ask: Why is every impulse not divine for everybody, since every impulse has its origin within? Because not everybody knows it to be so. The divine part of the impulse

1. Lecture given in the Virginia Hotel, Los Angeles, March 26, 1926.

is in knowing it. The moment you are conscious of the divine origin of the impulse, from that moment it is divine, although at all times in life it has come from within. It is the fact of knowing which makes it divine.

Mystics remove the barrier that stands between themselves and another person by trying to look at life not only from their own point of view, but also from the point of view of another. All disputes and disagreements belong to the misunderstanding between persons; and mostly people misunderstand because they have their fixed point of view, and they are not willing to move from it. This is a rigid condition of mind. The more dense a person, the more that person is fixed in that person's own point of view. Therefore, it is easy to change the mind of an intelligent person, and it is most difficult to change the mind of a foolish person once it is fixed. It is the dense quality of mind which becomes fixed on a certain idea, and that covers the eyes from seeing from the point of view of another. Many think that by looking at things from the point of view of another, we lose our point of view. But I would like to lose a point of view if it was a wrong point of view. Why must one stick to one's own point of view only because it is one's own point of view? And why is it one's own point of view? Are not all points of view the point of view of one and the same spirit? And as two eyes are needed to make the sight complete, and two ears are necessary to make the hearing complete, so it is the understanding of two points of view—two opposite points of view—which gives a fuller insight into life. A mystic calls this unlearning.

What we call learning is fixing ideas in our minds. Learning is not freeing the soul; learning is limiting the soul. By this I do not mean to say that learning has no place in life. I only mean to say that learning is not all that is needed in the spiritual path. There is something besides, there is something beyond learning, and you can get to it by unlearning. Learning is just like making knots of ideas, and the thread is not smooth as long as the knots are there. They must be unraveled. When the thread is smooth, you can treat it in any way you like. The mind with knots is not capable of having a smooth circulation of truth. The ideas that are once fixed in one's mind block it. Mystics, therefore, are willing to see from all points of view in order to make their knowledge clear. It is that willingness that is called unlearning, and I will give an example of it.

Once I was traveling on a ship, and there was a young Italian who was perhaps an atheist. And seeing me in a sort of religious robe, he thought I was a missionary who was preaching a certain faith. He began by saying, "I do not believe in anything." He defended himself and protected himself by this affirmation. I said, "That is very nice. But what do you believe? How do you say it in words?" "Well," he said, "I believe in eternal matter." I said, "Your belief is not very far from my belief. You believe in eternal matter, and I believe in eternal spirit. It is the same thing. Eternal matter, I call eternal spirit. I am willing to take your word as long as you believe in the eternal. You call it matter. I call it spirit. We shall not argue on words. What is the use? If you are pleased to call it matter, I am willing to accept it." And from that moment we became great friends, and a truth he would never have listened to, he listened to with great interest. He parted by saying, "Your religion is my religion."

That is the idea of the mystics. They see the superficiality of differences and the uselessness of it, and that they are only caused by a little ego, a little vanity, a little pride that my argument is right and yours is wrong. That is all. The sense of understanding is one and the same in all of us, and if we are willing to understand, the understanding is within our reach. Very often, what happens is that we are not willing to understand, and that is why we do not understand. Humankind has a sort of stubbornness. People go against what they think comes from another. At the same time, all that is learned has come from another; they have not learned one word from themselves. All they have learned is from others, yet they call it their argument, their thoughts, their view. There is no such thing; they have taken them from somewhere. It is by accepting this fact that makes mystics understand all, and it is this which makes them a friend of all.

Mystics do not look at reasons as everybody sees them, because they see that the first reason that comes to our mind is but a cover over another reason that is hidden behind it. They have patience, therefore, to wait till they have lifted the veil off the first reason and seen the reason behind it. But then again, they see that this reason, which was hidden behind the first reason, is a more powerful and great reason, but there is a greater reason still behind it. And so from one reason to another reason they go, and see in reason nothing but a treachery to cover reality. And as they go further, penetrating the added walls of reason, they reach a place where there is the essence of reason. By touching the essence of reason, they see the reason in every good and bad thing.

And now you compare a mystic with an average person who argues and disputes and fights and quarrels over the first reason, which is nothing but a cover. Compare the two. One is ready to form an opinion, to praise one and to condemn the other; and the other patiently waits till reality unfolds itself gradually. A mystic believes in the unknown and unseen, not only in the form of God, but in the unknown that is to come, the unseen that is not yet seen; whereas the other person has no patience to wait until that person knows the unknown and sees the unseen.

A mystic does not urge the knowledge of the unseen or unknown upon another, but sees the hand of the unknown working through all things. For instance, if a mystic has the impulse to go out and walk toward the north, the mystic thinks there must be some purpose in it. The mystic does not think it is only an imagination, a foolish fancy, although the reason for it that mystic does not know. But the mystic will go to the north and will try to find the purpose of going in the result that will come from going there.

The whole life of mystics is mapped on this principle, and it is by this principle that they can come to the stage when their impulse becomes a voice from within that tells them go here or go there, or leave or move or sit there. Therefore, while others are prepared to answer why they are doing anything or where they are going or what they wish to do, the mystics cannot answer, because they themselves do not know. And yet they know more than those who are ready to answer why they are going and what they are going to accomplish, for what does one know about what will come or follow? One makes one's program and plans, but one does not know.

"Man proposes, and God disposes"—many say this every day, and at the same time they make plans and programs and lay out their plans. A mystic is not particular about it. A mystic is working on the plan that is laid out already and knows that there is a plan. The mystic may not know the plan in detail, but the mystic is one who will know the plan—and if anyone does, it is the mystic. This again tells us something; the one who knows little, knows most; and those who seem to know more, know the least.

The outlook of a mystic is that of a person standing on the top of a mountain and looking at the world from a great height. And if you say, "But a mystic looks upon them all as one and not much different from the other; they are all like children to the mystic." But you see the same from the top of a mountain also: all tall and short people, all seem to be of the same size, they appear like little beings moving about. And an average person is frightened of truth in the same way as a person who has not been on a great height gets a fright at the sight of the immensity of space. So the truth is immense, and when a person reaches the top of understanding, that person becomes frightened and does not want to look at it. Many have told me that: "The Eastern philosophy interests us very much, but the conception of nirvana is very frightening." I say, "Yes, it is frightening; for one who is not accustomed to stand on the top of the mountain, it is frightening. But truth is just the same: truth is frightening, but truth is reality."

Besides, humanity is so fond of illusion that it, so to speak, revels in it. If a person awakens another person who is seeing an interesting dream, that person says, "Oh, let me sleep." People like to look at their dreams. They do not like to awake to reality, because reality is not so interesting as the dream. So among the students after truth, you will find one among a thousand who is courageous enough to look at the immensity of truth. But many others take interest in the illusion; and they are glad, out of curiosity, to see a mental illusion because it is different from the illusion of the physical life; and they are apt to call it mysticism. But that is not mysticism. No one can be a mystic and call oneself a Christian mystic, a Jewish mystic, or a Muslim mystic. For what is mysticism? Mysticism is something that erases from one's view that idea of separateness; and if people claim to be this mystic or that mystic, they are not mystics; it is only a name they are playing with.

People say that a mystic is someone who dreams and who lives in the clouds, but my answer is that real mystics stand on earth with their heads in heaven. It is not true that the wise person is not intellectual or that the wise person is not clever. The clever person is not wise, but the one who has the higher knowledge has no difficulty in having the knowledge of worldly things. It is the one who has only the knowledge of worldly things who has great difficulty in having the higher knowledge. It was very wise of Ford,[2] who told me the other day, "If you would have been a businessman, I am sure that you would have been successful." "Furthermore," he said, "I have all my life tried to solve the problem which you have solved." This again gives us an insight into this idea that a higher wisdom does not debar a person from having worldly wisdom, but worldly wisdom does not enable a person to have the higher wisdom.

2. Henry Ford (1863–1947).

And now, coming to the mystics' vision. People think seeing some colors or some spirits or some visions is mystical. I do not think that mysticism can be restricted to these things, and those who see these things are not necessarily mystics. Besides, those who can see and whose vision is clear, say so little about it. The mystics will claim the least of seeing wonderful things or doing wonderful things. It diminishes their vision, their power, as soon as they begin to feed their vanity by a claim to know or do things that others cannot do. Because the main thing that the mystics have to accomplish is to get rid of the false ego, and if they feel it on claiming such things, they lose all their power and virtue and greatness.

Besides that, friends, for a mystic, every person is a written letter, just like before an experienced physician, a person's face is a narrative of that person's condition. And yet, do you think a mystic would say, "In this person I see this," to another person? Never. For the reason is that the more they know, the greater trust is put in them by God. They cover all that is to be covered. They only say all that is to be said. Would you ever see a mystic say, "I understand your ways, I catch you!" Never. A mystic will know the most and will act innocently. It is the ones who know little who make a fuss about their knowledge. The more a person knows, the less that person shows to the world.

Do you think a mystic is ready to correct people for their follies and to condemn them for their errors and to accuse them of their foolishness? Mystics see so much of errors and follies and foolishness that they never feel inclined to do so. They just see life in its different ways, they just see this process that an individual goes through in life. It is by mistakes and errors that one learns in the end, and mystics never feel that they should condemn anyone for this. A mystic only feels that it is natural. Some are going rapidly, others are going slowly. Foolishness is just like light and darkness. It is through the darkness that the sun rises, and through ignorance wisdom will rise one day. Mystics, therefore, need not learn patience; they are taught patience by life from the beginning till the end. Mystics need not learn tolerance; their outlook gives them tolerance. It is natural for them. Mystics need not learn forgiveness; they cannot do anything but forgive.

Humankind loves complexity and calls it a knowledge. A great many societies and institutions, here and in the world, which call themselves occult and esoteric and psychic and different names, knowing the fact that everyone is interested in complexity, they cover truth. And instead of covering it in one cover, they cover it in a thousand covers to make it more interesting. Just like there was a custom in ancient times, that when people went to the wise, they said, "How shall we worship? How shall we have a manner of worship?" And the priest said, "How far do you live from the shrine?" And they said, "Two miles." And the priest answered, "Well, you must come on foot to the shrine and walk around it a hundred times before you come in." He gave them a good exercise before they were allowed to come in. And the same thing they do even today. When people say, "I want to see truth," but they want to look for truth in complexity, they cover truth under a thousand covers, and then they have the problem to solve. Are there not many interested in the mahatmas of the Himalayas? Are there not many seeking for the holy souls in remote places of Persia, looking for a master perhaps in the midst of Australia? Perhaps next year an article will appear in which it is said that a great soul is found in Siberia. What is it all? It is all the love of complexity, funny notions, and strange ideas which lead souls no further.

Therefore, very often mystics appear to be simple, because sincerity makes them feel inclined to put truth in simple language and in simple ideas. And because people value complexity, they think that what the mystics say is very simple and that it is something which they have always known; there is nothing new. But I repeat, there is nothing new under the sun, as Solomon has said.[3] Besides, truth belongs to the soul, and the soul knows it. And as soon as the truth is spoken, the soul happens to know it; it is not new to it, it is not foreign to it. If a person says, "This is something I have already known. It is nothing new; I know about it." But I say that even if the soul has known, it is never repeated too often for you. The great saints of the East have said, perhaps, a phrase: "God is one," for a million times in their lives. Do you think they were so foolish as not to understand the meaning, to say it only once? Why do they repeat it for a million times? The reason is that it is never enough. We live in the midst of illusion from morning till evening, when we go to sleep. What we do not know is the illusion in which we are from morning till evening. It is not the truth that we do not know; truth is all we know, if we know anything fully. The mystics, therefore, instead of learning truth, instead of looking for truth, wish to maintain truth. They wish to cling to the idea of truth, to keep the vision of reality before them lest it be covered by the thousand veils of illusion.

One may ask, does a mystic make any effort to reach the higher realization? Yes, it is an art that is taught from teacher to pupil; and so, from one person to another person, this art is handed down from ages. But one might think, if truth is within oneself, why is there a necessity for such an art? Art is not nature, after all. The animals and birds, they do not need an art; they are happy, they are peaceful, they are innocent, they are spiritual, really speaking. Yes, it is true, but they live in nature, their life is natural. We live far away from nature. We have made our own artificial world to live in. And it is therefore that we require an art to come out of it—and I do not mean to say that we must go out of life or that we must not have anything to do with life in order to be mystics. But we have to practice that art by which to get in touch with reality.

That art is concentration, in the first place. By concentration, I do not mean to close the eyes and sit in the church on

3. Ecclesiastes 1:9.

Sunday. Many know how to close their eyes and sit there, and their minds wander about, especially at that time when they close their eyes. Concentration means that every atom of the body and of the mind is centered in one spot. The next stage is contemplation: that is to be able to retain an idea that raises one's consciousness from the dense world. The third stage is meditation, and that is to purify oneself, to free oneself, and to open oneself to the light of truth, that it may abide in one's spirit. The fourth step is realization. Then the mystic no longer is the knower of truth, but truth itself.

49

Cosmic Language

BELOVED Ones of God, my subject this evening is cosmic language.[1] What is it that makes those who can know, know of the changing of weather before the time? The coming of the flood, the coming of rain? The changing of weather, all different changes in nature—there are some who know this beforehand. Of course, there are signs, the signs that become words for those who read them; and by those signs they understand about the coming events from nature. For them, therefore, it is a language of nature. For the others who do not know it, it is gibberish, *sons qui n'ont pas de sens*.[2] And what is it that those who know not only astronomy but what is called astrology—that by the change of the planets and stars they know about people's past, present, and future? This only shows that there are signs that indicate the past, present, and future to them as words would indicate, and from them they learn of coming events. There are, again, phrenologists who can see from the muscles of the head of a person. There are those who know physiognomy. They can see from the face of a person things that no one has told them, that they have never heard but that they know, and they read it from the face of a person. There are others who know a science that is as small as palmistry; but even for them, the sign of the hands are as loud words, as the form of a physiognomy.

1. Lecture given at the Sorbonne, Paris, December 22, 1924.
2. Sounds that do not make sense.

And now, coming to the natural conditions such as the parent knowing the language of the little child who has not yet been able to speak. The child's tears and smiles, its looks, explain to the parents its moods, its pleasures and displeasures, its aspirations and its wants. One has also known that the heart of the lover knows the pleasure and displeasure, knows the changing of the moods of the beloved, without having spoken one word. There are physicians who, by their experience in life, have become so advanced, that before the patient has spoken one word, they already have found out what is the complaint, what is the matter with the person. There are businesspeople who are so engrossed in business that, as soon as a person has come to their shop, they know whether the person will buy or whether the person will go without. And what does it tell us? What does it show us? It only shows us that whatever be the walk of life, whatever be our profession, our business in life, whatever be our occupation, through it all there is a sense in us, a sense which can understand the language without words.

There is also another question that is attached to it closely, and that question is that everything in life is speaking, is audible, is communicative in spite of its apparent silence. What we call the word is only the word that is audible in our everyday language. What we consider hearing is only what we hear with ears, and we do not know what else there is to hear. In point of fact, there is nothing that is silent. All that exists in this world, whether seemingly living or not living, it is all speaking. And therefore, word is not what is audible to us, but word is all. This argument is supported by the Bible where it says first was the Word and the Word was God.[3] But I would repeat again, that it is not only that first was the word, but always when there was anything, it was the word, and always the word it will be.

The real meaning of the word is life. And is there anything that is not life, whether silent or whether living? For instance, a person not knowing the secret of the planets, not knowing

3. John 1:1.

their influence, their nature, and their character, what do they say to that person? Nothing. That person knows that there are planets, and that is all. As far as the science of astronomy, a person who has learned astronomy may say the planets have a certain influence upon the weather and upon the season. But the astrologer perhaps hears a louder sound of the planets, and can say that the influence of the planets has a certain influence upon the individual and so has a certain influence on their life. What do we understand by this? We understand by this that to one, the planet does not speak; to another, it speaks whispering; and to the other, it speaks loudly. It is the same thing with physiognomy. To one, a person is a mystery; a second knows something about that person; and to a third, that person is like an open letter. For one physician, it is necessary to make the examination of the person with all different machines and mechanisms. Another physician would like to ask the patient about the patient's condition. And a third physician looks at the patient and knows perhaps more about the patient than the patient does.

Is it not the same thing with art? When we see one person go in a gallery, looking at different pictures and thinking that it is different colors, red and blue, and different lines—that person is very pleased to see different colors, and that is all. That person knows nothing more about it. There is another person who sees historic fact behind the picture and is more interested in it, because the picture has spoken to that person a little more. But there is a third person, and for that person, the picture is living. The picture which that person sees, which that person appreciates—that picture is communicative, for the person reads in there meaning that was put in it by the artist. It is revealed to that person by looking at it. Therefore, by the mediumship of the picture, one person's thought, one person's ideal is known to the other person.

And in the same way, to one person, music is a noise, perhaps a harmonious group of notes. For that person it is a pastime, it is a certain amusement through which that person is going. To another person, there is some joy coming out of it; that person is enjoying some pleasure and feels the music that is coming to that person. But there is a third person who sees the soul of the one who is performing the music, who sees the spirit of the one who has written the music. Even if it is a thousand years ago that the music was written, that person hears it in the music.

Is this not all communicative? If it be art or science or in whatever form, life expresses its meaning. If one was only able to understand it, one could always understand. The one who does not understand this, will not understand it. That person's sense is closed. It is just like the ears being deaf. In the same way, the sense of communicating with the thing has become dull; that person does not understand it. But if one does not hear, one may not say that a person is not speaking. And in the same way, if one cannot sense the meaning of life, one must not say that life has no meaning. The word is everywhere, and the word is continually speaking.

There is a belief, a belief of the ancient people, and that belief is that the word was lost and then the word was found. And out of this thing a great mystery was made, a mystery that until now exists among the people of the old civilization. Until now they are looking for that word, that word which was lost; and in gaining that word they consider it the fulfillment of their life. And there are many who have tried to mystify this idea, and mystify it so much that a person may go on and on and never come out again. But the truth is not found in mystification; the truth is to be found in simplicity, because there is nothing more simple than the truth. Simply, the idea is this: that all that exists has come out of the word and goes to the word and, in its own being, is a word. Besides the quotation of the Bible that I have given to you, there is a quotation of Qur'an which says that: "God said 'Be!' And all became."[4] And there is, again, a word from Vedanta, which perhaps comes from scriptures

4. Qur'an 2:117.

that existed many thousand years before the Qur'an and the Bible. That scripture says Nada Brahma, which means that in the word you will find the creator.

By *word*, I do not mean a word that is audible to the ears. By *word* I mean what is conveyed to you, all that is expressed to you and that comes to you as a revelation. I feel that what you hear by your ears, what you smell by the nose, what you taste, and what you touch—by all your different senses, by all that becomes intelligible to you—that is a word. In other words, that life's mission is to convey something to you. And all that it conveys to you is a word; through whichever sense you experience it, through whichever sense it is conveyed to you, it is a word. But now, it is not only depending upon the five senses—taste, hearing, seeing, smelling, and touching—that the word depends. For these five senses—we call them five senses, because through five different organs we experience them, but in reality there is only one sense: a sense that experiences life by the vehicle or mediumship of five external senses. And because of these five different directions of life, therefore, the experience of life becomes divided into five different experiences. For the word becomes, or life becomes, visible to us, touchable, audible, smellable, and tastable. But besides these five aspects in which we are accustomed to hear the word, there is another aspect of hearing the word that is heard independently of the five senses. And that way of hearing the word is called the intuitive way. When a person comes before you, whether you are satisfied with that person or dissatisfied, whether this person has given you sympathy or antipathy, you cannot say this by seeing that person or hearing that person—you have recognized that person. You can only say that you had such and such an impression of that person. And this shows that there is a language, a language which is beyond the sense, and a language you are capable of understanding if the sense was open to a certain degree.

There is not one person who has not experienced this. It may be that some have experienced it more, others have experienced it less. Some are conscious, some are unconscious, but a feeling comes, a feeling when a disaster is coming, a sorrow is coming, a failure is coming, a success is coming. No doubt a person with a tender heart, a person with a greater sympathy, a person with love awake in the heart is more capable of experiencing this sentiment. And it is this feeling that may be called intuition, something which does not depend upon reason. A woman feels it more perhaps than a man. Very often a woman can say to the man that, "I feel it. I feel that it is going to be a success," or, "it is going to be a failure." And when he is asking her, what is the reason, because man is very reasoning, she will still say that, "I feel it." There is a language that she understands; the man has not heard it.

Then there is another experience. It is not only that the spiritual people or most advanced people know about it, but it is an experience that is known even to a scientist, to a material person, to an inventor. One may not believe it, but at the same time this experience comes: a sense of an idea how to work out an invention or how to form a system, how to make a plan, how to write poetry, or how to arrange a thing that one wants to arrange. However much a person says that these great inventors have studied mechanics, they have studied technology, and that it is the outcome of that which gives them that ability, there are thousands of students who study mechanics, but not everyone is an inventor. And there is one who accomplishes, and that one surely accomplishes by the help of inspiration.

You will also ask all sorts of artists—a painter, a drawer, a singer, a dancer, a writer, a poet—you may ask them, "Can you always do the work that you wish to do so perfectly, so excellently as sometimes you are able to do?" The answer will be, "No. I never know when it will be done. It comes, and sometimes I am able to do it. It comes, and I know not when and where." A poet may try for six months to write a poem, the poem that the poet's soul is longing for, the soul's desire, and yet it has never been finished. And yet it may be finished in six minutes if the moment comes, if that time comes. The poet cannot imagine how a thing should come in six minutes' time—something that is wonderful, something that is complete in itself, something that gives the poet the greatest satisfaction, something that is living. The great musicians have not written their most beautiful compositions, their masterpieces, in six months' time. All that they have written in a long time is of little importance. It is those moments when they have written and finished in five minutes—it is that which is living and will always live.

And it is the same thing with all different aspects of art. Creative art depends upon inspiration. And mechanical art may be developed, and a person may be most qualified, but it is a dead art. The only living art is the art that comes from a living source, and that living source is called inspiration.

And then, what is inspiration? Inspiration is the same word of which I have been speaking all this time. It is the hearing of that word which comes from within; and a person hears it and expresses it in the form of line, in the form of color, in the form of notes, as words, in whatever form. But the most interesting thing, and most wonderful thing in connection with this subject, is that the same inspiration may come to people. It is the same word that is coming to four people. One person is drawing it in the form of line. Another person is putting it into the form of notes. Another person writes it as words; another person paints it as colors. This shows that artistic inspiration, inventive genius in every form in which the meaning of life wishes to express itself, has within another aspect from what we see in the outside life. Then what is inspiration? A word that we already know, a word that is the soul of inspiration? Where does it all come from? It is a beauty in itself. It is an energy in itself. It is a wisdom in itself. It is a harmony in itself. It is energy, because it gives the greatest joy when once expressed by an artist, by an inventor. It is wisdom, because it comes with an understanding of accomplishing it. It is light, because the thing that one wants to make becomes clear to one; there is no sign of obscurity. It is harmony, because it is by harmony that beauty is performed.

There is another form, a form that people attain by a greater enlightenment, by a greater awakening of the soul. And that form is to be pictured as people going through a large room where all things are exhibited, and yet there is no light except their own light—a lantern of searchlight. If they throw their light on music, music becomes clear to them, note and rhythm become clear to them. If they throw their light on words, the words become clear to them. If they throw the light on color, all color comes near. If they throw the light on line, all lines, in most harmonious and beautiful form, come near to them. This searchlight may become still greater and may reach still further. It may be thrown on the past, and the past may become clear, as it has been clear to the prophets of the past. It may be sent on the future, and it is not only a sense, a precaution that a person might have, but a glance in the future. This light may be thrown upon living beings, and the living beings may become before a person as written letters. This light may be thrown on objects, and the objects may reveal their nature and secret. And when this light is thrown within themselves, then the self would be revealed to them; they would become enlightened on their own nature and their own character. And it is this form of experience, it is this way of knowing, which may be called revelation. And it is in the knowing of revelation that one accomplishes the purpose of life.

And the mystics have said that the word which was lost is found. Friends, every child is born crying; a crying which conveys that it has lost something. What has it lost? It has lost the word. And that is to say that all that a child sees, it knows not what it is. It conveys to it nothing. The child seems to be lost in a new country where it has been sent. And as the child begins to know a little, either the parent or those around it, the colors and the lines and all things of this world begin to communicate with the child a little, to speak. In this way the child begins to foreknow something a little, with the eyes, ears, nose, mouth; and it is in this way the child begins to know the word that is within. And it is this communication that is the sustenance of life. It is not the food or drink that keeps humankind alive. It is that communication through the different senses, and to what extent one understands what they have to say—it is this that makes humankind live.

And when we think of our life, and when we compare the pain that we have in our life to the pleasure, the portion of pleasure is so little. Besides, what little pleasure there is costs also, and therefore, it resolves into pain. If that is the nature of life, how could we live in this life if there was not this communication, if there was not this word, which in a smaller or greater extent we hear from all things, from nature itself? And it is in the fulfillment of this communication that no wall nor any barrier may stand between us and between life, within and without. It is this that is the longing of our soul, and it is in this that revelation comes. It is in this that is the fulfillment of our life.

Thank you all for your sympathetic response.

May God bless you.

50

Spirituality, the Tuning of the Heart

BELOVED Ones of God, it is my great privilege to give the address before the people of this city on the subject of spirituality—the tuning of the heart.[1]

The tuning of the heart must be looked at, in the first place, as the tuning of the self—what they call in English language "pulling oneself together." Most often what happens is that we are occupied in our everyday life, and every influence from within or without has an effect upon us; and that effect, so to speak, breaks a person to bits. And when a person is upset, disturbed, out of rhythm, then a friend says, "You must pull yourself together." That means you must tune yourself. It is just like a string of the violin becoming loose. By tuning it to the pitch where it ought to be, you get the whole violin in tune. Apart from others outside one's own life, even for one's own self, one's own peace and rest and illumination, it is necessary that the heart must be tuned.

And now one may ask, what do you mean by heart? *Heart* is a word of the dictionary, and very few really understand the meaning of it. Some think it is a piece of flesh in the breast; other times the heart is an object of the fairy tale in which it is so often said that it is love and imagination and feeling! But it is only a fairy tale. For many people, it is not clear what the word *heart* means. If I were to explain it in simple terms, I

---

1. Lecture given at Casa de Mañana, La Jolla, California, March 11, 1926.

would say the depth of the mind is the heart, and the surface of the heart is the mind. The reasoning faculty is the surface of the same object, the depth of which is the faculty of feeling. And therefore, it is not true that the heart is enclosed in the physical body, only that there is a seat of the heart in a certain part of the body, as there is a seat of thought in another part of the body, just as, according to modern science, the brain is everywhere in the body at the same time. The seat of the thought is called brain, and the center of the brain is the head. And so naturally, one points to the breast when there is a thought of the heart. Really speaking, it is not the body that envelops the heart, but it is the heart that envelops the body. There is a saying of one of the great poets of Hindustan who says that if the heart was large enough, it could accommodate the whole universe. When the heart is developed and becomes living, the physical body seems too small and too limited in comparison with it, for there is no comparison with the physical body and the heart. The relation of the heart with the outside world—for instance with conditions—is so great that it is the condition of the heart that influences one's life's affairs. When the heart is out of tune, everything goes wrong; it makes the whole atmosphere out of tune.

Once a lady told me, "Some bad luck has come to me this week." "What is it?" I asked. She said, "Many things are lost or glasses break; everything tears, breaks, and becomes destroyed." So I said, "There is something wrong with yourself: you yourself are out of tune, especially this week. Something has upset your rhythm." And on thinking on the subject a little more, she found out that, yes, it was so. Now, what effect does the heart have upon the outer conditions? But you will see, the more keenly one watches life, the more one will find that the heart has an influence upon failure and success, rise and fall, favorable and unfavorable conditions in life. No sooner has the heart been tuned than conditions in life become better, ill luck is averted. The wrong reasoning of people who become tired and discouraged with things going wrong, losses—all these things disappear no sooner than the heart becomes tuned. But at the same time, how difficult it is to keep the heart tuned when it is so difficult for a delicate instrument like the violin to keep always tuned! The heart, which is incomparably more delicate, is the instrument upon which the soul, the spirit, plays. It is the heart on which the model of the harp that we know has been made. The ancient artists have given the harp or lute into the hands of angels. Symbolically, it means the heart: angels mean the heart, the heart quality.

Besides this, the reason why the heart has an influence upon our life is because the heart is as the seed out of which that plant has grown that we call our self. The fruits and flowers are the effect of heart; the same thing is produced that is already in a person's heart: thought, speech, and action. For instance, people cannot conceal their feelings always; one may play to be a friend, one may play to be a brave person. But whatever one plays, one is able to sustain, to maintain so long and not longer, because what is in the heart must come out some time or other in the form of action or words, from the lips or in the expression or in the form of atmosphere. But the heart never fails to express itself in some form or other. And what does it express? What it possesses, what it is. A person may be our bitter enemy and for a long time may try to hide it; in some form or other it will come out. If a person may be our friend and likes to show indifference, in some form or other that person's love will leap out. If a person has something against you or has admiration for you, it cannot be hidden. People will close their lips, not show anything in their actions, and never say it; but even through the eyes it will come out, through the expression it will show, through the atmosphere it will manifest. The heart will speak louder than words.

Now, for the relation of the heart to those we meet. This relation is so great that in the life of industry, business, profession, science, in politics and domestic life, in every aspect of life, the people you meet are influenced and affected by the condition of your heart. If the heart is out of tune, let a person go into the office, to the factory, at home, among friends, in the club, in society gatherings, whatever that person will say or not say or do, still that person's very presence will upset the condition wherever the person will go. Therefore, the secret of magnetism, the mystery of attraction in a person is solved in the study of the heart. Very often you are uncomfortable in the presence of someone, or the presence of someone draws you quite near without that person having said one word. One may feel in the presence of someone as if one had always known the person, as if one had always been friends. What is it? It is the condition of the heart of that person. If one is in tune, one tunes others also. But if a person's heart is not in tune, then anyone in that person's presence goes out of tune. That is the mystery of attraction and repulsion. But very often one will see that people attract one day, but perhaps next week or a month or a year later, there is repulsion. The reason why that person attracted for a moment, was that person's heart was in tune. But then, after a week or a month or a year, that person's heart has become out of tune. It is therefore that one who is attracted once will feel repulsion another time; and because one does not know the reason, one always blames the other. Human nature is such that one sees oneself last. Especially if one comes to blame, one never thinks of oneself; one first blames another.

And if we go still deeper into this subject, then we shall find that not only with human beings but with the atmosphere, with the weather, with the climate, there also is the tuning of the heart. With all those things that come, even so much with nature, there is the tuning of the heart. Even flowers feel it. Many people can keep flowers in their hands; and with others, no sooner they have touched a flower than it fades. The fading of the flower means that it becomes out of tune.

We have stories of the sages in the East that some of them, after having left that place of rest and peace where they were staying—perhaps under the shade of a tree or in a village in a certain place—after they had left for ten years perhaps, when they came back the place was in a bad condition. But the moment they had come and their presence was there, it became fertile, and the place was flourishing again. What does it mean? They are in tune. You may have heard in the stories of the East of what they call the philosopher's stone: whatever it touches it turns into gold. But there is no such a thing as the philosopher's stone. If there is, it is the heart of humanity. If the heart is in tune, whatever it touches it turns into gold. The sages have not only healed people but tuned people, because all ill-luck, sorrow, failure, disappointment—all these things come from one reason, and that is the heart being out of tune. The moment the heart is tuned, one rises above all these things; conditions begin to change.

And if we go still further, we come onto a religious ground—not on a religious but more than religious—a spiritual ground. And that is the effect of another person's feelings on us. Very few in this modern time know, as occupied as they are in worldly affairs, what effect the feeling of another person brings upon us, what influence it has upon us. A central teaching of all religions and the philosophy of all prophets and the philosophy of all things has been one and the same, and that was consideration of the feeling of another. And if anyone has touched this true religion, or if anyone has understood the mystery of all mysteries, it is this one thing; and that one thing is regard for the feeling of another. The life such as we live from morning till evening—busy, occupied, and interested in our own motives, persevering to get our object accomplished—we become regardless of the feelings of another. Sometimes the others do not say it, and we become still more ignorant of this.

There is a fable that once there was a dispute between a man and a lion. This dispute was on the question of who was superior. The lion said the lion; the man said man. So they said, "We shall find out. We must ask three beings." So they first came near the tree, and they asked the tree, "What have you to say: Is lion superior or man?" The tree said, "Lion is much better than man. Men walk when journeying under our shade, and they sit under our shelter. And when man is rested under our shade, then his first thought is about the fruits. Then he throws stones at us. He is ungrateful. He does not think that we are standing in the sun and that he has had his rest, but he throws stones at us and gets our fruits. He never thanks us, he never thinks about it." So the lion said, "Now, look here, here is your praise." Man said, "Come to someone else." When they went further, there they meet a cow. And both asked the cow what it thinks: Is the lion superior or man? The cow said, "Please do not talk about man. When I was young they cared for me and I gave milk; and my little calves were taken and used on the ground to work. And when they died, man used their skin for his purpose; for his food, he has used the flesh of my children. My milk has been taken by him. And when now I am old and of no use, now he throws me away in the forest, where any lion or tiger may meet me and eat me one day." And there was another proof.

When we begin to think about and study human nature more, we begin to find that there is no creature as selfish as humankind can be. With all the intelligence and goodness and greatness, if there is any creature most unjust and inconsiderate, it is humankind. And as such, for one who is a naturally talented person, whatever one's motives be—whether wrong or right, small or great—one very often is inconsiderate about the feeling of one's fellow human beings—with a relative who depends upon one, who waits upon one, who cares for one; someone who relies upon one's word in any case. People have always their motives, their conveniences, their joys, their objects before them; all else is aside. Always people are victims to their inconsideration. They do not know that it all means failure, ill luck, difficulty, trouble, problems, anything they have to face, very often because of their inconsideration. And you may ask, what do I mean by inconsideration? Friends, we have so many debts to pay in life, and not only money to pay, but there are obligations to those around us, obligations to those who expect something from us—thought, consideration, love, service, justly or unjustly, foolishly or wisely—our obligations toward friends and acquaintances; and obligations to pay to strangers. And today the life we live keeps our mind so much at work that it takes away that thought from us. Every day we become less and less considerate, less and less thinking. Therefore, the unknown influences that come upon us and bring about changes in our life are such that we blame this person or that person or stars or planets or different things. But in reality, it all belongs to the world of hearts. As soon as we know it, then we consider our relation toward another our duty, our interest. Our virtue in the world is to be thoughtful, to be considerate about every word we say, every thought we think, every feeling we have, thinking what influence it will have upon another, if it will bring pleasure to another. If there is any religion or spirituality, it is in this.

Education today begins with the children by teaching them figures, how to count money. And when they are grown up, they are best qualified to guard their interest. If that is the only education, we cannot expect a better time to come in the world. There is no longer religious education. No doubt the absence of religious education has broken down, to a very great extent, the error of creeds. Nevertheless, there is nothing to take the place of it. And children come to youth and become men and women, and what has there been in their education that has something to do with the heart quality? There is an old saying of Persia that a good manner brings good fortune, a bad manner attracts bad fortune. I was wondering about it, how far it can be true. There are so many ill-mannered people, thoughtless, with little feeling, who are well-off in the world, but by studying human nature and life, I found it is quite true. In the first place, one cannot judge if a person, being rich or in a high position, whether that person is happy. I think to have good fortune gives more happiness than to have a great deal of money, and we really are deprived of good fortune. What is happiness? It is a flourishing condition of the soul, and it is never there in outside life. For a child who has begun to be ill-mannered, hurtful, and destructive, the same power it attracts and the same things come to it. What it gives is rebounded, and it takes the same which it gives. And if the child goes on giving, the same things it gets back. How many are ignorant of that fact? People never think that they can be hurt by their own words or acts or thoughts or by their feelings. They go on doing, and at the same time it comes again to them, sweeping them off from the ground of happiness.

And now coming to the religious. What do we mean by prayer or meditation or concentration, or by praying with the congregation or by sitting in the church? What is gained by the prayer? The same thing: the influence of prayer is the tuning of the heart. What is gained by concentration? Again, the tuning of the heart. By meditation? Again, the tuning of the heart. All different ways given by religion or esoteric sources in whatever religion, it is all given toward that accomplishment: the tuning of the heart. So long as the heart is not tuned, whatever form of piety we show, it has no meaning. If it is not done with that object, it has no meaning; nothing is accomplished. Are there not many millions of people, apart from those who do not believe in prayer, who pray every day at least once? But not knowing the fact that it is the tuning of the heart, they are not directing their hearts toward it; and therefore, they get a very small benefit. If they do not know concentration, they may sit in the church at least once in a week, they may sit there week after week, but they have not accomplished that of which concentration is only the first knowing, if they do not know the object of concentration, which is again the tuning of the heart.

There is a story of the Shah of Persia. He used to spend most of the night in prayer. Once his minister begged him and said,

"King, there is so much to do all day long, for you to pray so much time of the night is not right." And he said, "Please do not advise me on that question. You do not know. In the night I pursue God, in the day God follows me. In everything I do, there is God with me." That is the meaning of the tuning of the heart. When the heart is not tuned, then no prayer is of any use.

In the Muslim prayer there is a custom that the leader stands before the people and leads the prayers. During the time of Aurangzeb, the last Mughal emperor of India, a very great sage was compelled by the state to go and join in the prayer. He always said, "Leave me alone in my solitude." But they forced him to go among the people, and they said, "No, no. You must go, follow the example taken by the others." And he went and stood there. And in the midst of the prayer, this great seer went out of the mosque. And the police brought him into the court, saying, "He ran away in the midst of the prayer." And when court asked, "Why did you do this sacrilege?" "Oh," he answered, "I could not stand there. The leader went home, he had forgotten his keys. So I had to go home with him." The mind of the leader was in his keys, and while conducting the prayer his mind was in his pocket. The seer knew and ran away. Is it the closing of the eyes and sitting in a religious attitude that makes concentration? Very often people think that to recite a certain form with closed eyes is concentration. This is the absence of knowledge of concentration, and it deprives one of progress.

Now, one will ask what is the way of tuning the heart and how to do it? There are four different ways. The first way is the stilling of the mind. Those whose minds are not still, whatever be their qualifications, they are incapable of accomplishing anything. They will always show to be restless, thoughtless, and full of errors. It is too much activity of mind that works against it. And how is stilling of the mind, how is it to be accomplished? By concentration. And how is concentration to be done? Very often people, not knowing the way of concentration, strain their minds too much, and instead of accomplishing, they destroy. They become weak because their minds are strained too much.

For instance, the other day in San Francisco I saw Rodin's statue of the *Thinker*. It amused me very much to see how Rodin has given it a hard expression and a stiff body. And then he made the remark that it means "thinking hard." By hard concentration, much is spoiled. And very often, among a hundred persons who concentrate, there are at least ninety persons who think hard. Then there have come others who, instead of doing it themselves, take a sensitive, nervous, fine person as a medium, and make that person concentrate. They wreck the medium's brain, and then think they have accomplished something.

Besides that, by taking an object before us, we do not only accomplish concentration but partake something of the object, just as it is according to the point of view of the mystic about diet: that everything we eat has not only an effect upon our body but also upon our character. It is therefore that the Brahmins had a certain idea of food. They did not touch other food that had a bad effect upon the character. The Muslims, the ancient Jews, they all had a certain way of eating. They did not eat all things; they knew what effect it has upon the character of humankind. Today we do not think about it; today we have gone so far that we do not question about food. What comes free is taken without knowing what it contains. It is the same thing with concentration. What we concentrate upon has a similar effect upon us. If we concentrate upon a flower, a rock, a stone, a tree, a living or a dead thing, whatever we concentrate upon, that effect one draws from it, whether it gives power, inspiration, spirituality, or stupidity and cruelty.

Besides that, there is the natural way of doing things. If one concentrates longer than one should, one loses by it. It is just like people strain their voices if they sing too long. The master singers always say, "Do not sing any more than so much." Very often people say they have bad effects from concentration or from any meditative practice. It is because they do not do it under a certain direction. What is happening today is that people take books to guide them. They find it is much easier than a teacher. They ask where to find a teacher to listen to, a teacher that they do not want. Then what do they want? What they want is to ask for a book or something that can give guidance. Do you think that in the East any sage publishes a book, writes in a book about the way of attaining spirituality? Never. They never make such a thing. It is not so cheap as that.

With the Chicago Exhibition,[2] where all the world religions where represented, Vivekananda[3] came from India, and the word *yoga* became very well-known. Others wrote some books, and now many who want to know something go to the book as to the drugstore, and according to that book, they begin to practice. If everyone went to the chemist and bought medicine, there would be no necessity of the physicians any more. And in such a delicate, important matter as spiritual attainment, the tuning of the heart, if one took the aid of books, where will it lead one to? It does not mean that books are not inspiring and a great help on the path, but at the same time, when it comes to practice, it must be done under the personal instruction of someone who knows and to whom one can give all the confidence one has. Besides that, the present age has lost one great quality that humankind always had and valued, and that quality is patience. The quicker activity becomes today a great virtue, and people have anything but patience.

It was so amusing the other day. There was a ferry going from one post to the other in San Francisco, crossing the bay, and so many automobiles had to stop for one minute. And every person was blowing a horn—a thousand motors not staying one moment, all together blowing horns. What is it? It is collective impatience. And where will it lead? It may show a great quality: it is a sign of great strength and energy, an outbursting of energy.

2. The Parliament of World Religions held in 1893.

3. Swami Vivekananda (1863–1902).

But at the same time, everything has a limited purpose; and when something is not under control, especially human nature and character, some day or the other it must get loose. And when it has got loose, it will result in a great disaster.

For instance, who could, for one moment, think that such a war as this[4] could have come in this time of great civilization, when there are so many universities and colleges, when there is so much spoken about goodness and kindness, uniformity and humanity. With all this progress, how could it come? That it has come is due to collective impatience, a lack of general spirituality. And if it goes on like this, perhaps there will be still greater scientific inventions, but what is it? It is going forward in one way but going backward in thinking and in feeling.

The other day a genius came to me to have my blessing. I asked him, "What do you want" He said, "I want to make a cannon that can destroy the whole town." I said, "I give you my blessing, but no blessing on this. From this day direct your mind in constructive work." And the reason of this is that, from the first day when education begins with the child, what is taught is to guard your interest and not to take every step with thoughtfulness. Besides this, the other way of tuning of the heart is in cultivating a sympathetic nature, and that is cultivated by a regard for another.

The third way of developing that heart quality by which the heart is tuned, is to be able to judge oneself. And so long as one judges others, one is not able to judge oneself, because then one is so full of the faults of the others that one never has time to judge oneself and is always unjust. Besides that, the most amazing thing is that you will find the foolish one more ready to judge than wise one. The more thoughtful, the more wise the person, the less that person judges, because one has so much to judge in oneself that there remains very little to judge outside.

Besides that, there is a way of seeing from the point of view of another; and so long as one has not cultivated that faculty,

4. World War I.

one has nothing for another but blame. And praise and blame do not depend upon what a person is, but upon the heart being favorable or disfavorable, and upon the outlook on life. Besides this, a person who sees with one eye has not a complete vision. In order to have a complete vision, two eyes are needed; and in order to understand a certain idea, a certain point of view of another as well as one's own is needed. Your own point of view is not uprooted. If that is the case, it is not right. But it is by looking from the point of view of another that one completes vision. That is also tuning of the heart, because when two persons meet and when there is understanding, at once there is friendship established. It does not take long to become friends if there is real understanding. But if there is no understanding, and if there are barriers between people, if they are divided from one another, it is by the lack of understanding. If anything brings people together, it is by understanding one another. Therefore, in having understanding of every person we meet, we tune our heart.

And now, coming to the conclusion of this subject, I shall quote the saying of Christ, "Seek ye first the kingdom of God, and all these things shall be added unto you."[5] That is the best idea one can find anywhere: that by getting in tune with the God-ideal—in other words by getting in tune with one's divine ideal—one will become so attuned that one will find a way open to the heart of every person one meets, and one will find a connection with every condition and with every object, and realize at-one-ment with the Absolute. And it is this achievement, it is this attainment that one can call spiritual development.

God bless you.

---

5. Matthew 6:33.

51

THE FOUR PATHS WHICH LEAD TO THE GOAL

MY beloved Ones of God, I would like to speak this evening on the subject of the four paths that lead to the goal.[1]

There is one path that may be called the way of the intellectual. When an intellectual person has risen above intellectuality, then that person may be called an intelligent person, for a difference can be made between an intellectual person and an intelligent person. An intellectual person is one who has gathered knowledge by impressions, by studies, and is the ruler of the domain of one's intellect. What one has learned, what one has studied, what one has experienced, that is what one has in the book of one's mind, and that is one's world. No doubt it makes a person captive to a limited horizon of knowledge, and it is rising above that knowledge that may be called intelligence. But, no doubt, it is the intellectual person who is capable of being intelligent. The intellect is a cover over intelligence, and when this cover is taken off, then a person becomes intelligent. Intelligent are those who perceive for themselves, who learn for themselves, who understand for themselves, who recognize things by themselves, who are pupils and who are teachers within themselves, at the same time.

When once people have risen above the boundaries of their limited knowledge, then the higher knowledge begins to come to them by itself. They begin to learn more in one moment than an intellectual person would learn after having read all the

1. Lecture given in Summer School, Suresnes, France, August 23, 1925.

books in the library in six years' time. When once intelligent people have got an insight into the hidden laws of nature, they begin to see a way opening and the higher knowledge. Their reasoning changes its nature; it becomes the essence of reason. They do not see things from the reason they have learned from the world, but they begin to see the reason of all reasons, the reason that is covered by ordinary reasoning. There is a question: How can one be intelligent? The answer is that human beings are born intelligent; it is afterward that they cover their intelligence, and they are glad to call it intellect. Then they are recognized to be learned and think they have got some knowledge. And it is at that point that they make their intelligence limited; and as long as the intelligence is limited, so long they cannot see further than they see.

There is a time in people's lives when they are learning. And there comes a time when they themselves are the knowledge. It is at the time when a soul becomes knowledge itself that it begins to have glimpses into the hidden laws of nature. And this illumination may develop so that one may see the whole manifestation, clearly and fully, in the light of intelligence.

The Qur'an says, "God is the light of heavens and of the earth."[2] And if there is any spark of God that could be found in humanity, it is its intelligence. Naturally, therefore, when this divine light that is hidden in humanity is once brought to blaze, is once risen as a flame, it illuminates one's path to perfection.

And the other path to perfection is the path of righteousness, is the path of duty, is the path of good action. People may not be intelligent but may be conscientious in what they do and what they should do, so that they may always use their good will to do righteous action; and by doing so, they are fulfilling that law of harmony that automatically raises the soul to perfection. Very often one wonders about friends and relations whom one thinks are goodness itself, and their actions are righteous ac-

2. Qur'an 24:35.

tions, and yet they never seem to show any tendency toward religion or meditation. And often a person thinks: "What a pity! Will they arrive at spiritual perfection?" The answer is yes, it is possible that they will arrive at that perfection before the seeker who makes too much fuss about it and does little. They will arrive at that perfection before the person who talks too much about spiritual things and knows little. They will arrive sooner to that perfection than the person who is clinging to the outer things of religion and spirituality, merely by righteous actions and by good deeds. They may not know it, but automatically it must work because they are taking the path of righteousness that surely will lead them to perfection.

The third path is the path of discipline. It is in the path of discipline that concentration is necessary, that meditation is necessary, that contemplation is necessary. All different forms of discipline are necessary in order to bring about the realization that is the ultimate goal. The path of meditation enables humankind to experience different planes of life, but not always the way people say: by classifying, by saying this plane and that plane, this grade and that grade.

The real experience of the inner life cannot be very well classified. For instance, to a meditative person, if another person asks if there are seven planes of existence, the meditative person says, "Yes, it is so." But the other person says, "I have read in a Greek philosophy that there are nine planes of existence. Can it be true?" "Certainly." But another one comes and says, "I think that there are only three planes." The meditative person says, "Certainly, I do agree with you." The meditative person does not tell this to please the other; those who meditate are able to see planes of existence as five, nine, seven, in as many forms as you like to see it, because they actually see them. For instance, go to a beginner in music and ask how many notes there are. The beginner says there are seven notes, and then there are semitones besides. Yes, but to very experienced musicians who have perhaps given all their life to music and have come to understand the essence of sound, if you asked, "Is it not true, as the Chinese say, that there are twenty notes in the octave?" They say, "Yes, it can be true." But if you say, "But Indians say that there are twenty-four notes in the octave," they will say, "That is true, too. It is as you look at it." It is not that the octave has twenty-four notes. It is as you look at it; therefore, you see it that way.

All that people learn intellectually of metaphysics keeps them limited to book learning. They derive no benefit but a passing interest to be surprised, to know that there are so many different planes of our being. They do not go beyond. If people have to see them to know what they are, they cannot see them; but by the way of meditation they can realize them. And by this realization they can give interpretation to any philosophy. Whether it is Buddhist or ancient Greek philosophy or Vedanta philosophy, to any philosophy you put before them they can give their interpretation, for they know what they have experienced through meditation. No doubt the way of self-discipline is a very difficult way. It is a way of mastery. It is the way of power, but it is a hard and difficult path. Imagine, if you practiced discipline by sitting in one pose or in postures, how difficult it is to keep doing it for a long time. Imagine if you make a vow—I will not eat fruit, sweet or sour—how difficult it is. Imagine if you make a vow of silence, of fasting, a vow of standing so many hours or walking or keeping up at night—for part of the night or the whole night—it is not always easy. Self-discipline is learned by going against one's inclinations, one's own inclinations. One might ask, are they not natural inclinations? Why must one go against them? The answer is that one cannot say which is one's own inclination. All inclinations are borrowed here, and what one calls natural is that to which one becomes accustomed. The word *natural* is a word that one can study for years and years and years, and one will find, at the end of the study, that there is no such a thing as natural.

There are natural inclinations to pleasure and comforts that clash with the still greater inclinations and deeper inclinations we have for greater power and strength, for more light, and for more life. So the inclinations can be divided into two aspects: the innermost inclinations and the inclinations that one feels in everyday life. There is always a conflict between them. The innermost inclinations are sometimes undermined by the outer inclinations. And by learning self-discipline, one learns to suppress the outer inclinations in order to give a way for the inner inclinations to rise and to flourish, which in the end culminates in what we call mastery.

The fourth path to perfection may be called the path of devotion, a path that cannot be compared with any other path in its value, in its depth. For the reason is that devotion strikes straight to the spirit of God. Not everyone is capable of this path, for in some persons the heart is closed by the head quality, by intellect. And in some persons the heart quality is foremost. The first step in the path of devotion teaches selflessness. It makes one unselfish. And if I were to explain what devotion is, I would say that devotion is the tuning of the heart to its natural pitch; in other words, the healthiest condition possible in a person when devotion has blossomed. It is devotion alone that covers the false self from a person, be it for a human being or for God. If truth is ever to be seen, it is in devotion; for the world of the heart is a different world than the world where all live. Its law is different, the weather there is different. Its sky is different, its sun and moon different. The nature of that world is different; it is a world in itself. By devotion, heaven is brought to the earth. And yet how very often a person says, "But is it not a simple devotion?" It is in simplicity that the greatest subtlety is to be found.

For it is the heart of the devotee that is liquid, compared to the others whose hearts have become crystal. It is wakened to sympathy; it is open to appreciate all beauty. Krishna has said

"I am with my devotees."[3] And therefore, if one asks: "Where is God? Is God in the sixth heaven or only in the seventh heaven or in a certain paradise or certain palace in which people imagine God to be in?" The paradise or the palace or the dwelling place of God is in the heart of the devotee. No doubt, for a person to rise to a devotion to God is not easy. It is therefore that by the Sufis in all ages, devotion was practiced gradually by their sympathy for their teacher, by the devotion for the divine, and by the culmination of that devotion in God. It is devotion that raises the object of its devotion or its ideal to the highest heaven. It is by devotion that rocks have been turned into gods. Someone asked a Hindu. "By the worship of a god made of rock, what do you gain? Is it not a god that you have made?" "Yes," said the Hindu, "my hands have made this god of rock, and my devotion has given life to it. If you believe in the formless God and have no devotion, you have not yet reached God. God is far away from you. My God is before me. Your God is away from you." As the Bible says: "God is love."[4] If God is to be found anywhere, God is to be found in the human heart. And when is God to be found? When the heart is awakened to sympathy, to love, to devotion.

God bless you.

---

3. Bhagavad Gita 10:9–13.
4. 1 John 4:7–8.

52

Intellect and Wisdom

BELOVED Ones of God, my subject this evening is intellect and wisdom.[1] Often people confuse these two words: *intellect* and *wisdom*. Sometimes they use the word *intellect* for wisdom, sometimes *wisdom* for intellect. In point of fact, these are two different things altogether. The knowledge that is learned by knowing the names and forms in the outside world is the knowledge that may be called intellect. There is another source of knowledge, and that source of knowledge is within oneself. Saying it is within oneself might confuse some people. One might think that within oneself means inside of one's body, but this is the ignorance of humanity of itself. Humankind has a very poor idea of itself, which keeps it in ignorance of itself. If one only knew how large, how wide, how deep, how high is one's being, one would think, act, and feel differently. But with all this length and width, depth and height, when one is not conscious of it, one is as small as one thinks oneself to be.

The essence of milk is butter, the essence of the flower is honey, the essence of the grapes is wine, and the essence of life is wisdom. Wisdom is not necessarily a knowledge of names and forms. Wisdom is the sum total of that knowledge that one gains from within and without. Intellectuals are those who will argue and will dispute, but very often upon a subject that they themselves do not know fully. And very often you see among those who dispute and argue, that they dispute for the very

1. Lecture given at the Sorbonne, Paris, February 25, 1924.

reason that they do not know it fully. Their argument on the outside makes one feel that they know it, but the very reason that they argue shows that they do not know it. Those who know do not need to argue; they know it. For the very reason one knows, one is so satisfied that the satisfaction does not give one the hunger of that person who argues.

In the first place, the trace of wisdom in nature can be found in studying instinct: the art of weaving and making a nest among the birds; the art of swimming among the fishes; the art that exists in nature; and besides that, the science that exists in the animals and birds who know their medicine when they are ill. In the ancient traditions of the Oriental people there exists a belief that the first medicine was learned by the bear. The reason is that the bear knew when it was ill, where to go, and what to find as an herb or as a remedy to take in order to bring about a cure. By a deep study of this idea, no scientist will deny the fact that among the birds and animals there exists an instinct that, in their illness and distress, they too find the medicine.

Therefore, what we call intellectual study is a collection of knowledge that has been given to humankind as a study to learn; and one understands it as an intellectual study, something to depend upon. But that is not all the knowledge; that is a limited part of knowledge. There is another fact of knowledge that can be drawn from the essence of life. That which is called instinct in the animals and birds in the lower creation, is the very instinct that, when developed in a person, becomes intuition. It is not true when the psychologist says that all the child knows is what the child has learned—whether a favorable attitude or an unfavorable attitude, whether a good manner or an ill manner. If two children were brought up from different parents and different races without being trained in manner or wisdom, you will find that both will show their manner and tendencies differently. If one were to think how much one learns from the outward world and how much one learns from within, it would not be an exaggeration if I were to say that ninety-nine percent one learns from within, and one percent one learns from without—if one learns. It is not true that outwardly the learned person becomes the great person or personality in the world. It is the inward learning that helps one to become that. By this I do not at all mean that outward learning is not required. Outward learning is the qualification of expressing the learning that one gets from within in a better form. But at the same time, it is from inner learning. If anyone has ever learned anything, one has learned from there.

And now the subject comes of how one has to pursue this. How does one pursue the wisdom that is within? By first realizing that intuition exists in oneself. It is not every person who perhaps even believes in an intuition. And among those who believe in intuition, they are not all those who trust in their intuition. No doubt they have a reason not to trust, because many times an intuition seems to be a futile knowledge. But if I were to say what is the reason that intuition proves to be wrong, I will say that it was not an intuition but that it was thought. Every person is not able to catch the first impulse, and the activity of mind always goes from one thing to another. Therefore, as soon as from within there comes one thought, it goes to another; and therefore, mind thinks it has thought an idea. And therefore, one thinks that: "I thought like this"; but really speaking, it was not an intuition. But after an intuition, one goes a little further in thought, and one thinks one has an intuition. In this way one begins to distrust intuition, and when one distrusts one's own intuition, one has no confidence in oneself. And to me the meaning of faith is self-confidence. The one who has no confidence in oneself, whatever be that person's faith or belief, it is not substantial. If a person would come to me and would say: "I believe in you, I trust in you, but only I cannot trust in myself," I would say: "I appreciate very much your trust and belief, but I cannot depend upon you."

But if another person comes and tells me: "I trust myself and do not know yet if I can trust you," I should say that there is a hope for that person. For I will know that person has taken the first step already. The person has to take the next step. Those who cannot trust their own intuition are perplexed; they do not know what they want. They will always depend upon outer things that give them reasoning; and the things of outer life, which are subject to a continual change and all subject to death and destruction, are not dependable. These things are called by the ancient Hindus an illusion. A person who thinks that: "I am a positivist because I depend upon outer reason," is depending on something changeable and subject to death.

But now a question comes: How are we to know that it is an intuition? The thought waves are just like voice waves. It is quite easy and possible that a thought of another person happens to float in that horizon in which one is conscious. And one hears it and thinks: "It is my intuition." Very often what happens is that a person feels a depression without any reason, a person feels humorous without any particular reason. Very often it is a kind of floating thought or feeling of another person that passes through one's own mind and being, and for that moment one begins to feel happy or unhappy without any reason. And it happens very often to all people during the day, that there come thoughts and feelings and imaginations that they have never thought or that they have no reason to think. It would then not be right to call these things intuition. Water that is to be found in a little pit is not the water that is in the depth of the earth; and therefore, the thoughts that come and go, floating on the surface, are not to be depended upon. Real intuition is to be found in the depth of one's being. In the first place, one must learn to believe in the existence of such a thing as intuition. The next thing is to be able to follow one's intuition, even at the cost of something valuable. Even if one were deceived for some time after, one will not continually be deceived. Therefore, in the end, one will find oneself on the right path.

But the third thing is to make the mind one-pointed by the help of concentration, which would help one to perceive the intuition properly. Just as in hearing the ears are so made that the voice waves make a resonance and become clear, so also the mind must be made a kind of accommodation or mold in which the intuition may become clear. The difficulty is this: that outwardly the work of the ear is different from the work of the eyes. The mind does both kinds of work: seeing and hearing at the same time. But besides this, the mind is perceptive and also creative. But it cannot at the same time both perceive and create, for creating is expressing and perceiving comes by receptivity. In the Sufi terms there are two temperaments among humanity: the *jalal* temperament and the *jamal* temperament. The jalal temperament is expressive, and the jamal is receptive. And the temperament that at the same time, is receptive and creative, that temperament proves to be without result. It is this temperament that is called *kamal,* a temperament that has no result. That is why many people would like to hear, and there are many other people who would like to speak. There are many people who would like to act and be active; there are others who would like to see others act, and sit.

The one who works is pleased with working. The one who is sitting is pleased to sit. Both enjoy what is akin to their temperament. Therefore, that one is creative who acts; the other is receptive who sits. But one can master one's life by taking these two different faculties in hand and trying both: at times to be creative and at other times to be receptive. The one who is creative needs, no doubt, an action and a knowledge of action. But the one who is receptive wants concentration and the attitude of mind that is receptive. The mind can become a receptacle of knowledge that comes from within. If we look among people, we shall find that among a hundred persons there are ninety-nine who are creative by nature, but only one among them who is receptive enough to receive from intuitive faculties.

The difficulty with the mind is that when one wishes to receive, the mind wishes to create. When one wishes to create, then the mind wishes to receive. For Hindus, the mind is like a restive horse. A horse, unless you have put a rein upon it, will not be controlled and will not take the direction that you want it to take. Therefore, in order to attain the wisdom that is as the essence of life and that is to be found within oneself, it can only be attained by first making the mind obedient. And the mind can be made obedient by concentration. People have easily understood when you tell them about voice culture, and how necessary it is, in order to sing well, to produce the voice. Also one can easily understand what it is to learn physical culture in order to make the muscles strong. But when it comes to training the mind, in the first place a person asks: "Is there a mind? I thought that there was only a brain." And if it happens that people believe in the mind, they do not know what can be done with it. Anything else they will find more valuable than the training of the mind. They might think that it is the work of the lazy people, who have all sorts of luxury to give time to it. It is the greatest mistake that one makes by keeping away that culture, which is the most necessary to begin from childhood, as a training. And sometimes a person asks the question: "Does a child not learn concentration when it goes to school?" And my answer is: "Quite the contrary. Children mostly lose their concentration in school." When little children begin to learn mathematics and go from one to a hundred, they lose their concentration. Children have never an opportunity to sit quiet for one moment. They have not often an opportunity to think of one thing for a moment. What, therefore, becomes of them? Children become nervous. Today one sees that nervousness is to be found everywhere. If people have equipped themselves with a certain amount of education, they are found to be nervous. Besides, after the education, the education has to be made use of. If the mind is not under one's control, how can one use it? It is one thing to learn, and it is another thing to make use of learning. It does not suffice the purpose to learn a song. By that, one cannot be a singer; one must learn to produce one's voice also. And so it is with intellectual knowledge. A person has become a qualified person by studying for a long time, and if that person cannot use a knowledge, what is the use?

There is a sufficient number of learned people. What today we want is people with masterminds: those who do not only see the life without, but within; who do not only draw inspiration from the life without but also from the life within. Then they become the expression of this perfect being, which is within, hidden behind this life of variety. I do not mean by this that everyone learned becomes a kind of super-being. I do not at all mean that a person should be able to perform wonders or to perform miracles. I only mean by this that a person may live a fuller life and may become a human being in order to bring about better conditions in the world. What do we want? We want human beings. It is not necessary that all people must become most religious or most pious or too good to live. We want wise people in business, in politics, in education, in all walks of life—those who do not only live on the surface, and those who do not only show belief in matter, but those who believe in life within and without. It is such souls who will produce beauty. It is these souls which will harmonize the world, who will bring about the condition that we need today. We want not only the knowledge of matter or spirit, but we want it living in all walks of life—in one's business, in one's effort, industry, in every art or science one is busy with—that one might use the wisdom that is perfect in oneself. When the individual and the multitude will find beneath their feet a solid foundation on which they stand, from that day we will begin to say that now we can hope for a better condition in the world. It is toward this ideal that every effort of the Sufi Movement is directed. It is to attain to this mastery of mind that the facilities have been given by the Sufi Movement to those who wish to study and practice in their lives.

53

THE AWAKENING OF THE WORLD IN THE NEW YEAR

BELOVED Ones of God, my subject of this evening is the awakening of the world in the new year.[1] By circumstances and by the time that is to come, the East and West, world's two poles, are awakening and are coming together. The East is awakening to life's needs, the West is awakening to life's purpose. The East is changing its sides, and the West is rubbing its eyes. The East is realizing the need of commercial and industrial development, and is considering social and political problems. On the other hand, the West is thinking, wondering about occult and mystic science, and is trying to awaken to the religious and spiritual ideals. You may call it involution or evolution, or you may see it as the East going downward or the West going upward, but it is a circle, and only action makes a step forward in evolution.

Now, taking the circumstances before our view, we see that all such things as wars and disasters and conflicts between nations and races, which the world has experienced recently, all these things have awakened humanity to think and to pursue the deeper side of life. No doubt the all-prevailing materialism and commercialism, as they are today, keep people still absorbed in their daily occupations so that they have not sufficient time to attain something their souls crave after. Nevertheless, the people in Europe and in America, whatever be their occupation, more or less, they are inclined toward the spiritual ideal. No

1. Lecture given at the Lenox Theater, New York, January 3, 1926.

doubt, very often seekers after truth who give their precious time to spiritual things become disappointed before they come to realization, and when these things are not presented as they ought to be. And when they find that it is not real, what they were seeking after, they think: What is reality? Worldly occupation is not real, and under the cover of something real there is also falsehood. Then where is reality? A wise person who has become disappointed says, "I shall pursue my material life. I am craving for reality, but I give it up. Perhaps someday I shall find myself."

It seems that there are four different kinds of persons who pursue the spiritual path. The one kind is those who are after phenomena. They think that in order to strengthen my faith in the hereafter, in the soul, in the deeper side of life, I must have some proof. They are willing to make any sacrifice or to pay any price for it. But when once they see a proof that there is something wonderful and something different from what they experience in everyday life, they meet with people who are clairvoyant or mediumistic or who have some such occupation as to tell the future or fortune or to see at a distance. They sometimes think it is true, and sometimes they are disappointed. But at the same time, nothing of all these things bring them nearer to reality. They keep people on the surface; people remain groping at the surface. Or perhaps their patience becomes exhausted, and they have found nothing. I spoke with people who give a greater importance to phenomena, who tell me that this day, when materialism is prevailing, it is best to give belief in the spirit and in the hereafter, to give some proof of the life of the other side, and that we can give this proof by spirit communication. And what has happened is that many have become curious—ten times more curious—and perhaps after one year they are still more curious. And where does curiosity end? It ends in outer communication. They communicate with a relation and then with a king and then with a prophet.

There is no end to it. And when there is one proof, there are ten mistakes; and in this way it goes on. And those who are not ready to believe, after having a thousand messages they will not believe in the soul and the hereafter. And if only spirit messages and plays and phenomena could attract a wise and serious person, it would be different. But that is not so. It is the sincere seekers who are the first to doubt; and before they come to the right thing, they have perhaps met ten wrong examples and are finished with them.

And there is another kind of person. This kind is wanting a certain knowledge, a knowledge that these people do not find in ordinary learning such as is given in colleges and universities. These people have finished learning grammar and all the books concerned with knowledge and learning. Now they want another learning of an intellectual type: that in the moon, there is a shrine; and on the top of the Himalayas, in a remote place, there is a deserted sacred center; that there are planet influences over the world; and that before a thousand years humankind had a different sense, and after a thousand years humankind will get still another sense; that the features will change, and humankind will become quite different. Then they believe more in the book than in a living person; and that which tickles their curiosity, they are pleased with it. This kind must have something to think about that is not everyday knowledge.

And, friends, there is a third kind of person: for these people the letter counts; for them, what is first is the law. They want to know about different religions, dogmas, and principles, and fixed virtues and sins, and what is right and wrong as it is written on the record; and this belief is better than the other, and that great teacher is not so great as another teacher; and the other teacher is different from another teacher. These people prove it by their lives, see their differences from what history tells them, or they see it from one book or another book. This is something they consider spiritual knowledge. Besides that, the meaning of different symbols, which, perhaps if ten wise people were asked, each wise person would give a different answer. These things interest this kind of person. They consider that as spiritual knowledge. Out of this, what they can find is nothing but the difference between the aspects of wisdom, which is one and the same. You'll find these people very often learned and well versed, knowing all the differences that exist between different religions. This knowledge we will call the classical knowledge of spiritual things.

And there is a fourth kind of person, and these people have no interest in all those things. They say, "I only see the need of the world and I am waiting, waiting for an extraordinary event to occur." Either they are looking to the sky, that from there should drop something from space that not everybody had seen; or they are expecting that something will happen so that everybody would be shaken, and everyone would kneel down and would begin to pray. But these things never happen. Jesus Christ came and spoke to a few fishermen and has gone. Muhammad fought and was driven out of his country and lived. Moses taught and gave the law, but the world did not know him. Nevertheless, what they have given has reached the world directly or indirectly. Some must suddenly be changed in a moment. It is a good ideal, but it is a question if it comes true. They are waiting and will wait.

And then there is a fifth kind of person who really thinks rightly on the spiritual subject: that what is the need of the world and of every individual is that the spirit may waken to reality; that the latest inspiration and power may manifest; that humankind may find eternal life within; that every possibility of expanding one's sympathy and love may be attained. It is by this ideal, that if people will proceed in the spiritual path, they will fulfill the words of Christ, "Seek ye first the kingdom of God, and all these things shall be added unto thee."[2]

2. Matthew 6:33.

Now, to tell you how does one pursue the right spiritual course. In the first place we must find out that physically, what are the possibilities of experiencing the inner life as closely as one experiences the outer life. Then comes the spiritual culture: that these very eyes, which only can see things of matter, are then able to see beyond. There is a quite different sensation, a liberation. There is one experience that one makes with the physical body, which one calls sensation. Any experience which is made by the senses is called sensation; but that experience which is made by sense, that which penetrates and reaches further than the ordinary senses and touches deeper than the every sensation, is the experience that allows one to attain the first step in the spiritual path. Never think that these two eyes can only see what they see. No, they are capable of seeing further than what they see, if only one were to explore the truth of life. Besides that, for the physical organs, such as the head and the body, one thinks that the head is for thinking and the body for working. But one does not see the other possibilities in the physical body, that the body is so constructed that the study of ordinary anatomy is not sufficient to understand it. There are nervous centers that are finer than material instruments and can examine and feel. And there are finer fluids. There is a finer life that can be experienced, there is a joy, there is a peace, there is a greater knowledge that can be obtained by the help of some particular organs situated in different places of the human frame. And this shows that, as people are capable of acting outwardly with the organs of the body, so they are capable of using their physical frame to make intuitions and inspirations clear to themselves.

One knows from a scientific point of view that the brain registers thought forms, impressions; but that is what comes from without. But humankind does not know that there are centers in which intuition is born, instinct is born—not in the human being alone, but also in the lower creation. What teaches fishes to swim without sinking and birds to fly? It is instinct. And where does it come from? That which in humankind we call intuition, and which in the lower creation is instinct. The source of both instinct and intuition is to be found within and not without. And the body that is made as capable as it is of working outwardly, so capable it is to perceive intuition. And when that sense is overlooked, naturally one lives but a half-life, and a certain part in one becomes blunted. When people can no more feel intuition, they no more can believe that they have something like intuition. Therefore, the real source of knowledge is stopped, because their intuitive faculty does not work. Then they find knowledge outside in books, in discussions. But no words can give that knowledge that one's self can teach, but can only teach when intuition is awakened. For the great gurus and teachers of humanity, the knowledge they have given is little, but their work is to awaken the knowledge that the real teacher from within may teach.

Now, coming to another aspect, and that is the faculties of the mind. The mind has five faculties: memory, thinking, judging, feeling, and reasoning. Feeling is the most important faculty; therefore, that part of mind is called the heart. Thinking comes on the surface, and that part is called mind. Heart and mind are one and the same thing. It is the surface of the heart that is the mind, and the depths of the mind that is the heart. When a person says, "I feel in my mind a great affection," it is in the heart. When I think very highly of someone, it is their mind. A great mystic of Hyderabad said in his poetry that the whole cosmos can become as a bubble in the heart of humanity if it is sufficiently enlarged. If there is such a possibility that the heart can become like an ocean in which the universe may seem to be a bubble, how great and how mysterious is humanity itself. Humankind's pursuit after little mysteries is in vain. Humanity is a mystery itself and such a great mystery—if only one can explore one's mind, dive deep into one's own heart, and see the phenomena. Then the whole life becomes a phenomenon, and every moment one would see nothing other than phenomena. No other wonder in this world would surprise one, for this wonder in oneself is much greater.

And then there is a moral world, which is greater still and which is to be explored within oneself also. If one only knew what a bitter feeling makes and what an affectionate feeling makes, how it separates and how it expands and penetrates through the space, and what it brings about, one would marvel in life. You see so many living beings, people moving about with eyes open, and yet their heart is closed to this truth. There is a psychological action that is caused by every person in the whole cosmos. Every little thought and feeling arising in the heart, before it is materialized, manifests on the surface and has its action in the inner world. Whether it is joy or sorrow or harmony or disharmony in the inner world, it all acts on those who know and do not know. People may feel and not say; or they may say, and it may not be heard; or they may do something, and it may not be seen. And yet what is done has its effects, whether it is a wrong or right or good or bad effect. Does an individual think that it is one's individual action or thought or feeling that can have an effect upon the whole cosmos? One never thinks about it, and yet it is so. A person may do something in the North Pole and then may go to the South Pole, and it is waiting there for that person. With all the thieves and criminals and treachery and deceit in this world, can you say with open eyes that anyone in this world can get away with anything that was not one's right, that did not belong to one? Perhaps on the surface. But then there is the government, an inner government, and that government has officials everywhere who will catch one wherever one goes. Every grain of food we eat and every drop we drink, every breath of the fresh air we take, all has its tax that we shall have to pay. That is the moral phenomenon that so few think about. We live in this world, intoxicated by what we do and want to do, and that intoxicates us so much that we do not see further. And there is much to be seen that is worthwhile.

And then we come to the spiritual aspect of our being to be explored. And that aspect is connected with our source and with our goal. Call that God or call it spirit or call it our real self or the absolute—it is one and the same. And by knowing that relation we can know and understand many things. We can understand why we have come here, and why we go back, and what there is to fulfill in this world, and where lies our real happiness and peace. We can understand the meaning of truth that words can never explain, and the relation with and the difference that kept us distant from God—what distance there is.

If humanity explores the faculties that can be explored in the body and in the mind, and the moral effect and influences, if one can realize this, then one can attain to the spiritual bliss that connects one with God, and which keeps one connected while on earth with the heavens, and which makes one an entity which is connected with the whole cosmos. It is with this realization that one lives a fuller life. We need not live the life of a wonder-worker or of an empty, curious person. What is needed today is for us to live a fuller life by discovering inspiration. If that is our occupation, it is the part of our occupation in life that we ought to think we have come here to accomplish.

God bless you and Happy New Year.

54

The Spiritual Significance of Sound and Color

IT seems what science arrives at realizing in the end, mysticism reaches from the beginning, according to the saying of Christ, "First seek ye the kingdom of God, and all will be added."[1] When one hears the present discoveries about sound and about color from scientific directions, one begins to be surprised; one says, "What a new discovery, something we have never heard." It is something quite new, and yet when you open the Bible, there it says, "First was the Word, and the Word was God."[2] And if you open the still older scriptures of the Vedanta, you read that in the Creator there was that word or that vibration. And when we come to the Qur'an, we read there that first there was the word "Be," and then it became.[3] The religions of the world, the prophets and mystics who existed thousands of years before knew it then.

Today someone comes with a little plate, a photographic plate, and says, "Here I have a photograph of sound." That shows how important is vibration and its action upon the plate. That person does not know that it is something which has always been known to those who knew it and has been spoken of, but in a spiritual term; and therefore, of what has been spoken that person does not think about. What is being spoken is thought of as something new, but as we realize, as Solomon has said that

1. Lecture, Switzerland, January 1925. Quote from Matthew 6:33.
2. John 1:1.
3. Qur'an 2:117.

there is nothing new under the sun,[4] then we begin to enjoy life, seeing how, time after time, the same wisdom is revealed to humanity. The one who seeks through science, the one who searches through religion, the one who finds it through philosophy, the one who finds it through mysticism, in whatever manner they seek the truth, they find it in the end.

I was very amused once when I was introduced in New York to a scientist, a philosopher, and the first thing he said about his accomplishments was, "I have discovered the soul." It amused me very much that all scriptures have spoken about it, that thinkers have spoken about it, mystics have spoken about it, the prophets have spoken about it, and the man comes and says, "I have discovered the soul." I thought, "Yes, that was the new discovery that we were expecting, something that we never knew."

Such is the attitude of mind today, the childish attitude. When one sees into the past, the present, and the future, one sees that it is eternal, and what one can discover is that which has always been discovered by those who seek. In the first place philosophy or science, mysticism or esotericism will all agree on one point if they touch the summit of their knowledge; and that point is that behind the whole creation, behind the whole manifestation, if there is any subtle trace of life that can be found, it is motion, it is movement, it is vibration.

Now, this motion has its two aspects. There are two aspects for this reason, that we have developed these two principle faculties: sight and hearing. One aspect appeals to hearing, the other to our sight. That aspect of movement or vibration which appeals to our hearing is the aspect which we call audible, and that which we term sound. The aspect that appeals to our sight, we call light, we call it color, and we call it visual. In the point of fact, all that is visible, all that is audible—what is it in its origin? It is motion, it is movement, it is vibration. It is one and the same thing, and therefore, even in that which is audible, that which is called sound, those who can see can trace color

4. Ecclesiastes 1:9.

in it. And those who can hear, to them even the sound of the color is audible.

Is there anything that unites these two things? Yes, there is. And what is it? It is harmony. It is not a particular color which is harmonious or which lacks harmony. It is the blending of that color, it is in which frame it is fixed, how the color is arranged; in accordance to that it has its effect upon the one who sees.

And so it is with sound. There is not any sound which is harmonious or inharmonious. It is the relation of one sound with another sound that creates harmony. Therefore, harmony is not such a thing that one can point out that this certain thing is harmony. Harmony is a fact, harmony is the result of the relation between color and color, the relation between sound and sound, and the relation between color and sound.

The most interesting aspect of this knowledge is how to different persons different colors appeal, and how different people enjoy different sounds. The more one studies this, the more one finds its relation with the particular advancement of human evolution, because one will find that at a certain time of one's evolution one had loved a certain color and then one lost contact with that color. With one's growth and evolution in life, one begins to like some other color. It also depends upon one's emotional condition, whether one is emotional, whether passionate, whether romantic, whether warm or cold, whether sympathetic or disagreeable. Whatever be one's emotional condition, in accordance to that one has likes or dislikes in colors. It is therefore that which makes it easy for the seer, for the knower, to read the character of people even before having seen their faces, by only seeing their clothes. Their liking for a certain color expresses what they are like, what is their liking. Their liking for a certain flower, their liking for a certain gem or jewel, their liking for a certain environment in their room, the color on their wall, that all shows what people are like, what is their fancy. And as people evolve through life spiritually, so their choice of color changes. With each step forward they change, their idea about color becomes different. And there are some to whom striking colors appeal, to others pale colors, and the reason is that the striking colors have intense vibrations, the pale colors have smooth and harmonious vibrations, and it is according to the emotional condition of people that they enjoy different colors.

Now, coming to sound, everyone, whether one knows it or not, has a choice of a certain sound. Although every person does not study this subject and, therefore, remains ignorant of that idea, each one has a certain liking for a certain sound. It is therefore that there is a saying, a belief among people, that everyone has a note. The thing is that each person has a sound, a sound which is akin to that person's particular evolution. And besides that, with all the divisions that the singers have made of tenor and bass and of baritone, everyone has a particular pitch, and everyone has a peculiar note in which to speak, and that particular note is expressive of a person's life's evolution, expressive of the soul, the condition of feelings, of thoughts. And besides this, it does not only make an effect upon children to hear certain sounds and to see certain colors, but it also makes an effect upon animals. Colors have a great effect and influence upon all living creatures, animals or birds or human beings. Without their knowing it, the influence of colors works in their lives, turning them to this or that inclination.

Once I was visiting a house which was taken by a certain club, and they said, "It is a very great pity. Since we have taken this house, in our committee there is always a disagreement." I said, "No wonder, I see it." They said, "Why?" I said, "The walls are red, they make you inclined to fight. Striking color from all around gives you the inclination to disagree. The emotions are touched by it, and certainly those inclined to disagreement are helped by it."

And it is these things in view, and it is from this psychological point of view that in the ancient customs one finds in the East, especially in their weddings, that a certain color is chosen for the time of wedding and for other different times in different festivities. It has all its meaning, it has a psychological significance behind it.

Since both color and sound are perceived differently, and we have different senses to perceive these, we have distinguished between visible and audible things. But in reality, those who meditate, those who concentrate, those who go within themselves, those who trace the origin of life, begin to see that behind these outer five senses there is one sense hidden, and that sense is capable of doing all that which we seem to do or to experience.

There are our external five senses. We distinguish five senses because we know the five organs of sense. In reality there is one sense. It is that sense which, through these five different organs, experiences life and distinguishes life in five different forms; and they call it five senses, but there is one sense. And so all that is audible and all that is visible is one and the same. It is that which is called in Sanskrit *purusha* and *prakriti*. In the terms of the Sufis it is known as *zat* and *sifat*. The manifestation of it is called sifat, the outer appearance. It is in its manifestation as sifat that one sees the distinction or the difference of that which is visible and audible. In their real aspect of being, they are one and the same. In that plane of existence where they are one and the same, according to Sufi mystics that plane of existence is called zat, that knowledge of the inner existence in which one sees the source and goal of all things.

Color and sound are a language, a language which can be understood not only in the external life but also in the inner life. For the physician, color has a great significance; for the chemist, color has a great significance. The more one goes into the science of medicine, into the science of chemistry, the more one recognizes the value of color—that each element and the development of every object, or the changing of every object is distinguishable by the changing of the color. The physicians of old used to recognize diseases by the color of the face and form. And even today there exist physicians whose principal way through which they recognize the complaint a person has is from the color in the eyes, on the tongue, on the nails, on the skin. In every condition it is color which is expressive of the condition of the person. Also in objects, the changing of the object is recognized by the changing of colors. The psychologists have recognized the condition of things, of objects, by the sound, and of people by their voice. What a person is, whether strong or weak, what is that person's character and inclinations, what is that person's attitude toward life, outlook on life, all that is known and understood by the voice.

But color and sound are not the only language by which one communicates with the life without, but also the language with which one communicates with the life within. One might like to ask: How is it done? The answer is that we today see some scientific experiments. Some make certain plates and, by speaking near their plate, make with the sound and vibrations, marks upon that plate. And those marks make either harmonious forms or inharmonious forms. If that is true, then every one, from morning till evening, by what they say, is making an invisible form in space. They are creating invisible vibrations around themselves. They are, therefore, introducing an atmosphere; and it is therefore that some people come into the house, and before they speak you are tired of them, you wish to get rid of them. Before they have said or done anything, you are finished with them, you would like them to go away, for they are creating an atmosphere; there is a sound going on, a sound which is disagreeable. There are other people with whom you feel sympathy, to whom you feel drawn, whose friendship you value, whose presence you long for. There is harmony which is continually created through them. That is a sound too.

If that is true, then it is not only the external signs, but it is the inner condition also which is audible and visible. Though not visible to the eyes and not audible to the ears, yet it is audible and visible in the soul. We say, "I feel the vibrations, I feel the person's presence"; either, "I feel sympathy" or "an antipathy against that person." But there is a feeling, and the person creates a feeling without having said anything or done anything. Therefore, a person who is in a wrong vibration, without doing wrong, without saying wrong, creates the wrong atmosphere; and you find a fault with that person.

It is most amusing and very funny to see that in life you meet people who bring to you a complaint, "I have said nothing, I have done nothing, and yet people dislike me, and yet people are against me." That person does not know that it is not saying or doing but what you are that speaks louder than what you say. It is being, it is life itself which has its tone, that has its color, that has its vibration. It speaks aloud, and one may think, "Where is it, and what is it, and where is it to be found?" And the answer is that what little people know about themselves is only about their body. If you tell them to point out where they are, they will point out this arm, this hand, this body. They know little further than that. There are many whom you ask, "But where do you think? Is your body thinking?" "Yes," they say, "my brain." They limit themselves in that little physical region which is called body, thus making themselves much smaller compared to what they really are.

The reality is that the human is one individual with two ends, just like one line with two ends. If you look at the ends, it is two; if you look at the line, it is one. The one end of the line is limited, limitedness; the other end of the line is unlimited. One end is human, the other end God. We forget that end and know only this end of which we are conscious. And it is the consciousness of limitedness which makes us more limited, otherwise we have a greater scope to approach that unlimitedness which is within ourselves, which is only the other end of the same line, the line which we call or which we consider to be ourselves.

And when a mystic speaks of self-knowledge, it is not to know how old I am, or how good I am, or how bad I am, or how right or wrong I am. It is to know the other part of one's being, that deeper, subtler aspect of one's being. It is in the knowledge of that being that the fulfillment of a life depends. And one might ask, "How can one get nearer to it, how can one get closer to it?" The way that those who searched after truth, those who sought after God, those who wished to analyze themselves, those who wished to sympathize with life have found is one way, and that is the same way of vibrations. It is again the same way of old, that by the help of sound they have prepared themselves. They made these physical atoms, which in time became deadened, live again by the help of sound. As Zeb-un-Nisa says continually, "That sacred name will make thee sacred." They have worked with the power of sound. The Hindus have called it mantra yoga. The Sufis have termed it *wazifa*. It is the power of the word which works upon each atom of the body, making it sonorous, making it a communicative medium between the external life and the inner life. What first one begins to realize as the first experience of one's spiritual development is that one begins to feel communication with living beings—not only with human beings, but with animals, with birds, with trees, and with plants. It is not an old tale that people tell that the saints used to speak with the trees and with the plants. You can speak today if you are in communication. It was not only the ancient times which were blessed. The blessing which was ancient is here today, but the old one is not today old, it is new. It is the same that was, that is, and that will be, and no privilege was ever limited to a period of the world's history. Human beings have the same privilege today if they will realize that they are privileged.

When people themselves close their hearts, when they make themselves covered by the life within and without, they no doubt become exclusive, they no doubt become cut away from this whole manifestation, which is one whole and which is not divided. It is human beings themselves who divide themselves; if not, life is undivided, indivisible. And it is by opening communication with the external life which makes people wider.

Then, to their friends, they do not say, "These are my friends, I love them," but say, "These are myself, I love them." That is the time that humans can say that they have arrived at the realization of love. As long as they say "I feel sympathy with these because they are my friends," sympathy has not yet been fully wakened. The real wakening of sympathy is on that day when people see their friends and say these friends are themselves. Then the sympathy is wakened.

Then there is the communication within oneself. A person does not close only the self from the external reality, but also closes the self from the inner reality, which is a still more important part of one's life; and that inner reality is also sound, the inner reality is light. And when one gets in touch with this sound and this light, then one knows that language which is the language of heaven, a language which is expressive of the past and the present and of the future, a language which reveals the secret and character of nature, a language which is receiving and giving that divine message which the prophets at times have tried to reveal.

Additional Lectures on Kinship

1

Universal Kinship of Humanity

ALTHOUGH the word *kinship* seems to be easy, there are several points of view.[1] If it were as simple as it seems the world would not have gone through the great catastrophe that it has gone through.[2] The cause of all the trouble is the lack of realization of kinship and that this kinship was taught by the great teachers of humanity. If the great teachers have given a message to humanity, it is no doubt the message of kinship. In plain words: God is love; you must love your enemies.[3]

No doubt simple things to human beings are too simple; too many people who have studied think that they must no longer learn anything. It is too easy; yet if they would study it closely they would see it is the most difficult thing in the world. The necessity of life is a spiritual necessity from a metaphysical point of view. In other words, kinship is the nature of humanity, and the secret of kinship is centered in the idea that like attracts like. Some animals go in numbers; they are attached to each other, and they abide in harmony. But other animals, such as lions, tigers, do not like to be together; their passion is their own enemy. They are never contented because they have not that spirit of harmony for which every soul longs. Human beings show that tendency more pronouncedly by living together in villages or cities, by marrying people of their own nation, and,

1. Lecture given in Brussels, January 1922.
2. World War I.
3. 1 John 4:8 and Matthew 5:44.

no doubt, in this way are born virtues like family pride, which sometimes engaged families in long quarrels. In the traditions of East and West, humanity is the same and has shown virtues that seem right and wrong—both are so close together that it is very difficult to distinguish which is which. Family pride developed into native quarrels. The old traditions of Persia explain those quarrels between people, tribes, and so on. For instance, if the chiefs of two different tribes were struggling together, the stronger one became chief of the two tribes; yet as long as the feeling of kinship remained, it was a virtue in itself, and it was living. All that is moving is living, and that which is still is dead; and that which is dead is useless in life because it brings about death. In the great war we have gone through there was a dead element. The patriotic spirit, so long as it was progressing, was a virtue; but when it ceased to expand itself then it became contrary to what kinship should be. Any individuals in society have to trouble themselves about their own interests. A greater virtue is the care for a whole family, the endeavor to do all one can to please one's friends. But that virtue is surpassed by those who do not only think of themselves and their family, but also of the people in their own village or town. One may even see some considering themselves as nothing, because their outlook is greater and they consider the nation first. As long as that heart quality is progressing, there is a great blessing in society; but as soon as that spirit becomes still and is not given a chance to progress, then it ceases to fulfill its purpose. It is hindering the progress of human life, and, if it cannot expand, it brings about the greatest catastrophes that have been experienced in the world.

From a philosophic point of view, the whole world is one family; and, if we look at the way in which the world is working, we see that all are seeking their own interests. Human beings, however, are interdependent. A person living in a family cannot expect to be happy so long as one member of the family is unhappy. According to a mystical point of view, the whole world is one body; and, if there is a weakness in any part of a body, the whole body will be affected by it.[4] Life, at the present time, is like a child's game; every child is trying to get the other child's toy, but does not know how to keep it. Things in the world are changeable, they are not to be relied upon. People see the vanity of the world, but if they do not see a reality in contrast, they remain intoxicated by the unreality and try to get some pleasure from their life, even for a moment. The happiness of this world is something we cannot keep; it is just like the horizon—the nearer you go, the farther it goes. As soon as you get it, you see it is not the thing you wanted. That discontent continues its work till we have found and understood the manifestation of God, in which is hidden the divine spirit. God cannot be sought in temples, for God is love, and love does not live in temples but in the heart of humanity, which is the temple of God. The true religion would be to recognize it so, and to tolerate, to forgive, and to love each other. No doubt there are difficulties; we are not angels, and we cannot expect to act like them. Many have no clear vision before them as they are indulging in the life of intoxication. Perhaps the time will come when everything we depend upon will be taken from us. The best would be to consider life from a philosophic point of view, and then we really should be able to smile at life. Today this thing is most necessary.

4. See Sa'di Shirazi, *Gulistan*, 1:10.

2

The Problem of the Day

THE most important part that the ideal of kinship has to fulfill in daily life is not only to bring about a better understanding between different classes, nations, and races, but to create a moral ideal in every individual.[1] Those conscious of the principle of kinship can consider the interest of their fellow beings. In the schools the most essential teaching of kinship must be that a child should grow to recognize in the other children its brothers and sisters, and that the child's obligation to them is as its obligation to its own brothers and sisters. Children with their development in life grow to recognize in the family their obligation to their brothers and sisters without being especially taught, only the fact that they know they are their brothers and sisters; and therefore, naturally that knowledge produces in them a sense of duty to one another and a sense of honor to care for the honor of their brothers and sisters. If the same sense was developed in children to look upon the children of another also as brothers or sisters, to stand by them in their troubles, and to guard them in their difficulties, and to consider their honor one's own honor, the world would become much better. When they would grow to adulthood, they would have a different outlook on life. They would move about in this world as a human being, as an adult. Besides, in business, one would realize not only one's material interest but also one's duty to those with whom one has to deal in business.

1. Lecture given September 11, 1922, at an unknown location.

In one's profession one would not only think one has to obey the laws of the professional unions or observe their etiquette because one is forced by one's profession to do so, but one would feel the interest and honor of the others as one's own interest and honor if the feeling of kinship were developed. Business causes people to have necessary laws, etiquettes, forms of politeness, and outward kinship; and yet there is always something absent that is most necessary in life. The moral of kinship must be realized by understanding the meaning of kinship. Kinship does not only mean a name. People may say outwardly "brother" or "sister," and yet may talk against each other. The word *brother* or *sister* has something sacred in it. It is not only a word, but life; there is something living in it. When one calls someone else one's brother or sister, one stands by that person for all one's life. A brother or sister is just like one hand to the other hand. When one hand is hurt, immediately to its rescue comes the other hand. When one hand is trying to do something, the other hand helps it. When one hand is tired, the other hand is ready to take up its work; and the rest of both hands is when they are united together. When people want to rest, they clasp their hands. That unity is symbolical of kinship. If people name the members of a certain institution or society brothers or sisters, it means nothing. Instead of members you call them brothers or sisters.

Kinship is realized by the recognition of three ideas. One idea is that we are brothers and sisters because our source is one—our divine parent is one. We are family because we are working on this earth hand in hand; conditions have brought us together. Our interests are common in their depth when we in this world are so linked together with one another. If we could only see it through another's eye, then we would find that the unhappiness of one individual has its effect in some way or other on all; and the happiness of one individual has its effect on all—more on those who are around them and a little less on those who are distant. Everyone pulled or pushed in life has an effect upon the whole of humanity. The pull is a pull on the whole humanity in proportion. If only humanity were to understand this living doctrine of metaphysics, which has always been taught by the prophets—if only the scientists had been able to tell this, the world would have been quite different.

And the third idea in which one can realize kinship is that our goal is the same. Through whatever way we may reach, through heaven or hell, it is the only goal. It is not a settlement, it is the final goal we have to reach. And therefore, we have to meet again. This shows that in the beginning we are brothers and sisters because of the source; and we are brothers and sisters in the midst of it because we are living on earth, the interest of one depending on others; and in the end the goal of all is the same.

What keeps humanity ignorant of the ideal of kinship is the outward nature of creation, which is of a dual nature. It is the idea of separation—"You are different from me. I am different from you." And that difference and distinction in character, in ways of thinking, in the way of living, in all different forms, are dividing humanity into different classes, different nations, different races, and the difference that exists between people in their way of looking at things and in their ideas. This impresses one with the thought "I am a separate entity and in no way connected with another." In spirit one is not aware. The only actions one is conscious of are the outward ties, such as relationship or some partnership in business, or when there are collaborators in certain work, in learning at school; some occasions like this make people feel they are connected with one another. But these outward actions do not awake the spirit to the inward connection that is stronger and closer and binds one soul to another. All these outer connections make people think there is no inner connection. When an outer tie has been broken a person says, "I have nothing to do with that person." One thinks it is finished, but it is not finished. You have that person in you, and that person has you in them. It is not finished. And if one could see the beginning, where it has begun, then one would never believe that it finishes. It is always there. It is only the outside links that one recognizes as a relation; the inward connection, which binds every soul to one another, one does not understand.

What is necessary just now is not only for kinship to be taught as morals, but for kinship to be taught as spirit, as a spiritual idea, as the mystery of the whole of metaphysics and philosophy. In all ages prophets and sages and seers have realized this law, and yet there is so much in life that works against it, that covers it from human eyes. Human sight is so limited that people see no further than they see. And they remain in an illusion, in a mist, not knowing with whom they are connected and with whom they are disconnected, only recognizing the outward little connections that seem to bind them here and there, and yet not realizing that this whole manifestation is one whole working mechanism, wherein every soul fills in its place, where every soul has its purpose to accomplish, and where every soul stands in connection with all souls.

The more you look at the world from the mystical point of view, the more your outlook on life becomes keen, the more you find that every person you meet, every person who goes your way in life, has something to do with you, and you have something to do with them. And it is this kinship that must be realized, this truth of the whole universe; and by awaking the consciousness of this kinship in the world, the ideals of the spirit of kinship will come to manifestation.

* * *

Question: *What will be the ideal work, the ideal relation, between the work of the different sexes in the future evolution? Is it not wrong that women try to do the work of men?*

Answer: Well, there are two questions in this. I will first answer "Is it not wrong that women should try to do the work of men?" The question is, what is the work of man? Very often the work that man is accustomed to do and may be seen doing is considered man's work. The work that woman is not seen doing for a long time, people consider not to be woman's work. What woman has been seen for some centuries doing, people think is woman's work. But I should think, that according to the metaphysical point of view, considering woman and her life, the fine work must be for woman, and the rough work must be in the charge of man. But besides this it all depends upon the evolution of man and woman. If woman is evolved enough to do a certain work that wants art and intelligence, why must she not do it? No doubt it is a very great pity to see, especially after the war, women having taken the work of the laboring men that does not in any way suit the life of woman, and that has destroyed many lives, from their youth, for their whole life.

Now, coming to the next question, what would be the ideal of work for men and women in the future? Just now we are in a period of reaction, which is coming from the woman's side and which is caused by man's negligence in the past of the life of woman; and therefore, the conditions today are not normal conditions. Life in the world just now, considering the work of man and woman, is not balanced. Just now it is a revolt or reaction coming from the side of woman in answer to negligence that has passed before, but there will come a time when the conditions of life in the world will adjust themselves, and an ideal time will come when man will realize that as there is cooperation with woman in the home, so there will be in all directions of life, even in the state.

Question: *Has not the promise of heaven and reward an egoistic purpose?*

Answer: Call it egoistic if you will. Very often a child is induced to work better if it is promised candy. You must remember that humankind is always a child, if not in one way, in another.

Question: *How many souls that realize the message are wanted to fulfill the work?*

Answer: As far as I understand this question it means those who have realized the value of the message—how many of them are needed to fulfill the work of the movement? We shall never have a sufficient number, and therefore, every individual must bear in mind that if life permits one to offer one's time, life, and work, that it will not be too many.

Question: *In what way can we bring this ideal of spiritual kinship to humanity?*

Answer: The first way is understanding for yourself, making it clear in your mind. The next process will be to try to explain it to your fellows, and when you find that you have succeeded in making an impression with the ideal in which you sincerely believe, then you must proceed to spread this idea in a wider circle. But note at the same time, that it is the will of God that this be known to the world, and souls who will become channels of this have this as their life's privilege. Therefore, we must consider that there is no doubt that it will spread—only that the contribution of our efforts is a life's privilege.

Question: *If the source of all souls is one, do they all proceed from the same source at the same point in time, or are there younger or older souls in humanity?*

Answer: There is such a large variety of younger and older souls, and the souls are so numerous, that it is most difficult to fix a standard of younger and older souls. Every soul, however young, can find a still younger soul; every soul, however old, can find an older soul. God is unlimited, and so is manifestation.

Question: *What is the reason that enlightened souls must come from the East, and why cannot they come from the West if their message is for the West?*

Answer: One cannot divide the wisdom of the East and West. In fact, the wisdom does not belong to the East or West. The idea is that among many other reasons there is one reason why the East has remained as a cradle of thought from very ancient times. One can see, in all traditions of the Aryan race in ancient times, that it went out to spread throughout the world; and especially those who wished to make experiments in the inner life sought, for their place of meditation, the land of India. Therefore, for thousands of years the people of that country have devoted their lives to this end.

Humanity must progress in some way. Life cannot exist without progress. And when people think that the Orient has not progressed, that the people of the East have not improved as have the people of the West, it is true. When you compare the present civilization of the West, its order and system, the great progress which the West has made, it is incomparably greater than what one can see in the East. Perhaps just now you can see in the uncivilized parts of the Western countries some forms of Eastern life, and that shows how much the Western world has gone forward in one direction. But at the same time, while vast progress in some direction or other—and it is the direction of the multitude that individuals take—when we come to the metaphysical view the whole of life is a balance. The sun, moon, the moving of the world itself, are all a balance. If there was no balance, the world would drop down. If the East had progressed in the same direction as the West, how many more wars would have come. In the first place, there would have been guns and cannons all over the world; just now this is only in this part of the world. God has busied all those in the East and West in a certain work. But, no doubt, the world will become more balanced if the East will partake of all that is required from the West, and the West will partake of what is required from the East. The more exchange there is of thought and idea, the more balanced the world will be and the greater comfort will come to humanity.

Question: *Does the recognition of kinship tend to keep people in contact even on the physical plane?*

Answer: Yes. If the spirit of kinship is understood in the way I have explained in my address, it would not only keep people conscious of their contact on the physical plane, but people would realize their contact with one another in the spirit.

Question: *What is the meaning of the Virgin Mary standing upon the crescent moon? The same symbol is also found in India.*

Answer: The crescent moon is the symbol of womanhood, as the sun is the symbol of manhood. The crescent moon is the symbol of responsiveness, which is the female attribute of the soul. The crescent moon also is the symbol of the Messenger, for the message is received by different prophets in response to the voice of God.

3

The Ideal among Nations

Ideal among nations, in principle free,
Child but wide awake,
America blessed be.
Thy heart is open to all, old and young alike;
High note of brotherhood, indeed thou dost strike.
Thou hast inherited
the knowledge from all,
And thou givest the same
to those who on thee call.
O desire of nations, in thee we all meet.
Blessed America, thee I humbly greet.[1]

BELOVED Ones of God, my coming to the United States at this time, when the world has not yet arrived at its normal state after the great strain of war, is to awaken in souls the consciousness of kinship, on the principle of which this great nation was founded. The central theme of the formation of the Constitution of the United States of America and the undertone of Abraham Lincoln's noble reform, was kinship.

The nation which was nursed with the milk of the ideal of kinship from its infancy, is the one to be attuned to its predisposition at this time of the world's greatest need. In spite of the wonderful phenomena that science has produced through modern civilization, if a sober-minded person reflects on the question of whether we are really progressing, an answer will

1. Lecture given in New York, February 1923.

come: not altogether. If we ask ourselves what is missing, we shall realize without difficulty that it is the ideal which expands the limited soul to perfection, which raises the mortal to God.

It is the all-prevailing materialism and the flood of overwhelming commercialism that have drowned the ideal. The nations of today stand in the quest of their own material benefit, regardless of other nations, in the same way as one today who is called a practical person proves to be best qualified in guarding one's interests in life. This has made the world a battlefield of continual struggles, where life is nothing but a chaos in the world that was purposed to be the place of aspiration, rest, and peace.

Education today tends to teach the youth the best way to acquire, own, and possess all the goods of this earth; and naturally, the more souls become qualified by this education, the greater the struggle of life becomes. The competition that exists today in trade and profession seems to lead humanity to the tendencies of the primitive human being. As relations between nations are only based upon their material interests, so in the same way relations between individuals exist. It has blunted all the fineness and beauty of unselfish, friendly devotion.

In order to bring humanity to the realization of the law of beneficence, it is not necessary that a new religion be taught. It is the light of truth thrown upon every religion that will bring to human perception wisdom, which is the underlying stream behind all the great religions of the world.

The good tidings that the Sufi message brings to the world, is the recognition of the divine in the soul of humanity. The knowledge of living right is the only religion which will answer the need of the world. The efforts of the Sufi Movement are directed to bring humankind to understand that the real well-being of each depends on the well-being of all. The whole humanity is as one body. All nations are its different members, and the pain and injury caused to one nation, in time, develops into the disorder of the whole.

The Sufi message is the answer to the cry of humanity, for it warns souls to unite beyond all differences and distinctions between caste, creed, nation, and religion.

May your ideal of liberty expand to the liberty of nations. May your principle of freedom rise to the height of freedom of souls. May the message of God reach far and wide, illuminating and making the whole humanity one family, in the parenthood of God.

4

The Work of Our Movement in the Line of Kinship

THIS line of work is, really speaking, the fulfillment of every activity of our movement.[1]

One activity of our movement is the esoteric school in which people are initiated, and they advance grade by grade, individually developing the soul toward the attainment of spiritual realization. There is another activity, which is a devotional activity and which is called the Church of All, or the Universal Worship, and it is a religious activity—religion not in the sense of a sectarian activity, but on the contrary, a religious activity that brings souls to the true religion that stands above all sects. But whether we strive in the path of religion or we journey through the path of mysticism, it is for one object: that we may be best fitted to live the ideal of kinship. If one were such a great mystic that one was the greatest master, or if one were so pious and religious that one was the greatest saint, and yet if one did not live the ideal of kinship, it would be of no great importance if spiritual realization were not also realized in the practical life by observing the ideal of kinship. At this time, when the world needs the ideal of kinship more than at any other time in the history of the world, it is our privilege and destiny to do all we can to bring about the ideal of kinship in our own lives first, and then to spread it outside in the world. Any problem or theory or doctrine intellectually studied is of no value unless it is practiced. Ten thousand people crying

1. Lecture given in Summer School, Suresnes, France, July 15, 1923.

out "kinship!" and one person living it is equal or even better. Kinship is not a materialistic ideal here, it is a spiritual ideal. The materialist cannot understand what kinship is in the real sense of the word. For the reason is that the materialist can go as far as saying "Another person is as good as me, and therefore my happiness is in sharing all the good with another." But the spiritual person says, "Another person is me. That person's happiness is my happiness," and therefore, this highest ideal of kinship, which spiritual realization can teach, materialism cannot teach. Therefore, in spite of all this activity that is going on in the world just now to bring about a world family, it is not being successful, because the life of kinship, which is its very breath, is the realization of the same God in oneself as well as in another. The work of the spiritual ones is to forget their false self. And what do they realize by forgetting? They realize the true self, the realization of God; and that self is not only in themselves but in their neighbor also.

There is no doubt that every person, more or less, loves the ideal of kinship. I do not speak of those who are not in their right mind, but a normal person cannot deny the ideal of kinship being the only idea that can be called religion or spirituality. But the question is in practicing it. It is easy to know it intellectually, but when it comes to practice it, it becomes very difficult. It needs sacrifice, it needs humbling, it needs endurance, it needs patience, it needs forgiveness, it needs that brotherly and sisterly sympathy for every soul who stands next to us. And it is the power of love alone that will raise humanity through the pettiness, the smallness of human nature, to rise to the high ideal of kinship that is the true aristocracy of the human soul.

Now the question is: How can we set to work on it? We have only taken our first step in this direction; many steps more we have to take. The first step is that wherever our movement is established, there we have one day or two days in a month when we have such meetings of world kinship. In this meeting we have the lecture given by our own members or by our friends, a lecture on the problems of our everyday life and its relation to our spiritual ideal. Therefore, this meeting platform gives scope to members and to friends who have some ideas to suggest for the welfare of humanity, that they may bring their ideas before their friends. And in this way, by hearing the ideas of different friends on these most important questions, we shall be able someday to make our thoughts more distinct as to the working of this idea. And thus we shall be able to set forward our blessed movement in order to accomplish our sacred ideal, the service of humanity and God.

5

A Kinship Meeting 1

BELOVED Ones of God, I have a great pleasure and happiness in opening today the Kinship section in Geneva.[1] I would like to tell my murids what a responsibility it is, and what an opportunity it is to be on the soil of Geneva to work for this cause of kinship. This place, the soil of Geneva, is not only the place that is chosen by all the nations to form a League of Nations to work for humanity and for peace, but also destined by God that the center of this universal harmony and peace, from a spiritual point of view, may also be formed here. It is therefore our privilege, which is our blessing, to be here together and to think of forming that league of friendship beyond all the differences and distinctions of faiths or beliefs.

What is the meaning of the word *genève*? The meaning of the word *genève* in the Sanskrit language is the sacred thread.[2] And who must prove the meaning and the value of this sacredness? It is for us, who are serving in that sacred cause, to bring about harmony and peace for humanity. We unite here on the soil of this land, coming from different countries, being born in different lands, and yet come here with that brotherly and sisterly love to do good for one another; and we are welcomed by the people of this land with open arms to discuss the affairs of the world and the affairs of humanity, for the benefit of which all the people are anxious and eager.

1. Lecture given in Geneva, October 7, 1923.
2. The sacred thread is called *janeu* in Sanskrit.

Now, what benefit is there in store for our movement? From the spiritual point of view it is destined, it is promised that the message must spread, that the message must reach in all the parts of the Earth. But the other benefit which is attached to the center, to being here on the soil of Geneva, is that people coming from all different nations with the idea of uniting the world—bringing about better understanding, harmony, or peace—the atmosphere that we shall create of love and of sacredness and of spirituality will envelop all the souls coming here or passing here from the north to the south, or from the south to the north. The benefit that we have in store is this: that we shall create that atmosphere of love and harmony and beauty that will envelop those coming here to work from all nations, and those coming from the south going to the north, and from the north going to the south. Therefore, however small the number of our group, still its responsibility, its privilege, and its blessing is indeed great. But from a mystical point of view, number is not counted. It is the depth, it is the sincerity, it is the solidarity of the faith that is the thing and that is counted.

Now I should like to explain a little more what work we have to do in the movement of kinship. Is it political work? Not at all. We have the League of Nations here to discuss it; we do not need to discuss that matter. Our love for humanity, our goodwill, our desire for kinship, that itself will spread as an atmosphere congenial to those who will come to discuss matters at the League of Nations. Then are we to discuss socialism? That is also not necessary. There are several unions, and there are various movements working on that question. That is not our purpose, that is not our work. Then are we to discuss the difference of the faiths and religions? Not even that. The problem that is before us is that when that problem is solved, the divine light will manifest. And that problem is: What purpose is behind this whole creation? What purpose is behind the life of an individual? And how best we can solve this problem? That is the subject of our study. And it is the work of our practice. When one has studied—perhaps for one's whole life—psychology, when one has perhaps meditated all through one's life or been practicing all through life, what result in the end does one come to? One arrives at a stage, and that stage is the stage of kinship. What does it show? It shows that the first lesson that we have to learn in this world is kinship; and the last lesson, after learning all philosophy and mysticism, and after all our efforts, is kinship.

Then remember, my friends, that if you studied Sufism for twenty years, all the problems of metaphysics and philosophy, and if that spirit of kinship were not developed in you, you must be sure that progress has not been made. Or if you meditated for thirty years in solitude, and if you communicated with God, and yet if the spirit of kinship is not developed in you, no progress is made. A person who is loved by everybody in the world, and yet who has not loved anybody, has done nothing. A person who has possessed the wealth of the whole world, but who has given nothing, has not earned. A person honored by everyone in the world, but who has not respected, has not lived. What does it mean? It only means that what we gain is nothing. It is what we give that counts. What has been done to us is as nothing; if we only did all we wished to do, that is what counts. Either learning or wisdom, possession or power or wealth, all these things gained are very small compared with what one can give to the others. Therefore, my friends, it is not talking about kinship nor discussing this subject that does much good. It is living kinship and realizing the one source of all that is the divine Parent, and in whose family we observe kinship. Let us, therefore, all unite together in silence with the intention of doing what little we can in endeavoring to serve and promote the good work of kinship. And let us pray to God to bless us all to do our little part in this big scheme of life.

6

Three Objects of Our Work

THE first thing for the murids is to know the real object of our work.[1] We have three objects in view: one, kinship; two, the message; and three, the esoteric school.

The more we notice the condition of the world at the present moment, the more we will realize the necessity of human kinship. There has never been a greater need of human kinship than at the present moment. There are trade unions, political institutions, and socialist institutions; they all work toward the same object. Still there is a very great necessity of spiritual work to be done toward the unity of humankind. We are doing this work in different places in America, in England, in Holland, in Belgium, in France, and in Switzerland, where the center of the Sufi Order is being established.

No doubt we would prefer it if we could do the work without an organization or center, but it is impossible. It is just like imagining the soul to walk about on earth without a physical body. To be without a center means for a person to live in the cold and heat without having a house. Even the insects need a hole to live in, even the birds need nests.

There are reasons, both in favor and against, why the international center of the order must be in Geneva. But as one sees, Geneva is privileged at this time by the work that is done by the League of Nations, which, so to speak, forms the body of the worldly unity. Whereas our order, however small and humble

1. Lecture given in Geneva, October 1923.

in its infancy, rests here in Geneva, and also the spirit of that object of unity, which the League of Nations in its way works to accomplish.

The second object of the order is the spreading of the message in all parts of the world. And murids who really value the Sufi message and who recognize the destiny of our movement must try to help in every way. This main center, which is made to collect the message given in different places, is called upon to reproduce it, to circulate it, and to preserve it for the coming generations.

Whenever a spiritual message was given to humanity there has been a struggle between the people to whom it was given. A few recognized it, and still fewer understood it, but many opposed it; and it has always been difficult to find the authentic records of the messages, of the wisdom of God which were given at different times in the world's history. The murids cannot show a greater sympathy to their teacher and devotion to the cause than receiving the message, following it, giving it to the others, and preserving it for future generations.

The third work of the order is the study and meditation in the inner school, the Sufi school which originated from that ancient school of ancient mysteries—a school which existed even before Abraham, the father of three great religions: Christianity, Judaism, and Islam. Those who know Sufism from the superficial writings and sometimes from the translations of Arabic or Persian literature are apt to think that Sufism is the mystical side of Islam. In reality it is not true. Sufism existed before Muhammad, before Christ, even before Abraham. It is true that the mystics in the world of Islam are Sufis, but that does not mean that *sufi* means the "mystic of Islam." For instance, the green color is the national color of the Irish, but that does not mean that everybody who dresses in a green color is from Ireland. The green color existed even before people inhabited Ireland. There are initiations, one after the other, which are given as a trust to those who are sincere and who wish to tread the path steadily, full of faith and confidence.

The Sufis of all nations are one. They are a nucleus for human kinship. It is not our wish that all people in the world must become the members of our order, but it is our wish that we, the members of the Sufi Order, may be able to serve the world. Our movement, no doubt, is in its infancy. But the power that gives us courage is truth. There is no question about the success of the Sufi Movement; it is certain, since it is no man-made enterprise. It is the message of God, and truth must be successful. We, at the same time, do not work for success. We work for the sake of the work. It is the direction that we are given from above. We take it, and we shall go on through life, making a way until the message of God is fulfilled.

7

Religious Unity

BELOVED Ones of God, my friends and murids, words are too inadequate to express the joy and happiness that I feel to find myself again with my friends in Paris.[1] And it is a great pleasure and surprise together to have met with my friends in these new quarters, which are offered by the devotees of the cause. True it is, and it gives me a great joy to think, as our great and sincere worker Madame L. has said, that all the devotees of the great cause have contributed to it in thought, in feeling, in prayer, in every form they could, in order to make this realized. I cannot forget a friend whose thought is just now with me, our faithful friend Colonel Guillon, who is not here today, but I feel his spirit with us. But I am most delighted to find with us today Madame Baronne d'Eichtal, who has been our backbone for the blessed work in Paris; and the devotional work most beautifully carried, quietly and modestly by Reverend Cheraga Madame Detraux, has always brought exaltation in our group. And I do not need to say in words, as you all know and you have seen, the most valuable efforts that, from the beginning of the work in France, Monsieur L. has been doing, and to whose most earnest efforts we credit this joy of today.

You all know, as well as I, the present condition of the world and the need of a work of uniting the divided sections of humanity together. Our movement is not a new religion; it has no desire to form a sect or community. On the contrary, our

1. Lecture given in rue de Dragon, Paris, November 25, 1923.

efforts are to invite the followers of different communities and different religions to come and meet on one single platform where everyone professes respect for all religions.

Do we, therefore, call people to leave their own community or particular way of worship? No, what is studied in the Sufi Order is the essence of all religions, which brings humanity to the realization that there is one religion; there cannot be two religions.

At this present condition when humanity is divided into many sections, one section opposing the other—at this moment it is most necessary that a movement such as this, the impulse of which is directed by God, may work and work to its utmost to serve the divine cause. No doubt, efforts are being made by many different institutions, many different movements, in order to bring about kinship, a better condition; and we are perfectly in sympathy with any movement of this kind. Every effort made in the direction of unity in bringing this harmony and peace, which is the longing of every soul, is worthwhile and is worth being appreciated. There are efforts made through educational channels; there are efforts made through social and economic efforts. But it must be remembered that there is a certain work that religion can perform, that spiritual activity can perform, and that is the work to which our movement is destined.

And what is mostly needed in the world today is the spiritualization of the world, and it is toward this end that the work of the Sufi Movement is directed. No doubt, as in every work, there are difficulties. So there is no end of difficulties that we have to go through. And if we had no belief in that saying that there is no difficulty that cannot be surmounted, we would have given up such efforts long ago. But through all these difficulties I must admit that there has always been a divine blessing in one form, a tangible form, and that form is faithful friends, sincere workers under all conditions, with all the difficulties they have gone through. And they have proved, in the tests that very often came to try them, they have proved in the end sincere.

If we have any treasure just now, counting upon the treasure we have undertaken, the service of God and humanity, that tangible form is in only these sincere, faithful hearts. The phenomenon of this is seen in this accomplishment; and if there is any power behind, it is the power of God and our conviction of the power of the almighty God, whose responsibility it is, whose service it is, to whom we have all given our lives.

Let us, therefore, lift our heart in prayers before God, whose service we have undertaken to perform, and pray that God's blessing may remain and maintain this place of the work that we have arranged for God's service.

8

Our Service to Humanity

BELOVED Ones of God, I am asked by the kindness of our hostess to speak a few words telling about the service the Sufi Movement is rendering to humanity.[1] Friends, if I explain the history of the Sufi idea, I should like to say that it has existed in all ages, and we can very well trace, up to the time of Abraham, the esoteric school of the Sufi Movement. Even now there exist in different parts of the East different schools promoting the Sufi idea that trace their origin as far back as the time of Abraham.

And now, coming to the subject how Sufism has developed in the past, I should like to say that in Arabia, Palestine, and Syria it passed its childhood. Its youth passed in Persia. And in India it came to its fullest development.

And now to tell you what Sufism is. It only means "wisdom." Wisdom not in the ordinary sense of the word, but wisdom that comes from within, which is not dependent on the external experiences of life, a knowledge which is perfected by the inner illumination and this outer experience in life.

In Islam, in Buddhism, and in all occult philosophical and mystical ideas, it is there where Sufism flourished and, so to speak, became finished. If one would travel to inquire what Sufism has done in India, one may easily find that in every village there is either a tomb of Sufis or a little cottage, where Hindus and Muslims and Christians and Jews all rest; its door

1. Lecture given at The Hague, January 16, 1924.

is opened to all. At the tomb of the Sufis, people of all different creeds and religions go and pay homage to personalities who did not work throughout their lives for a particular creed or religion or sect, but who worked for humankind, whatever be the religion. It was the thing that out of that school a message came forth, an answer to the cry of humanity at this judgment. At this time when it started, a hatred existed between nations and had upset the whole of humanity. Thinking of all the misery humanity has gone through, one may not deny the fact that humanity stands before a similar [*text missing*]. It is good that life actually has thrown such an intoxication upon humanity.

The service of this movement, therefore, will bring a warning in the world to awaken people to a greater idea, a deeper truth of life beyond the idea of life on earth. No doubt, the object is laudable but most difficult, nevertheless. And the service of all persons must be blessed and must bless, by all powers to whom we render our humble service.

In 1910 the movement started first in America, beginning in California, where a very small number of students in Sufism was formed together and started to work. After which, for ten years the Sufi center flourished and began to spread in England. The wartime was the worst time for the work of peace, because the name of peace was a horror; it was a great crime to mention the word. Thanks be to God that we lived through it all.

And our work? Had not there been difficulties? There was no end of it. And if you wish to do a work, which you consider the greatest, and you are thwarted by human skepticism, it is hard upon that work. Commercialism and materialism are everywhere increasing, competition ever takes over. There were a great many difficulties to endure, but we went on. There were the faithful workers who sacrificed themselves and brought the enthusiasm of work that was waiting for its time, and Sufism began to be made known. You know the real peace has not yet come; therefore, the working in the movement is still continuing to establish that peace, that real peace. The movement has existed in France and is established internationally in Geneva, and now has spread as far as Italy.

And now to the question, what is the different plan of work of the Sufi Movement? We have three activities that have been principally working in the movement.

First is the work of kinship, to try and make the sense and feeling of kinship understood among people. One might object that there are many institutions working for kinship. Does the Sufi do anything special in that line of work and thought? The answer is, there are many differences, but a central theme is the kinship with God, in God, our source and goal—a kinship that nothing else, money or position or whatever else, can give. This is done by holding meetings in different places and, in whatever way we can, to find the ways and the means to help suffering humanity. We do not touch politics, thinking that the work we are doing just now, trying to harmonize the heart of everyone we come in contact with, will help to bring about purer politics too in the end.

The other aspect of the work is the devotional side. There are, just now in the Western world, three classes of people. The first class is those (and they are the smallest in number) who have their own particular faith or religion. And then there is another class of people who believe in God and who think that there must be something hereafter, and they look out for the secret of life. Then there is a third class of people, and their number is slight, who do not believe in anything, neither in God nor in the hereafter. At this time, our movement has been called to serve all these classes in one form, and this form is the Universal Worship, wherein respect is shown to all the great ones who have come to the earth from time to time. A regard is shown for all the scriptures that millions of people have received and find to be their most sacred possession. The practice of tolerance to followers of all churches we try to realize among ourselves. In every form it is possible to try to live and express it in everyday life. This may be called the symbol of our churches.

And the third aspect, and the most important one, is the esoteric school. It is not everybody who is interested in it or is ready for it or has the patience for it. And therefore, it is not open for anyone. In this school an initiation is given, and, as the patient must have trust in the doctor and the doctor must trust the patient, so the pupil trusts the teacher and the teacher trusts the pupil—else the teaching would be nothing and of no avail. One may ask, what is taught? No one has ever taught the truth to anyone. It is impossible to give the truth. Truth is so deeply in everyone's heart that the only the way to reach it is to realize it for oneself. It is not something one can give or that can be put into words. If there is any science of God, anything divine, it is this in itself.

Therefore, those who seriously wish to probe the depth of life and realize the life which is their innermost life—it is for those the school is meant. But beyond all this, the message is given every day to those who listen; it is given as a warning to waken for the higher ideal, to the greater truth. And it does not matter if those who have heard the message once do not come back to us, for the message is spoken. If people take home one word, and if they are going to practice it in their daily life, and that word they listen to, then they are working for and have received the message too.

9

A Kinship Meeting 2

BELOVED Ones of God, I would like to speak on the subject of the work of the Sufi kinship.[1] At this time, when one sees so many different movements working for kinship, one might ask what is Sufi kinship doing among all those movements of kinship? And in answer to this question I say if there were twenty thousand more movements of kinship, it would not be enough for the need of today. Besides, the point of view of the Sufi kinship, whatever is the form, whatever the society, this form, this society is our ideal. We think it a privilege to give our humble service in the great cause of world kinship. We do not think our kinship superior to others; there is only one kinship. No doubt one service will be done by different souls; we work according to our own individual method, so we are best able to serve humanity. We consider it absurd to say your method is wrong and ours is right. As long as we are doing our best, that is all we want and all we do.

And now I should like to speak a few words on the work and the ideal we have before us. There is no doubt that everywhere in the world there seems to be awakened a desire toward spirituality, and there is no doubt that all over the world lives a desire for kinship, for cooperation. That being the case, every effort, whether right or wrong, is made to answer the call of humanity. And as there is no apparent proof, as the proof is in the result, the right and the wrong naturally are confused. For

1. Lecture given in Geneva, April 5, 1924.

instance, instead of kinship, communities have become trade and business communities, who thereby fight and oppose each other because of their different thinking. They say, "We are against war," but they are making a financial war. Besides, they have only the name of the thought or the ideal, but mostly they fight one another. They have a disposition to fight.

This has occupied our thought for a long time. What is the way to avoid it? We have tried our best till now and will try always to avoid forming a community. Yes, we could not help forming a nucleus. As it is necessary to have a ship to sail in the sea, it is necessary to have a form by which you are best able to serve humanity. We tried to do our best to remain without a name, but even cats and dogs have names. People called it old, higher, new thought, and that became their name. But is there any new thought? Can there be an old thought? Every old thought is new. Besides it is difficult to discriminate between the higher and the lower thought. We have tried to do our best not to give importance to the name. As long as one has sentiment for humanity, we stand by their side.

But now the question comes: How must kinship be taught? What can help us to become brothers and sisters? In every house the parents teach their children to be brothers and sisters, and it is not even in their power to produce kinship in their own house. And preachers go out and say to become brothers and sisters. But it is not only by preaching that you become a brother and a sister, because you have a thousand arguments against it, even poetical ones, and grudges and prejudices. When each one will remember what has been done, how can anyone become brothers and sisters? It is useless to preach; even for years and years, it cannot suffice. Only one thing is necessary: to produce understanding.

And what gives understanding? We unite not through the knowledge of a fact, but through eternal truth. So we come to the essence of religion, to the thought of uniting in truth.

The central thing is that truth. In order to make one tolerant to another, we must not say it, but awaken, that they may understand.

This reminds me of an amusing incident. Once I had a new pupil to whom I was giving instructions, and the last thing was that, before retiring every night, the pupil had to send thoughts of love and compassion to all living beings. This pupil was instantly horrified at the idea and said: "Yes, all, but not my neighboring country." I did not resist, took it tolerantly, understanding the pupil's sore heart. Would arguing have helped? No. So I said: "You are quite right. Forget the neighbor while thinking of humanity." The pupil smiled; he had expected an argument. Yet he did not feel satisfied, and after six months he was able to think of the whole humanity. It is not preaching that is needed, but the hammering on the hearts, so that they naturally will understand.

Another abuse of this ideal is the desire to be spiritually awakened. But how do people want to be awakened? Do they want to see psychic phenomena, to have occult powers? But have we not seen great countries, ancient countries as Egypt and north India, possess magic, occult, and mystical conceptions? What did that do? The same in their way as with the scientific inventions during the war, they used the magic powers for the benefit of their own ego. Therefore, being absorbed in the attainment of the material world, trying to do things with magic to one another, has been the cause of ruined nations, of great distress to humanity in all ages. Prophets and saints of all ages have warned against it; in their words one finds simple things as could be taught to children. Therefore, today, to the intellectual seeker of complexities, the ancient scriptures mean nothing. The accustomed thought of today is the thought of the purse of gold and if the magic cabinet is favored with one. Imagine what great scope there is for evil to lead astray. It hinders true service, respect, love, and consideration for one another. But in spite of the difficulties, are we not trying to do our best? I am thankful to say that in different countries we have joined together in this humble activity, an activity nearer to our heart than anything else.

Now, the question is: What is the way of attaining to the truth that teaches, by itself, kinship? That truth is pictured in the symbol of the cross. The perpendicular line suggests diving deep in oneself, from the outer into the innermost consciousness, humanity reaching from the point of human to that point of the divine. And what does the horizontal line suggest? Expansion. That is the thought: "I and my neighbor are not only friends, we are one." Then there is no doubt that the same interest exists for the neighbor as for oneself. No doubt, without rising to that conception, it is very difficult to understand this. Humanity must realize it by meditation. When one touches the innermost self of one's being, then one sees in another person one's own self. And it is only then that real sympathy comes. It is as the love from a mother for her child. The mother naturally rises to that conception. She does not only know the child as her own, but sees in the child her own being. And she lives in the pleasure and the happiness of the child; in the absence of the happiness of the child there is no pleasure and happiness for her. What is it after all? The love of the mother developed without consciousness: it is the realized oneness with the child. From love and continual devotion is born unity, is born oneness.

Now, there is another question. A person may ask: Must we teach that, must we lecture about that which is difficult to learn? The answer is: outer knowledge is not enough. It is not sufficient to say my neighbor and I are one; that is only imagination. There are two things: conception and conviction. Conception is the crescent; conviction is the full moon. What is learned by study is conception, but that is not sufficient; conception must be deepened, as the moon rises. As conception is deepened, it results in conviction. The working of the Sufi Movement with students and workers is the idea of deepening the conception till conviction results.

God bless you.

10

UNIVERSAL LANGUAGE

I WISH to say a few words to the workers in kinship. Kinship meetings, which are conducted in different places, need a new force given to them, and that force comes by giving them a new ideal.[1] If month after month we held a meeting and read, according to the habit, the "Gathekas,"[2] that does not suffice our purpose. For besides these meetings, we ought to be active in doing something; and at this time the need of the world is so great that there can be never be too many servers of the cause.

There are many different things that we shall find to do for the betterment of the people. But some things, as there are before us at present, we always can think about and try what we can do to accomplish them. There is one great need, and that is a world language, a universal language. This is a matter to think about, to discuss, and to do what one can do in that way, because the need is very great to make the language of all nations one language. The misunderstanding that exists today is the lack of knowledge of one another's language, and this lack of knowledge of one another's language produces the lack of understanding of one another. The people of one land do not understand the psychology of the people of another nation. Imagine how many souls who could be your great friends, and by that friendship much can be accomplished. You cannot continue to be friends only because you do not know the language

1. Lecture given in Summer School, Suresnes, France, June 24, 1924.
2. "Gathekas" are esoteric study papers for murids.

of one another. By this, naturally, we become narrow; we only seek our own surroundings, those who understand our own language; we only know about the people who surround us. We understand them, we live with them the life of a turtle in the well, who does not know about the well, whose whole life is a well.

This can be accomplished by two things. One thing is to promote the desire among your friends of learning more languages. If the people in the East will learn the languages of the West, if people in the West will learn Eastern languages—what a great benefit it can bring to the world. Besides, those who are born and brought up in a country, if they know the language of their own people that is not enough. They must at least know one more language in order to communicate with the people of another country. But besides this, there must be a universal language to communicate with one another. For a world movement like ours, if all that is given in the form of literature was expressed in a universal language, the message, which might reach to the other end of the world in a hundred years, could then reach in ten years' time—a channel of communication would be open. It is deplorable to think that at this present moment, when we have communications of post and telephone and radio and wireless, yet we cannot communicate soul to soul, heart to heart, because of the lack of language. Because the living word has a great influence. No translation can convey the idea as the language itself can. It would centralize the education of all countries if there were one language. The quick development of Western music must be traced in that universal notation system that exists in all European nations. Composers of any part of Europe can convey their soul's expression to any part of the world. There lies the secret of the development of music that we see today. One cannot imagine how a great many difficulties will be solved and many great things will be accomplished, if once a universal language became prevalent in the world.

It is not we who are to decide that question; it rests with the world. But we can bring this question to the fore, making it known to the multitude in order that something, which may be accomplished after a long time, may be hastened by our humble efforts.

* * *

Question: *Would the Esperanto language answer the purpose?*

Answer: Yes, but I do not know how far that language has advanced.

Response of another person: *Many nations attend it already. It is a great success, they had lectures in Esperanto in the States; they have advertising for it. Esperanto is practically rejected as a universal language now no longer.*

Answer: It is a question, in the solution of which, there is a great accomplishment.

Question: *Must it be a new language? Cannot the language which has the largest number of people who speak it be taken?*

Answer: Yes, that would be the best, if people accept it.

Question: *What will you do with the national jealousy that is shown in the States? They argue on that very point.*

Answer: At the League of Nations this was also a question on the foreground. This was the only drawback why a national language should come to the fore. Therefore, instead of English they made it Spanish. I was very much surprised as I thought it was the least known in the world, but it seems that in those attending the League of Nations there was a greater number speaking Spanish.

Response of another person: *It is the business language.*

Question: *What would be the answer to people who say there are so many kinship meetings already. Why must we come to yours?*

Answer: If you have your own kinship, go to yours. Here is a universal kinship. If you will, you can come here. Besides, there is one thing, and that is, there cannot be too many kinship meetings. The need of kinship is so great that if there were a thousand kinship leagues it is never enough.

Question: *If we would choose one Eastern language to learn, would Arabic be best?*

Answer: Any language that suits you best. There are some minds that a particular Eastern language suits—some Sanskrit, some Arabic, some Persian. Therefore, one cannot recommend one language, but such as Sanskrit, Arabic, Persian, or Hindustani will be best for philosophical purposes.

Question: *In which would we get the largest Sufi literature?*

Answer: Persian. It would help our movement very greatly if some of us learned some Eastern languages.

Question: *Is Hindustani universally spoken in India?*

Answer: Yes. Sanskrit seems to be the most difficult. But I think it is the most easy to learn, because it is phonetic. Each letter represents a certain sound, and each vowel is an additional mark. There is no difficulty of spelling. It is musical. There is no need of—once when one has learned the letters—there is no difficulty of spelling. Arabic and Persian are most beautiful languages.

Response of another: *In the States you are using the gramophone to learn the languages.*

11

A FEW WORDS TO THE WORKERS IN KINSHIP

WHAT shall we answer if someone asked us if there is a certain principle on which to build a state, a community?[1] Today there seems to be everywhere a desire to form a community, to form a new state. The reason is that humanity is rebelling against the existing laws, against the existing customs, against existing conditions. The Sufi message has not yet directed its activity in that direction, and just now we have too many things already to give our mind to. Therefore, we cannot give our attention to this subject, but that does not mean for one moment that we are opposed to what they call communism or socialism or Bolshevism. How could we, with any thought, work against something about which we do not know fully? We, who are practicing in our everyday life, at least try to practice tolerance toward our fellow human beings. We, who understand that all different activities, however unjust, crude, and brutal in appearance, may have at the back of them perhaps some love for humanity, some good object, which we have not yet come to understand. Therefore, if we do not partake of these activities, that does not at all mean that we are opposed to them. We are only occupied, with both our hands full, with the little works that we have taken to accomplish. And if we can work in our own little things that we have undertaken to do and accomplish, we shall feel that we have been able to perform our duty. Are we not helping all movements that work for the welfare of

1. Lecture given in Summer School, Suresnes, France, July 1, 1924.

humanity, in wakening the spirit of kinship among people? Is it not a contribution sufficient to ask of us if we cannot do more?

As to my knowledge, the work of spiritualization is greater than forming people into a community. Communities will form and break if they are not spiritual, if they have not understood the right ideal, if they are not tuned to that pitch that is a normal pitch for a human being to be tuned to. There will always be differences; human nature is such that humanity really does not know what it wants. Humanity wants a rule of life and wants to refuse to follow it; both things it is anxious to have. Humanity is looking for a rule of life and continually is revolting against it.

Is communism the fad of today? It has always been. It has always been practiced in different ways, and then it has always been broken when degeneration sprung up in it, when they did not understand the full meaning of it. Therefore, it is not the act of forming communities which is essential; the essential thing is to wake that tendency of kinship toward one's fellow human beings, the desire for service. It may not seem to be a big work, because one attributes bigness to something complex. This is too simple. Therefore, it may not seem large enough, but this is the only thing there is to us. After all the philosophical knowledge one attains, after all the mysticism one understands, after all meditations and virtues one acquires in life, there only arises, as a result of all the blessing, one desire; and that desire is to be best fitted to serve our fellow human beings. If that is the last thing, then that is the first lesson also. It is first and last. It is simple, yet it is the essential thing in life to do.

The kinship movement can have one more activity, and that activity is to guide the youth of the present time without them knowing that they are being guided, and to offer one's services in their worst moments in a manner that what one hand does, the other hand does not know. Youth today are more in need of a service, a loving service, than at any other time, because today the hands of the parents have become feeble to hold their children. Education gives them something but not all things, and they are left open to all influences, with an ego left as an uncut diamond. Youth today are not willing to listen; they are not willing to learn from you; they are not willing to humble themselves. Youth today are not so responsive as youth were before, and therefore, their unripe condition attracts upon it many difficulties and troubles that the youth before did not have. And they lack the knowledge to answer different demands of life and to avoid different disasters, dangers, difficulties that might fall upon them. Your duty toward human beings and your inclination to serve people must give you the inclination to render your services to the youth who are needing help. Without any pretense of spiritual or religious knowledge you possess, just a friendly help, a word of advice, an act of friendliness in the time of need, here and there, will enable you to do a great work for our kinship movement.

* * *

Question: *Why are the youth of today so difficult to handle? Is it due to the parents?*

Answer: Yes, there are two things, the bringing up of youth is not the same as before. The conditions around the youth are not the same, and as the life has changed so the youth have changed. In one way they have become more responsible for themselves, but in the other way, there remains a kind of uncut diamond. Something that may be called an ideal, that seems to be lacking today, and the lack of which is a kind of pain to both men and women, and it is a loss to humanity in general. I do not say that everywhere it is the same case. There are exceptions, but generally it is so.

Question: *In families of position and great wealth I have noted a slackening of that maternal influence. The children were given into hands of governesses, to the influences of outside people. Will that not account for the irresponsible attitude of the youth to life?*

Answer: Yes. Besides, the parents have a certain part to perform in the child's education, apart from all in the school. That part is much more important than what they learn in the school. If there is no communication between those at home and the child, then there remains a kind of wall between two souls, whether it is a mother or father. And the child lacks that strength and inspiration which it could have otherwise had from its parents.

Question: *If these conditions as a whole are changing so rapidly, it is only the plan of God. There are certain new elements, characteristics, to take the place of something formerly that is not lost but is yet dormant.*

Answer: It is according to our attitude in which we look at life. It is all the plan of God; all that is happening for the best then reaches the ultimate end in time. But if we are seeing that things are lacking, and if we can perfect it and render our service in order to complete what is lacking, it is best. I am sure that I would rather take that point of view of yours, to think that it is all God's plan and working for the best; in each case I would not be able to perfect it. But in the case if I had the means or power or inspiration to help, then I would rather take the other point of view. What is lacking? Is there any means by which I can do something to help that lack?

Question: *Is it not something to do with the aftereffect of the Great War? All the lack of discipline and passions set loose then? Is not the movement of Boy Scouts and Girl Guides doing good work?*

Answer: I think what you say has a great truth in it. Such unbalanced conditions bring about unbalanced results. War is an unbalanced condition. Of course, there is another way of looking at Boy Scouts and Girl Guides. It is a very good thing to learn discipline, but something learned at home is something different, just as it is to make a cake at home or buy it from a *confiserie.*[2] But at the same time, wakening the parents as well would do some good; that those who can give some little attention to the children, they could do so.

Question: *Would this kinship of the Sufi Movement as such, would it not have a message in the economic or social line?*

Answer: In the future I do not know; at the present our hands are full with the duties we have. Therefore, we leave our murids free to take interest in any question of the world welfare; and they may do so, personally inspired by the message that they receive in the Sufi Movement. So in this way, through individual murids, a good work can be done. But at the same time, the movement cannot occupy itself with any more activities than it has just now at hand.

2. French word for a confectionery shop.

12

Kinship Work in Prisons and Hospitals

A FEW words on the kinship principle in which the workers may engage themselves, and by which they would be doing a very charitable work: to read the "Gathekas" to patients in the hospitals, to read the Sufi literature to the prisoners if they were allowed to go there.[1]

Besides, there are two objects some time or other for us to accomplish as a kinship activity. One object is prison reform; that those put in prison, sometimes in prison for the whole life and sometimes for part of their life, need spiritual help in order to endure the whole life sentence or to make the best use of the part of life that they live.

The work that can be done in the hospitals with the patients is the most blessed work that the kinship workers could accomplish, because when people are in the hospital all the time is their own; they can grasp things, their hearts are open owing to the suffering, they have time to contemplate upon it. And there is no medicine, no treatment that can help the person to the extent that the spiritual message can. Your work there will be more valuable than medicine and more important than treatment.

Besides this, in education, in the adult schools such as there are in England or in other private schools, if it was difficult to introduce it just now in the government schools, one could give an opportunity of going and getting an interpretation of

1. Lecture given in Summer School, Suresnes, France, July 8, 1924.

the message of unity. By this you will be doing a great service to the cause and, at the same time, to God and humanity.

There is one thing in favor of the kinship workers: that they do not go to the different places as religious missionaries. They go only as servers without any outward religious appearance. And those sensitive to a religious ideal, who would close their hearts otherwise, would in this case open their hearts when a kinship worker goes, because they do not go there as clergy or as a priest; they only go, as a friend, to entertain the patients in their time of suffering.

13

Questions and Answers

TODAY I wish to ask my workers in kinship to ask any questions regarding the continuing of the work.[1]

Question: *I want to ask you, if we, the cherags,[2] are going to you in the summer, then we cannot continue the service in our towns. People have expressed their wishes to continue. When will the time come that it is a greater need to continue the service?*

Answer: Of course, if you had left your service in order to go for an amusement or pastime, it would have been different. But you have left your service in order to come here, to take all that is needed for the service, and then to go and continue it again. So you are doing the service for your friends who are interested in the service just the same.

Question: *I think it is of infinitely more value to come here, but I think he has in mind their need also. They do not like it; it weakens our position.*

Answer: Therefore, we are trying to have more cherags in every city, that in the absence of two or three cherags, others may continue the work. If your co-workers in your city will continue even now, it would be a good thing. Although we consider two months of the year as a vacation for the Sufi Movement, we used to consider first August and September [*text missing*].

1. Session in Summer School, Suresnes, France, July 15, 1924.
2. Cherag(a)s are those who lead Universal Worship services.

Question: *In the States the service goes on just the same.*

Answer: Service must be continued if it can be managed to do so. But if in a place there is only one cherag, and that cherag has to come here, in order to receive, it is better that the cherag takes a leave of a month or two and comes here.

Question: *If there is no cherag, can the service be continued in an informal service?*

Answer: Yes, by taking the permission from the headquarters or from the national representative of the country.

Question: *So then it will become an informal service, or does one continue with the Universal service?*

Answer: The Universal Worship goes on always.

Question: *In regard of a practical question of kinship meetings: In New York, where there are so many different nationalities, would it be the work of kinship to invite teachers of other religions to talk of their religion in kinship meetings?*

Answer: Yes, you may call a Zoroastrian or Hindu or a Buddhist or someone who is an authority in some religion.

Question: *I have heard from cherags: "Yes, we have our service, but it comes that people come and ask of other religions. Then we are ashamed that there are other religions we know nothing about." I know that, by and by, we can learn. But is there not a manner to teach a class for cherags to learn the other religions?*

Answer: We are beginning now a study of comparative religions, a textbook among cherags, in order to present religions in their right form. Regarding kinship activity, if the person was known to the national representative of that country, any person who can speak on religions or philosophical subjects can be invited to speak at kinship meetings, because our kinship meeting always opens its platform to any speaker on philosophical or religious subjects.

Question: *Would there be any objection to having kinship meetings at which different speakers would be called, to make them interesting to the public at large and then have that followed by devotional service?*

Answer: Yes, sometimes it would be a convenient thing, but sometimes not. For instance, we invite people to a kinship meeting without thinking about their ideas. They may come there and be interested by it, and come four, ten times. The more they become acquainted with us, the more they will tolerate us. But if we begin to have before them a kind of Universal service, they will perhaps be horrified and never come again. Therefore, better first let them come to kinship meetings and acquaint themselves with our ideas, and then if they think, "What a pity there is not a devotional service," then they can be invited to come in and see what it is. But it is better that the kinship activities go forward to welcome people who are of different thoughts and ideas. This is the first thing to unite.

Question: *I do not grasp that the Universal Worship is—it is better that in the beginning it is so [*text missing*]*

Answer: The kinship has a special mission to acquaint ourselves with people, because strangers are always apt to look at you with suspicion and doubt, however good and correct it is. The first thing is that they will form an opinion. Really it is true that so many people will form an opinion without thinking; it is very easy to form an opinion at once before thinking. We shall be in that way exposed, which shall not be for our benefit. When in the beginning the plants are small, little seedlings, anyone can walk upon them; they can be destroyed. When the plants turn into trees, they protect themselves. They stand on their stem; it is strong, it is its own defense. In the beginning in the movement also, it must be regarded with special care. What we need most is the psychology of human nature—not of individuals but of the multitude.

Question: *Each town has a different psychology?*

Answer: Yes, but at the same time the first lesson that we have to learn is the one principle that is behind human nature. Then it becomes easy for us to study different towns. But the first thing is the psychology of human nature; that is the main thing.

Question: *When you yourself are not afraid as* [text missing]

Answer: Too much of everything is wrong. If you are too conscientious of what people will think and say, then you will also keep the movement back from furthering. If you ignore people's ideas and feelings, then you may also cause a harm to the movement, because you will do too much. In spite of Murshid's enthusiasm for the cause, there is not one word or action Murshid does without thinking what effect it will have upon the individuals and upon the multitude.

Question: *Sometimes people have asked me, why have you not told me that these services have* [text missing]

Answer: We must strike the happy medium—not to be too careful nor to be too neglectful—and that is the most difficult thing because it wants balance. We could do too much of anything easily—either be too careful and keep the message back from furthering, or be too eager to further it and thereby spoil it.

14

Noiseless Working

I HAVE very often spoken to my workers and friends—and yet I think that it cannot be spoken too often—of the subject of noiseless working.[1] The deep study of philosophy teaches us that life cannot tolerate living beings: no sooner a head is raised, than there is a knock upon it. If you keenly observe the picture of the forest and what goes on there, you will see the moving picture of it. No sooner the rabbit has lifted its head then the wild dog is waiting there and has grabbed it. It does not give its reason to do it; it does it because it wants to do it. Among birds, among animals, among all living creatures we see the same thing. We do not see it in humanity. It is not because it is not in humanity; on the contrary, this is more pronounced in humanity, but the life of humanity covers it. We, whose only motive is to render our services to our fellow human beings, we must think that it is of the least importance that anyone should know us to be something, or that we are working or doing some good. Why must they have nothing to do with our work? We can work more safely by working quietly than with noise. Besides, noisy people will accomplish little; their own noise intoxicates them so much that they are tired before the work is finished. They are exhausted before they have accomplished; they are disappointed before success is achieved. We see it in our everyday life.

1. Lecture given in Summer School, Suresnes, France, July 22, 1924.

If someone wishes to follow the main principle of Sufism and desires to become a real worker of the movement, this is the first thing to be learned: to do quiet work. We see in children the tendency of letting the whole house know if a dolly's bed is being made. And the same tendency is in grown-up people; they will make the whole town know first what they are going to do, and then they will begin to do a little thing. By that time they will have aroused sufficient antagonism against themselves, so that they will become a victim as soon as they have begun their work.

The devotion for the cause, the desire to work—all these things are appreciated and considered most precious. But to work tactfully and wisely, gently, and quietly, is the most important thing. What five noiseless workers can accomplish, five hundred noisy workers cannot accomplish. Often people think that there is nothing to hide. If our work is true and right, what is there to be hidden? Yes, it is true, but what about the psychology of human nature? Every fluttering of the leaves will make the wolf jump and see what is there. That is human nature. Souls will not wait patiently to see the results of your good work. The first impulse in a person is, "What is it? Why is it? I will strike against it." An individual does not want to stop to think, to see what it is. People have no time to stop, their life is too busy. Is every human being so thoughtful and wise as to see the results of human work? No. And therefore, you will have to create the results of your work before you appear, so that you will not appear with intentions but with results of your work. Let the world see you then.

Then comes a question: "Will it not paralyze propaganda?"[2] No, it only will put away the undesirable way of propaganda. It is not our claim that must make people recognize us; it is our work. It is our service that must prove the worth of our work. When people say, "I am doing good," in what little good they do, they can never prove to be sufficiently good. It is those who

2. In 1924, publicity was called propaganda.

say, "I am doing nothing," and do what little that they can, what little they will do will make it worthwhile. From every point of view the principle must be learned to make as little noise as possible. By that we shall be able to accomplish much more. Besides, it will help us spiritually.

* * *

Question: *It is only a question of attitude, not a question of how you make propaganda?*

Answer: Yes, it is so.

Question: *In other words, the propagandist is the propaganda?*

Answer: Yes. Now suppose workers went from here—I am just making up a story in order to explain—to Germany. They went and said, "You have been very bad people during the war, and that is why you have got this punishment. And now the Sufi message is coming for your safety, to save you from this punishment." And they went to the clergy of Frankfurt and said, "Religion was all right for so long, but now your religion is dead." Then they go and say, "All that material learning will do you no good; here is something we bring." So every good worker thinks, "We are not doing good work; here is someone who is doing good work." Others go quietly, see different things, institutions, learn from them what they can learn, and give what little idea they can for use. In this way they serve the cause in a better way.

When someone has a friend and begins to see from that person's own life a real devotion to a certain cause, one certainly begins to feel impressed that here is a person with balance and goodwill, who wants to do good in life. This example is something that we should follow; this person has a certain ideal. It is interesting; I should like to know about it. Then that person says, "This is the idea of unification of the religions, of bringing humanity together. We all can do it. It is not I, especially, but every person; we all can do in our little way." Naturally, a person will have a group of friends who will be most happy to share the study of the mysteries of life, for every soul is yearning for it. There is the desire in all to know more about their soul, their life. There is not one person who has not this interest. Our customers are everywhere, in every country. Here before you is the example. Murshida Martin[3] was coming from India in a ship. Some people met her, became her friends, were impressed by her ideal. She had not given a lecture or preached there, but they had met her. They told their friends in Switzerland, "We have met someone who interests us very much, whom we liked." That is the idea. A quiet, gentle work, done without very much noise and talk about it, is much better than making things rigid.

Besides, there seems to be a kind of revolt in many minds about organization. Of course, one can fight with them and argue, but it will continue, and it is not their fault. It happens that they only see the organization; they do not see its necessity. It wants a little more thought given to it: that it is not only a thing in itself, but a necessity; that without it a movement cannot develop. If that is the thing, then we must know that it is better. The less we bring up that aspect before people, the better it is; for the organization is for the idea, not the idea for the organization. And when people are interested in the idea, and when they are fully convinced of it, they will not mind organization; however much against it, they will see the necessity of it. But before one has known the idea fully, when the organization is brought to them, it is just like a stone given instead of bread. A person runs away from it.

For instance, a person came to see me in Belgium who seemed to be intelligent and tried to find out if there was some truth in such ideas. When this person came, if I would have told that person that the truth of this idea depends upon your organization, this person would have shown herself against it. The first thing was that I explained to that person the idea, for I saw that the person was in a great doubt, in a condition of doubt-

3. Murshida Rabia Ada Martin (1871–1947).

ing—that person doubted everything. I never said one word about organization. I thought if this person is helped with the idea, is it not enough for us? If the present need of this person is satisfied, our work is done. After having heard of the idea, the person became very interested and said, "If there was any rule of life, anything to observe or practice, I will do it." This person was given the practices. There was no mention of organization. After some time this person came by herself to me and said, "Is there any organization? Is there anywhere that I could feel that there is a center where I could find the source of this?" I said, "Yes." Now this person willingly offered herself to sympathize with a cause like this, to do what she can for the movement. But that came afterward. No doubt, one cannot always have the same principle, for every place differs and every individual also; but one must know when to apply which principles.

Murshida Martin: *We can extract help from sympathizers. Even if they never join us, still they can be great helpers by their sympathy.*

Answer: Very often they can be of great use, and they can be frightened like a bird if you tell them of organization. After they are acquainted with you, they themselves will offer their service. You need not ask them.

15

Kinship Work

MY murids and co-workers, have we heard from different sources that we might take interest in the actual condition of people?[1] Yes, as a kinship movement, no doubt it is our work and our aim. Only, as our movement is at present in its infancy, one cannot expect much from an infant. If an infant can exist and live a healthy life, that is something accomplished. It is not that we lack enthusiasm, courage, or hope. It is not that we neglect matters that should not be neglected. It is only that everyone does not see things from our point of view, and if we begin to consider every person's point of view then we are likely to lose our own point of view. People express their point of view from the spirit they have, from their own condition of mind, their own mentality, their own attitude toward life. If some people are agitated toward life, if they speak to us, they will tell us we are all wrong. If they go to the shop at the *confiseur*,[2] they will say all the cakes are bad. If they go to the market, they will say the produce is bad. The wrong is in them. If we take up another point of view where shall we end? There is no end to such things.

But the first thing that we have to consider is this: What is the length of our program? Is it a few hours, days, years, or centuries? And, in order to even see the length of our program, we ought to rise to the spirit of the message to see it. And accord-

1. Lecture given in Summer School, Suresnes, France, August 5, 1924.
2. French confectionery shop.

ing to the length of the program, things that ought to come in the middle or at the end of the program cannot be done. For even in the life of an individual there is a youth, childhood, and middle age. Every age has its special work to accomplish. A child cannot dream of what a middle-aged person does. A youth cannot think of things as does a middle-aged person.

On our side we are doing our very best. Every moment of our life, thought, and energy—as much as we can devote to it—we devote, as our life permits us. No doubt we cannot do enough in service; it is never enough. Nevertheless, we must see it from our own point of view. If we depend upon this person and that person coming to tell us how to do it, we are of no use. We had better not take up such a responsible work. If there is a responsible person, our responsibility is to know what is before us and how to meet it.

I have seen certain societies of occult or mystical work and how, in order to be successful, they have tried what they call in English catering: preparing every kind of supply for every kind of demand. And, for the time being, it seemed as if it would be a successful matter. But it was a momentary success and resulted in the destruction of the society, because the varied and many demands of human life ate up all that the society prepared, and their hunger was not satisfied. As every individual is destined for a certain purpose, so the message is destined for a certain purpose, and it is the main thing that the workers have to accomplish. And if results are not seen just now and not much is accomplished, it does not matter. It is not a program of two days. It is not a bubble that has come and will disappear. It is a process, as the English say, "slow and sure." Nevertheless, it is a question which we must think about. We must keep our eyes open. We must try to study for ourselves, that we may not have to depend upon others and have to say we are not acquainted with this quest.

I therefore ask my kinship representatives and murids to study the five questions of whatever class they can reach: the hygienic, social, moral, mental, and spiritual condition. We do not need to take all questions. Each of you may take one of these questions and study it, and be prepared with the presentation of the subject with an article on the subject, bringing to us a thorough information of your study.

For the next Summer School, all the kinship meetings that will take place there, every lecture given, will deal with the subject of the actual condition of humanity. And your lectures will be pertaining to one of these subjects. And those who can prepare papers beforehand may do so and will be welcomed at Geneva in the month of April, when we shall be having a meeting to discuss this question. And there will be an opportunity of reading such papers written after a practical study on these questions.

* * *

Question: *By that advice, choosing one special subject, you would do one thing well, and the kinship would accomplish some one thing definitely?*

Answer: For instance, one person goes and sees the condition in the poor class; another sees the conditions in good classes; another of the average health; another the moral condition of humanity; another the spiritual condition. That is enough for the present to work. We shall not yet touch economic and political conditions. It is not because we are opposed to that quest, it is only because we are in our infancy. There is much to be done in those realms. But if we do these four realms, those who cannot come to the Summer School next and to Geneva may send their paper.

Question *Just what realm do you mean by the social?*

Answer: The condition of people, the dealings of people with one another, between one individual to another, one class to another.

Question: *But the economical question comes very close to the social?*

Answer: By taking the economical question, we enter into deep waters. We are not yet prepared. If we could swim in the water we do not mind. Now we go just as far as the shores. We are too young just now.

Question: *Do you mind statistical study?*

Answer: Yes, that is what I mean by social.

Question: *What could one put under the head of spiritual? Religions?*

Answer: Yes, religion comes under it.

Question: *You meant only in the countries where we live in?*

Answer: Yes, or where we happen to be.

Question: *About the spiritual, you meant that we gave a statement of the different new religious forms?*

Answer: Yes, if your mind takes that trend, you may—or if you see among individuals or communities a kind of spiritual going back or forward. Just to write your own impressions and the details about the conditions that you see.

Question: *Is the idea more to gather information?*

Answer: The first thing that we can do is to gather information, then to discuss and see in what way the workers of kinship can work to better conditions. We must know first, before we can go out to help.

16

Wakening the Divine Spirit

MURIDS, friends, and collaborators, I would like to speak on the subject of our principal work in the working of kinship.[1] There are institutions for different kinds of social work already existing. It does not mean that we must not do the work, but it only means that we must specialize our part of service in the work of kinship. Besides social institutions, there are many kinship federations existing. They are all working for a greater ideal, all working for the best for humanity, and most of them working sincerely and earnestly to serve humanity to the best. Therefore, we are not only the one kinship that takes up all this work. There are others, also, but if we shall be conscious of our special work, we shall be able to render a service that is really worthwhile. And that work is the wakening of the spiritual ideal—in other words, of the divine spirit in humanity, which is the basis of kinship.

But you might ask if we can find intelligible methods for any other thing to work and in what way to proceed. For instance, if I told you that we must work to bring a little pleasure and ease to the sick people at the hospitals, then at once comes an idea how to proceed. And it is not very difficult then, for you to find out how to do it.

But one thing so simple as this, as it seems—to waken the divine spirit—is not so very easy to work out. It is easy in the saying; it is not easy in the doing. And the more you will do

1. Lecture given in Summer School, Suresnes, France, August 12, 1924.

this work, the more you will find that if there is anything that is most difficult, it is this. It is like digging the ground and not allowing the dust to rise. It is like carrying water and not allowing the pitcher to be wet. It is almost as impossible as that. And therefore, our task is not easy. When speaking it seems simple. It seems as if it is the best that one could do. But when we bring it to work, it is the most difficult thing to accomplish. It is not any particular method that I would give you that would help you very much, nor it is a particular method that you will adopt. It is accomplished in the first place by one's own spiritual unfoldment. And as one unfolds spiritually, so one naturally takes with oneself others who are inclined to come along the same road. It is just like a person with any vice can easily influence others who have a tendency to that vice and take them along with them. So it is that those spiritually inclined will take with themselves those who are inclined to the spiritual unfoldment. Besides, the power of goodwill always proves to be strong. People say might is right, but really right is might in the end. It might seem in the beginning that might is right, but it is never right; it is right alone that is might. Therefore, our strength is in the path of truth, which we follow. And our service can be most easy and at the same time most difficult—most easy, because we do not need to find a mechanism to do service. A word dropped here or there, a little kindness done to those who come in contact with us, a little sympathy shown to one in trouble—all this will waken that divine spirit in those we meet. And we shall be able to develop that sympathetic attitude toward one another, that loving attitude. If we can carry out that object, we really have accomplished a great deal.

* * *

Question: *Some of the people engaged in kinship work sometimes ask a question in relation to politics. I always say we can answer those questions in political point in the path of providence. In the path of providence is the ruler and governor.*

Answer: At the same time as I have said that, when we ask ourselves the question why there is not a satisfactory condition in the political world—why is it going on like this, with all the intelligent people that seem to be at the head of it, and all the leagues and institutions? Why do we not come to a better understanding?—you will give a thousand answers and dispute upon a thousand arguments, but where shall we come in the end?

The end is that politics must be spiritualized, economics may be spiritualized. How can it? By any method of spiritualizing it. Who is the judge? Those who judge, what power do they have? They can only try the judgment. Therefore, the main thing even to help the economic world or the political world, is to help humanity to spiritualize. The difficulty is that we say, but when? If we shall go on like this, calling one person in a few years' time, five persons, perhaps, come to us who have some real mission in the political or economic world to perform. By this, what is accomplished? Why not do something special? But there are many who are together doing something in the world. Many federations, institutions are working along these lines. They are not waiting for us; they are doing it themselves. Our part of work is different. It is such that outwardly it is perhaps a limited number of murids who are working, but inwardly the Absolute is working. Therefore, we must not be disappointed that we are so few. The Absolute is working toward the fulfillment of God's goal, to the spreading of divine wisdom. It may be that for two, three, four, five years we go on without any apparent result, and then you will find that suddenly a result has come out. No one knows how, but it is there. And since we do not seek any credit for our work, since we do not hold the fruits that will come out from this as our property, since we are willing to give the crops to the owner of the farm, there is no objection to how long we work. Our work is just like filling pitchers from the sea and putting it into the ocean. We do not know how much water we have taken, and how much we have put. It is taken from the sea and put into the ocean. And if we are content with this aspect of our work—that if we never saw in our lifetime a result—it is in this spirit we should work. We do not mind. As long as our conscience says we have worked sincerely and earnestly, that is sufficient for us.

Besides this, if one patient with the plague goes into a country, the plague starts and becomes an epidemic in that country. Do you think that an earnest worker of kinship will not prove to be a power in the end? The worker will take this germ, and the kinship worker's being there will be a marvel. I want my murids to waken to that spirit, that trust, that optimism, that our sincere desire to serve God and humanity must have its effect. Wherever we go, wherever we move, whatever country we enter, the seed of the message is thrown. It does not matter if we do little or more, for as we develop the spirit in ourselves, so much greater the phenomenon will manifest. It will develop of itself. Only we ought to be earnest, sincere about it, to trust in it, to have a faith in it. By that we shall find that the words of Christ are the ultimate truth, "Faith will remove mountains."[2]

Question: *What attitude have we as kinship workers to take toward socialism and Bolshevism?*

Answer: Our attitude must be compassionate and appreciative, friendly toward all. There is no religion, no church, no institution, nothing against which we stand. For we are friend of one thing, and that is a desire to do good. We do not stand there as the judge of their methods, because we have no right to judge. If people are earnest, leave them alone if they are democrat, aristocrat, or Bolshevist, as long as their motive is good. Because if we shall involve ourselves in trying to judge different methods, there come Bolshevists with their own ideas. Since I have been working, I have found many people who have made a whole method of how the world must be made better and brought it to me. I said, "Why not practice it?" They said,

2. See Matthew 17:20.

"There is the difficulty." I said, "Then, my friend, go back get that power and inspiration to your method. You have no faith in your own method. You must become something first. Become a living being; then any method you will take, that will take." We have to become living. In the Bible: "No one who is not born again will enter into the kingdom of heaven."[3] It is in their desire to be born again, to waken the spirit to the divine. We cannot go away from that main principle—"Seek ye the kingdom of God first."[4] In the social, political, and economic realms that give such power, such inspiration, faith, trust, and conviction, whatever be the method. In the first place, a wrong method will not appeal to you; therefore, method is not the first thing. The spirit of God is the first thing.

Question: *I have often wondered, in that spirit of tolerance that we have and in trying to see that all are working for good in their own way, yet in our way why should we make an exception?*

Answer: The reason is this, that we are an infant institution and we are living in the world and subject to the laws of the world. And since it is so, we do not wish to involve ourselves in the political struggles and troubles as many others do. Suppose here we are here and the French government asks us, what is this? We have to prove our argument to the French government. We are so few people. We have to prove our method to the millions of people who have perhaps not the same point of view and idea as we. What would be the use of it? It is only a line of conflict. We want to keep ourselves from taking a line of conflict and not conflict with the existing social laws. It does not mean we ignore it, because all these things are necessary for the world. But our work is purely spiritual. In order to do it well we must not have our mind troubled with conflict. As soon as we become worldly, the spiritual thread is loose.

Suppose politicians have read a spiritual work; have done their exercises, meditations. If they try to look at the point of view

3. See John 3:1–3.

4. Matthew 6:33.

as we try to, who knows that this point of view will not reach even politicians in two, five years' time? It might reach such heads that we do not know even. Then our service is done just the same. We are not asking for credit.

17

Tolerance

FAITHFUL murids and co-workers, during this summer season we have been speaking about the idea of our work in the kinship movement, and we have thought about various different things in which to take interest and various different ways in which to work.[1] But at the same time, when we think that there are so many institutions of social work and their number is ever on the increase, and when we think that there are so many philanthropic societies who are really doing a good work in doing what little they can to help humanity in its suffering and distress, we come to think that the things that different societies are doing are being done, more or less. Our special way of working must be peculiar to the Sufi message, even in an outside activity as kinship.

In order to teach religious devotion, the ideal of God, the truth of scriptures, the respect for masters, we have Universal Worship, our religious activity. In order to study philosophy and meditate and to understand the deeper side of life, we have the Sufi Order,[2] or the esoteric work. But in the work of kinship, what especially we can do is to bring forward one principle, and that principle is tolerance. The more we study life, the more we shall see that it is wanting, it is lacking. And we shall also see, after a keen study of life in general, that any work done

1. Lecture given in Summer School, Suresnes, France, August 19, 1924.

2. The Sufi Order is now known as the Inayattiya.

in the direction of bringing out that idea of tolerance is never wasted. On the other hand, it will have an influence on all different activities such as suggested to us by different friends: social work, economic, political. In all things this one principle will be a great help.

But, one might say, how can this principle be brought forward? In articles, in lectures, in teaching, in writing plays and dramas and stories. And those who can write, those who can bring into art the principle of tolerance, in their poetry to weave that principle in whatever way they can and bring it before humanity. And bring it before the children in the schools, before the patients in the hospitals, the prisoners in jails, one's friends and associates, before young people and elder ones—not in the way of preaching and teaching, but in such a delicate way that it could be interesting to hear and know about it. If not, it is natural that everyone says, "Do I not know that tolerance is a great merit?" As everyone would say, "Do I not know what love means?" and hardly anyone knows what love means in the world. The more one knows, the less one speaks about it. We can find out a thousand mistakes in our everyday life; this is something that can never be learned too much.

The more we develop this tolerant outlook on life and tolerant attitude in life, the more we shall find there is a place to fill. And it will stand as a spirit, a kinship behind everything that we do. And although, outwardly, tolerance is a simple teaching, at the same time it is the most difficult thing to accomplish in our life.

For human nature is such in its psychology that the more you learn, the more you find out this one thing that has kept the followers of different religions fighting with one another. Nations have prejudice against one another, classes have their distinctions and differences, and individuals stand against one another. All inharmony in every respect is mostly caused by intolerance. And there cannot be a greater moral and a better teaching for our kinship movement today than tolerance, and to bring it before the world, not in a religious form nor in spiritual form, but in one's own action, attitude, outlook on life, and to bring it in whatever way you can. If you are able, write newspaper articles; if you are an artist, then in your work of art; if you are a story writer, then in your story. In business, in industry, bring that idea of tolerance. If you think that it is a part of your kinship work, you express it; and in expressing it you are fulfilling your sacred work of kinship.

Further, I wish to add that the kinship movement gives us the scope of fulfilling the idea of ours that no other activity gives us, and that is unassuming work, noiseless work, a humble service without any pretense of being a worker. In this activity we have every scope of rendering a silent service to God and humanity, for in this work we come forward as nothing, and not as a religious teacher or as a religious preacher or someone who teaches a doctrine. We just come as friends, as servants. And by practicing this manner we have a greater chance of accomplishing our spiritual work, because for the real spiritual work what is most necessary is unassuming progress. If there has ever been a difficulty in the path of a seeker of truth or in a person who is progressing toward the spiritual ideal, there has been only one difficulty, and that is to keep one's ego from becoming vain of one's spiritual advancement. Those who have advanced and gone forward in the spiritual path, what they have shown in their poetry and writing is one thing: "We have found one great enemy on the path, and that enemy is our own ego. It becomes conceited, proud, vain of its spiritual attainment, of its goodness, advancement, greater knowledge, power." Naturally, the further one advances spiritually, the more one knows, the more powerful one becomes, and the more one begins to live. One becomes delicate, steady, strong, fine, and tender. And therefore, all that is beautiful and good and rich comes to one: and naturally, as it happens to be human nature, one becomes proud. And it is this one thing that holds one back. If ever one's progress was hindered, it is not by anything else outside.

Therefore, as spiritual workers or seekers after truth, as the servants of humanity, our greatest enemy is our self.

In the work of kinship we have that facility of coming before others as nothing, as their brothers and sisters, as their equals. We can speak to them heart to heart. And instead of teaching them, we can show by our own action and outlook on life—not to dispute or correct them, but by showing them gently by our own living and tolerance, which is the main principle of the message.

18

The Importance of Kinship

OUR kinship activity has a wider scope than any activity we have in the Sufi Movement.[1] As it is touching so many different departments of life, it accommodates all those who come to the Sufi Movement; and therefore, our work is to keep this activity alive in order to keep the fire of the movement lively.

There must be continual meetings taking place everywhere where there is a center of the movement. Even in places where there is no center of the movement yet established, if there is only one murid, even there, there is a scope for the activity of kinship. For in different religions and churches there are certain people who work, but in this movement every murid is a worker. If murids are isolated in a place where there are not many murids, they may begin the work of kinship there. They may interest their friends and acquaintances, and those who have inclination toward metaphysics and spiritual things may be invited. They immediately, by inviting others to the meetings of kinship, commence the work of the center. And since the membership in kinship has no financial obligations and is free, it opens its arms to welcome everyone interested in the matter. This gives great facility to an enthusiastic worker of the movement to interest a large number of people in the place where that worker lives.

By coming to these meetings month after month, people become interested in the question of life's purpose; and they begin

1. Lecture in Summer School, Suresnes, France, August 26, 1924.

their interest in the spiritual ideal. Often I have heard people say, "In the part of my country there is no interest. People do not respond. They do not listen. There are no possibilities." But my answer is that in the wild world of Siberia, if one went even there, one will find response if one knew oneself what one is teaching there.

Is there one human soul, however unevolved, who does not wish to know about life and its mystery? Yes, there are people who are interested in art, there are others who are interested in science. There are others who take interest in other subjects. But there is not one soul who will refuse to take interest in life's meaning.

If any refuse, there is some other reason. Maybe they have no belief in you. Maybe they are prejudiced against a name, mysticism, or devotion, or a spiritual thought. But in reality every soul is searching to understand the meaning of life, and when that happens to be our part of service, our customers are everywhere in the world. It is absurd to allow our mind ever to think, even for one moment, that this part of the world or that particular section of humanity or this particular race is not yet ready for the message. To know this, even the birds and beasts and animals and insects are ready. There is no living being who is not ready for light and for life.

It is the consciousness of our workers that must waken and realize what they wish to present to the world. Of course, till that is wakened, they will find difficulty. The difficulty is not with the people. The difficulty is with themselves. Kinship activity is the least frightening activity; there is nothing to frighten people. Other things have perhaps labels to frighten. The name of mysticism is frightening, the spiritual is frightening, but kinship is most innocent and simple work. You are always entitled to say to everybody that the work to come closer and to develop friendship is our work; that does not frighten anybody. Imagine, therefore, what a great field of work there is before us in kinship if we only realized it. Many of us are open to think that there is a vast field of work in the esoteric work, but it is because we think so; it is not actually so. Many may realize that a vast field of work is in the church work. No, it is the vast need of it, but there is not as vast a field as there is of the work of kinship. But besides this, which is the first need? Esoteric work is the last need. Religious work is a need that is necessary before esotericism. A person who is not wakened to a religious ideal will not take esoteric conceptions in a right way.

In my experience of so many years' work, I have found many who have come only for the esoteric development, lacking entirely the devotional aspect, and some not only lacking but also having a kind of contempt toward it. And I have found in the end that it was a vessel that cannot accommodate, because the religious or devotional aspect makes a person as a vessel. The esoteric idea then pours into the vessel what it must contain. But when the vessel is not ready, then what is poured in it will not stay there. But before these, two things are necessary. The first thing is a brotherly and sisterly attitude, the wakening of a friendly attitude toward one another. That is the first step. In religion, as in esotericism, in both, that is the first lesson to learn.

I wish, therefore, and hope that we shall, day after day, consider this activity more and more, and see what great importance this activity has for the cause. So far the Sufi Movement has been able to accomplish very little in that direction, and the more we shall waken to that, the more we shall find that in the furtherance of this activity lies the secret of the spreading of the cause.

19

The Message of God

WHEN we consider the past traditions, we find that whenever there was a divine impulse behind a spiritual movement, the message was carried by its exponents to the far ends of the world at such times when there was no train and there were no ships made, as there are now.[1] Traveling at that time was so hard that the idea of a person going on, traveling from a family, would create a panic immediately at the thought of that person's traveling. Now we are in the age when we can reach New York in a week's time, and we now hear that an airplane service has been established between Egypt and India. Now the world is not so difficult to travel as it was before, but what I wish to say is that, even at such times, there is nothing that kept the souls back who felt the inner call to take the message to the other end of the world.

There are many, we are thankful to say, in the Sufi Movement who are really desirous of doing all they can to serve the cause, although the object that is before us is so great and such a tremendous work that we cannot say for a moment that we had yet begun our work. It needs at least ten thousand workers to make a beginning of our work. At least there are some souls among us, if not many, who would be willing to make any sacrifice. If they had to leave their country, their people, their work, they would leave it and go in a country, in a place where

1. Lecture given in Summer School, Suresnes, France, September 2, 1924.

the message is to be given. But our need just now is such that the movement requires a great many souls to start the work. Imagine the worldwide field that is before us and the limited number, the small number that we have just now at hand. And if there is anything that can help us, it is the courage and willingness of that small number to be ready to answer the call. And this can only be done by the inner realization, for there is nothing outer in the Sufi Movement in the way of a big financial help or support or anything material to encourage and help us; there is nothing. If we have something, it is our faith, our unity, our harmony with one another, our strength in our ideal, our trust in God, our willingness to serve humanity. That is all the power and strength on which we depend, on which we rely, and with which we are willing to work.

Only I wish my murids and co-workers to be confident and to be sure that whatever wealth lacks in the way of the outside things, this will not discourage us for one moment. We shall go on. Nothing will hinder our work. And it is in this realization that we all unite in one ideal and work on this farm that is given to us by God. Our honor, our privilege, our duty, our religion, is in service; and if we are able to carry it out, in this will be the fulfillment of our lives.

Furthermore, it must be known that all kinship workers, wherever they fare forth, they must realize that they are taking there the message of God. Whoever they meet, they must know that they have a duty toward that person in regard to the message. Whatever they do, a social or a professional duty, or a domestic duty, that they do not forget that the message is the main thing to carry through. And in all different conditions—whatever they did it in the office, in the factory, in a club, in a society, in the train, in a ship, at the market—to deliver it in thought, in feeling, in atmosphere, in every way each one can, so that one may give the message of God at every moment of one's life, in every condition; and at every occasion the time might not be wasted.

Now the question, how to do it? You must never ask that question, for that question cannot be answered. If I told you in this way, perhaps tomorrow there may arise a need that you will have to give it in another way. Therefore, you must not trouble about this. It is God's message; you are not separate from God. You must try to hear the divine call and do God's service. What is asked of you is your willingness, your readiness, your continual desire of doing God's will. No doubt, your sympathy with Murshid and your devotion to the cause will be a help, and in the thought that we have the blessing of those who have done the work that God has meant them to do, and who have passed away—we have their help, besides the benediction of God. We are not swimming against tides; we are swimming with the tides. Therefore, the success of the message is sure, though it is not for the success that we work. We work for the sake of the work. It does not matter if we do not see the fruit of our labor in our lifetime, for the greater the work, the longer it takes to be fulfilled. We are workers; we are concerned with our work. The harvest belongs to the owner of the farm.

* * *

Question: *Is it not dangerous to talk to some people about Sufism?*

Answer: It is not at all dangerous, but we must understand the psychology of human nature: to whom to talk and to whom not to talk, when to talk and when not to talk, and what to talk of and what not to talk of.

Question: *Under the form of philosophy, can it not be given to [*text missing*]?*

Answer: Yes, when a person knows the psychology of human nature, then for them working becomes easy. But if a person has all the enthusiasm, devotion for the cause, and yet not the knowledge of human psychology, no doubt that person would find it difficult. And even when this person would find it easy, it would be still more dangerous. But if I may say a few principles which may be remembered about the psychology of human nature, it would be perhaps advisable to remember them.

The first thing we must understand is that human nature is most sensitive, and everything you tell a person, unless that person is especially seeking for it or ready for it, jars upon the person.

Another principle is that humanity is proud, and if there is anything you say without knowing that hurts people's pride, they will reject it. For instance, if you say that, "The Bank of France has opened a department. If you go there and give your name, they will give you a thousand francs as a guarantee," people will leave their pride in their pocket and go there and get it. But if you say, "There is a department open in a certain place; if you will go, you will find some sense," it will hurt their pride, it will not interest them. The first thing they will say to you is, "Am I senseless?" When a person says to someone, pointing to another person, "Listen, listen to this person, What this person says is right; you are wrong," it is finished. One has made a wall between the two just by saying, "You must listen to this person." Instead of doing good, one has done harm.

The third thing is that human nature is jealous. When you say to your dearest friend, "I like this thing," or "I like this person; in this person I find a great knowledge," the other person says, "Not at all." That person does not know it, but that person is jealous. Humankind is jealous of another person; and especially in regard to the person whom one likes—one's brother, sister, wife, or husband, or anyone—one would go too far.

There is another idea, that, "The one whom I like will go too far." It is not one case, I have seen thousands of cases: friends, relations. They do not like their relatives to go further but want them to be where they are. When the relatives want to go further, they say, "This is not the right way. Only because I do not want to go further, you must not go further, too."

Then you will find that anything new is very startling to many people. They have got a kind of fear, for anything new is very startling to many people. Especially anything mystical or philosophical or psychological is even more horrifying because they do not know whether it is a ditch or a pit—where is the person going to? If you plainly say, "It is a geographical society," it is quite clear, it is all right. But when you say, "It is mysticism," that person is mystified. For years that person cannot find out what is it. If you say, "It is a football team," then one understands what it is. Or, "I am going to see a boxing match, cricket, or tennis," then what interest you have is quite plain. They do not think it is wrong. But as soon as you say "mystical" they are horrified. They do not know what it is; they cannot understand.

So you see our way is very difficult. It is so difficult that the more we see the difficulties, the more disappointing it is. But at the same time there is another side of looking at it, and that side is very helpful. There are certain people who are fond of sport. There are certain people who are fond of art. There are certain people who are fond of science. But there is not one soul in the world, wise or foolish, who is not interested in understanding the meaning of life. Imagine, is there any business, trade, shop, art, or science that ever has so many customers as we? All human beings are our customers if we only knew how to approach them. Besides that, there is not one place in the most civilized countries or in the most uncivilized countries where the spiritual awakening has no place, where a spiritual message is not needed. Yes, some will say that, "In my village I find it most difficult"; "In each town where I am working it is impossible to further it"; "In a place where I have gone nobody listens." Yes, I have experienced it myself. Now it is for twelve years that I have traveled throughout the States and throughout Europe, and I have seen the difficulties in working. But has it discouraged me? In spite of all disappointments, I have greater and greater courage. For what I had believed, I have seen actually: that there is not one place where the spiritual is not wanted. There is not one soul who is not interested in the mystery of life. One may admit it or not. Either on the surface or at the bottom of one's heart there is a continual craving to understand the meaning of life. And what is the message? The message is the answer to it.

20

UNITY

THE tendency of kinship is instinctive in living beings, not only among humankind but even among birds and animals.[1] In the lower creation, where the ego begins its work and where the ego rises against its sibling, even in that stage there are birds and animals that can be brought together. At the same time, by studying the lower creatures we can understand that in the lower stages even the destructive creatures can unite; and that gives us an idea that even in the lower stages there is already a tendency toward a higher stage of evolution. When we think of the higher creatures, we see this kinship can be developed, and this kinship has developed in humanity. The proof of this we see in the life in towns—that people would rather live together than live scattered in the forests. There are large cities such as New York, London, Paris, where there is difficulty in finding housing accommodation—and, on the other hand, the vast open spaces, woods, and forests. Yet people prefer to live together. This is, however, no virtue, for nothing is a virtue that is not consciously acted up to. Therefore, when human beings must live together this is no great thing, but when they consciously live together, then begins the tendency toward human kinship. Now, the conscious recognition of kinship requires a link, and that link awakens a feeling of kinship. For instance, in ordinary language, when someone says, "This is my brother, my sister," it means only that the other is born of the same parents.

1. Lecture given in 1924. Location and day are unknown.

There can also be a kinship of professions; there can also be a kinship in ideas, and a kinship of those born in one city. And to the extent that a person is conscious of the link that binds one with the other, so far will one realize kinship. If people do not feel conscious of that link, even if they are siblings, they will feel strangers. So the strength of kinship does not lie in the claim, but in the consciousness of that link; not in the profession that kinship exists, but in the conscious recognition.

The idea of kinship has manifested differently in the East and the West. In the East it has manifested in unity in God; in the West, in national feeling. It has appealed in the East to religion and in the West to national feeling. But at the same time, in the East, when Hinduism was predominant, especially in India, religious restrictions were taught in connection with hygiene, so that eating and drinking came to be separated, and so that the wife even had to prepare her own food separately. Things are different in the West, where there also exist hygienic questions; and life is different from that of the East, where it did not prove in the end the ideal life. And the degeneration of the Hindu race began when the different limitations began. There were four castes among Hindus: *brahmans*, *kshatriyas*, *vaishyas*, and *sudras*: the caste of the student, the caste of the warrior, the caste of the merchant, and the caste of the laborer. Nobody can deny that there was great wisdom in this division, for there are four different tendencies in humankind. But in the end it resulted in disaster. The people became weak owing to these divisions, and the link of kinship was destroyed. This example of the Hindu race is, in itself, an example for human beings in the reconstruction of the world.

In ancient times, Arabia and Persia were split up in parts, each part with its own gods and goddesses, and many different gods and goddesses. And as the Hindu race was most blessed by Shankaracharya, their teacher,[2] so the Arabs were enlight-

2. Adi Shankaracharya (788–820), Hindu philosopher.

ened by the coming of Muhammad. And one can see that even fifteen hundred years since, there existed the tendency of forming a human kinship by the teachings of Muhammad, which tended to form a universal kinship. The various families among the Arabs began to live together and began to eat together, to shake hands, and worship together in the same house of God. There is a story of the khalif 'Umar, that he was greatly hated by a certain criminal. And on a certain day this man came to the town and asked where 'Umar was. He was told that the khalif was in the forest, looking after his cattle. The assassin thought this a splendid opportunity to accomplish his plan. As he approached 'Umar, he saw no warrior there to protect him, but he was sitting alone, clad in a worn-out robe. The assassin could hardly believe that the khalif was so near and within his power; he could not trust his eyes that the khalif, whom he had pursued so long, was now so near and unprotected. But the nearer he approached, the more nervous did he become, so much so that when he was quite near, the dagger fell out of his hand. 'Umar said, "Peace be unto you, what do you want?" to which the assassin answered, "Tell me why I tremble before you." 'Umar said, "Just as I tremble before God when I think of doing wrong, so dost thou tremble before me."

Another story told about 'Umar is that after a war, at the peace negotiations, 'Umar represented the armies of Islam. The enemies were told by their astrologers that they must make peace when 'Umar arrived. But as the enemies had never seen him before, they asked, "How shall we know him?" The reply was, "You can recognize him when you see a slave on the camel, and 'Umar walking at the side." In fact he came as had been foretold, and the first question put to him was, "Why were you walking and your slave on the camel?" to which he replied, "I have not walked all the way. The first part I rode, and the second part it was my slave's turn to ride and mine to walk." And when one thinks of this, one realizes the beauty of the human heart, this perfume that resides in the human soul.

There is another example of human kinship. When the Prophet Muhammad was waging war against some people, the Prophet was compelled to flee three times from Mecca. And each time a great deal of harm was done to his family, and even he himself had scars and was bleeding from various wounds when he fled. But later, when the Prophet was victorious, these enemies were brought before him, and he asked them, "How shall I deal with you?" They answered, "Deal kindly with us." Muhammad said, "Yes, I will deal with you in the same way in which Joseph dealt with his brethren." And at once they shook hands and were friends, and all the feelings of hatred were forgiven.

By this I wish to say that it is not the intellectual teachings of the great ones that we need, but the example of their lives, which is so important to us. Now, the effect of that example can be seen even down to this day in the peoples of Arabia. The Bedouins, who spend their lives in fighting and robbery, and are found everywhere in the deserts of Arabia—if two of them are found fighting and on the verge of killing each other, and if a third person says, "Unite, in the name of the Prophet Muhammad," immediately they throw away their weapons, shake hands, and become friends. How much do we wish that what such wild people do would be followed by us, the so-called civilized nations! If people can only move from one country to another and cannot find the link that binds them to each other, what use is that to us? This does not mean that we have to ignore national distinctions, but that we have to ignore the narrow boundaries of the nations.

Any person with some heart will wonder, and say, "Will there ever come a time when the hearts will become united, and the barriers be removed, and humankind will become united in some higher link that binds us all together?" Considering the question from the psychological point of view, we shall find that no family can be happy where there is a difference of feeling or a feeling of reciprocal ill will. The atmosphere of such a house can cause all manner of diseases and all sorts of misery. Where there is disagreement, disharmony, perhaps one is in a better position than the other, but the suffering will be divided among them all, and each will have to bear a share of it. The old stories and legends that there came down fire from heaven, that there came floods and volcanic eruptions, show us that these disasters came as a result of disharmony. Now the national disharmony is more prevalent than ever before on earth, for the small communities have now become nations and peoples, so that they can now have a greater power for evil or good. From the psychological point of view, all the nations are one family, so that the consequences of what one nation does against another, the whole world experiences; so that the actions of races and communities are the same as the actions of individuals of the past. Every nation only interested in its own affairs, ignoring the conditions of the others, is equally responsible for the suffering and troubles that they suffer. Just think of the great suffering and pain that the larger part of humanity is going through in different regions of the world today.

If it were not for the fact of illusion and the blindness of humankind for others than themselves, the world would be in a different condition from what it is. But to see life as a whole is not the work of everybody. Each one has too much to think of in one's own affairs, one's own worries and troubles. Today is a time such as the world has never seen before. Humankind is divided, ignoring the truth that we depend upon one another. To the person who would think from a humane point of view, even the wise and clever are acting as children. What is required today is this: that some souls, unselfish, strong, confident of the truth of their ideals, should join hands in serving humanity—not that there are not some hearts and heads who see life from different points of view, but it is such as these that are required. The Sufi Movement is devoted to this ideal, and is an answer to the call of the earth to the heavens. It is not necessarily a religion or a philosophy, but it is the essence of all religions and all philosophies. It is an understanding that will unite humankind, and its great link is wisdom. It is not the claim or wish of the Sufi Movement that this shall be the only movement working for the kinship of humanity, but that the work be shared by everybody who feels called upon to take part in this task. The Sufi Movement does not make restrictions upon people coming from other religions—Christian, Buddhist, or Jew—because it looks upon all as one, coming from the same divine source. Everybody is welcome in the Sufi Movement, whose aim is to unite people in that feeling of the unity that is their source and life.

21

FRIENDSHIP

BELOVED Ones of God, I wish to speak this afternoon on the subject of friendship.[1] It is a word that we all use in our everyday language, and yet it is something that could take the whole life only to realize its meaning. However much learned a person may be, however much pious or spiritual a person may be, however more experienced a person may be, if one has not learned the nature and the character of friendship, one has not learned anything. This is the first thing we have to learn, and this is the last thing we have to learn. We so often make use of this word, calling every acquaintance a friend or professing to be somebody's friend, but the more we realize the meaning of it, the less we are able to claim to be a friend. For everything we are tested in life, we are examined, we are tried; but to go through this examination of being a friend is the most difficult thing in the world.

And what is the reason of this? Why is it so difficult to be a friend? One could think that it is the easiest thing in the world. The reason is that there is in ourselves something that is always against being a friend. And what is it? It is the self, the ego, which the Sufi calls *nafs*. So long as this ego is standing and it lives, a person cannot claim to be anybody's friend. And as one is not anyone's friend, one is not even one's own friend; for one learns friendship by being a friend to another. Selfish people

1. Lecture given on June 21, 1925, at unknown location.

may seem to be a friend to themselves, but it is on the surface, not in reality. They have not learned yet how to be a friend, so they cannot be a friend to themselves also.

In our pursuit after truth we are inclined to learn a great many things—the nature of life, the secret of life, the character of life—and to understand the meaning of friendship. It seems so easy, so simple, that we never trouble to think about what responsibility it is to be a friend. The great error we make in our lives is that we begin to claim friendship before we have learned the meaning of friendship. In this world of illusion, where in the end of examination we find all things of little importance, of little worth, if there is here a sign of reality—something that one can depend upon and something in which one can recognize a sign of eternity—it is in the constancy of friendship.

As people are absorbed in the active life of the world, they have a desire for friendship, but they never practice it. But this tendency can be found even among the animals. I have heard this story as a personal experience of a hunter, that one day he was shooting at little birds in the forest, and there were two birds sitting on a branch of a tree. One bird was shot and dropped on the earth. And as this man was at a distance, it took him a little time to arrive there; and during that time what he saw was that the other bird, the mate, which was sitting on the branch, came down on the earth to look at the other bird, its mate. And it touched it with the beak and found that it was dead. By the time that the man arrived, he found both birds dead. "From that day," said this man, "I gave up hunting, for I have seen friendship among birds that one cannot find among humankind." It is a simple lesson, and it is a lesson that we have to learn. And today, when nations are against nations, and races against races, communities against communities, one religion against the other religion—at this time friendship is so much needed. Besides, the first lesson of spirituality that one can learn is friendship. One says, "But friendship, a personal friendship, means nothing. A person does not become spiritual by a personal friendship." And the answer is, yes, one begins one's spiritual accomplishment by learning how to be a friend. For a person who is really treading the path of friendship needs not go anywhere to learn morals. Friendship itself teaches sincerity, gratefulness, tenderness, sympathy, appreciation. All these things that we must learn in this world, friendship teaches us. And once a person begins to learn these things by friendship of one person, naturally that person shows the same virtues that have been acquired by going through this path to the others. Naturally, the one who has learned how to sing beautifully will sing every song that is given to that one beautifully. A person who has cultivated the heart by friendship will naturally be inclined to be friendly with others. It is not the belief in God that leads us to the goal, nor it is the analysis and the knowledge of God that brings us there; it is the friendship of God. For one who learns the lesson of friendship in this world, this lesson develops, in the end, in the friendship of God. But when a person exacts from a friend all that the person does for the friend, then it is not friendship, it is business. It only means I give you a shilling, and you give me twelve-pence.[2] When people judge their friend in their heart, the spirit of friendship is not wakened; a friend never judges. When people talk to another about their friends, when they blame the friends and criticize them, those people do not know what friendship is; the meaning of friendship is too sacred to realize. All other relations and connections in this life are empty if friendship is not at the back of it to strengthen it. Between mother and daughter, father and son, brother and sister, husband and wife, teacher and pupil, all these connections need a spirit behind it, and that spirit is the spirit of friendship. When a daughter says, "O, I am friends with my mother," there is something beautiful about it. Besides the connection of a mother and a daughter, when she says,

2. In English currency at that time, twelve pennies made one shilling.

"She is my friend, she is my chum," it is a different, thing; it makes that connection living.

In every relation it is the same. When there is friendship to bind the relation, it makes it secure, it makes it lasting; it is that which gives it a life. It is true that love is life, and life is symbolized with water. Water is the symbol of life. When one wants to bring water from the ground, one has to dig it, and the first thing that one finds is the mud. And if one was disappointed that: "Oh, by digging for the water I have found mud," one has fooled one's own self. For at the bottom of the earth there is water. It can be found, but one must have patience to dig it, dig it deep enough to find the water.

If someone has made a friend, it is not something that one has made to order, that must just fit in according to one's expectations, according to one's wishes. Every person has individual characteristics, and as long as the spirit of forgiveness is not developed, friendship cannot last. It is a continual forgiveness that helps friendship to endure. Much can be learned by study, but not unselfishness. Unselfishness can be learned only by one thing, and that is by treading the path of friendship; and it brings a beauty in life.

A friendly person, whether in business or profession, in what capacity that person stands, gives you a feeling of warmth; in other words, an atmosphere of life. You are always glad to meet a friendly person in a shop, in a factory, in an office; in what position that person stands, it does not matter. When this spirit is wakened, you can feel that person in the person's words, in the voice. You can feel it in the expression, by the atmosphere, that this is a friendly person. There is something that goes out to meet the other person, a continual tendency to harmonize with another.

Once this spirit is developed, this ever-complaining tendency vanishes. If not, then this world is full of thorns; everywhere where one wants to lean one's hand against, there are thorns that prick. One will have no peace, no happiness, whatever position in life one may be. If we want to make our life easy, if we wish to create happiness in our life, we must try to crush that ego, that nafs, that thought of self which keeps us continually obsessed in our own thought and in our own affairs.

By rising above it we will learn the spirit of friendship, and then, for us, the same world that is full of thorns will become full of roses. For some souls the same world is heaven that can be as hell to many others, for friendship changes one's point of view. Unfriendly people, as soon as they see another, see the other person from their own critical point of view. They have their preconceived ideas, and therefore, they are not allowed by providence to see the good side of the person. But for those in whom a friendly spirit is wakened, they always overlook little errors, faults, little mistakes. They naturally rise above, for their sympathy and their love help them to rise above the faults of humanity. That story of Jesus Christ, the friend of humanity, before whom the greatest sinners were brought—the attitude of the Master was forgiving. Those who brought them were unfriendly, the Master was friendly.

The life is as we look at it. If we wish to find faults, we can find faults of the best person in the world; and if we wish to find good points, we can find good points in the worst person of the world. It is as we see life. Someone went to Jami,[3] the great seer of Persia, and asked if Jami would accept him as his disciple in the spiritual path. Jami asked him, "Have you loved, have you learned the manner of friendship?" He said, "No, not yet." Jami answered, "Go in the world again and learn it. The first lesson in the spiritual path that you have to learn is the manner of friendship. Once that is learned, then all other parts of the spiritual journey will become easy."

Friends, all these difficulties, such as wars, revolutions, disagreeable experiences in nations, fights among parties—where does it all come from? It all comes from that one thing, and

3. Nur ad-Din 'Abd ar-Rahman Jami (1414–1492), Persian Sufi poet.

that is the lack of friendship. And the most wonderful thing is this: one party is against another party, fighting for years perhaps, but if you investigate the particular ideas of that party, even they are not friends because of the unfriendly spirit developing in them, by fighting against the other party. They cannot be friends, even among themselves. It is a kind of intoxication. But when this is gone, then they fight among themselves in education, in religion, or in any other way that is possible. The best thing one can do is to introduce the spirit of friendship. But you will ask how can we introduce it, because this is something that cannot come by only reading some books about it. If not, there are so many societies and institutions of kinship that everywhere one hears about it every day, increasing kinship; but they prove to be everything else but kinship. Therefore, that is not the way. The way is that an individual must be brought to understand fully that the essence of morals and of religion and of education is one, and that is the manner of friendship.

Sufis of all ages have named it *sulūk*, which means "beneficence." If there is a best education, it is beneficence: how to bring a pleasure, a happiness to another. And one can begin to learn it by understanding fully, and by practicing, at the same time, friendliness.

God bless you.

22

World Kinship

THE word *Sufi* comes from the Greek origin, *sophos*, which means "wisdom."[1] And today we confuse the two words *intellect* and *wisdom*. Sometimes we use *intellect* for wisdom, and *wisdom* for intellect. No sooner do we distinguish between intellect and wisdom than we come to another consciousness: that intellect is one thing and wisdom another.

It is the same with the words *pleasure* and *happiness*. Often we confuse pleasure with happiness, and happiness with pleasure, but pleasure is a shadow of happiness. And when we come to the words *wise* and *clever*, there also sometimes we confuse. Very often we use the word *clever* for *wise*, and the word *wise* for *clever*. Cleverness is worldly wisdom, but when coming to wisdom, it is a higher, a greater idea from what we call cleverness. At the same time, pleasure is covered in happiness, and cleverness is covered in wisdom. Intellect is that side of knowledge that we gather from our study and experiences of the outside world. The knowledge of names and forms, all we learn from books, from experiences of life, all these impressions gathered together in our thoughts, which we call knowledge, are intellectual. But wisdom is the essence of what we have learned from the outside world and what we draw from the inner world. The knowledge we gather from the inner and from the external world, knowingly or unknowingly, makes wisdom.

1. Lecture given at the Twentieth Century Club, Detroit, May 15, 1926.

And we have conceived in our minds to be as such and such, for instance what we call false, true, good, bad, high, low, also harmonious, inharmonious—all these are different conceptions that we have made. There comes a time that we unlearn them, that we begin to see that in the same conception there is also the opposite of it, only covered in it; and it is by the process of unlearning that we may begin to come to the realization of things, which life [*text missing*] differently. Our outlook on life becomes quite different. But it is not only an intellectual attainment that must bring us closer to spiritual attainment; it is also the development of a sympathetic nature. Today one misses in modern education the culture of the heart qualities. The other day in Switzerland I met a professor of the university. He said, "Yes, we are studying all different religions, but at the same time we must be neutral. We must not look at these scriptures sympathetically; we must just study them." Therefore, I said, "If for a thousand years you study intellectually, you will not get at the depth of it, because these are the words of the holy ones." It is by sympathy that we can live into these words, get their true meaning. Religion and spiritual attainment apart, to understand, to know one another—all this is only one religion, and that is the development of sympathy.

Book learning, therefore, is not necessarily the attaining of wisdom. I have seen myself a man who had studied in the British Museum all the books on occultism and esotericism and mysticism, and perhaps wrote about fifty books himself. But when it came to the understanding of spiritual wisdom, he said, "I do not know what I am looking for." Particular learning is not necessarily wisdom.

Today we hear from every side that humanity is moving more, after the war, toward spiritual realization. One wonders if it is true. In some respects it is true. There are many who have come from the war after having seen that horrible thing, having gone through that horrible experience, after having seen such catastrophe and tragedy met at this time of civilization. Naturally, from every side, it seems that there is a desire to attain to a greater knowledge, a higher knowledge; and yet the means that people take in order to attain to higher knowledge is very often the wrong means. There are some who think that by intellectual studies one can attain to spiritual wisdom. It is not possible; on the contrary, it needs unlearning. One can get the knowledge of all that is in the world by studies, but one cannot get the knowledge of the unseen world by study. You might ask what I mean by unlearning. I mean by unlearning to forget all the impressions that we have gathered in life.

Our great poet of Persia, Rumi, says that the heart of humanity can be likened to a mirror. The mirror is made clear by sympathy. Every soul that stands before it is reflected in it, and it sees that soul clearly. One need not practice arts as clairvoyance and clairaudience. Once the heart faculty is developed, the natural culture helps one to be inside in every soul one meets. Every soul becomes as an open letter; one can see through the soul clearly.

Spiritual attainment is not necessarily a certain knowledge. It is the changing of the outlook, of the attitude, a spring of the consciousness, the deepening of inside experience, of that peace; and it is enjoying the happiness that is the natural heritage of every soul.

God bless you.

Appendix

Sufi Movement

Rules for the World Brotherhood

THE Sufi Movement is intended to work for the reconstruction of the world at the present moment.[1] The Sufi Message is the reform of the time to be introduced in the world, the peace of which is disturbed by the lack of ideal and absence of Brotherhood.

The Sufi Message was borne to the Western world in 1910 by Inayat Khan who has since then carried this Movement through the world.

The Ten Sufi Thoughts

1. There is one God, the Eternal, the only Being; none exists save He.

2. There is one Master, the Guiding Spirit of all souls, who constantly leads his followers towards the Light.

3. There is one Holy Book, the sacred manuscript of nature; the only scripture which can enlighten the reader.

4. There is one Religion, the unswerving progress in the right direction towards the ideal, which fulfills the life's purpose of every soul.

5. There is one Law, the law of reciprocity, which can be observed by a selfless conscience together with a sense of awakened justice.

6. There is one Brotherhood, the human brotherhood, which unites the children of earth indiscriminately in the fatherhood of God.

1. Original copy as given by Pir-o-Murshid in 1923.

7. There is one Moral, the love which springs forth from self-denial and blooms in the deeds of beneficence.

8. There is one Object of praise, the beauty which uplifts the heart of the worshipper through all aspects from the seen to the unseen.

9. There is one Truth, the true knowledge of our being, within and without, which is the essence of all wisdom.

10. There is one Path, the annihilation of the false ego in the real, which raises the mortal to immortality, in which resides all perfection.

Besides the esoteric side of the Movement, there exist two exoteric activities: 1. Religious and 2. Social. The social activity of the Movement, namely the World Brotherhood, has three objects, as follows

The Three Objects of the Sufi Movement

1. To realize and to spread the knowledge of unity, the religion of love and wisdom, so that the bias of faiths and beliefs may of itself fall away, the human heart may overflow with love, and all hatred caused by distinctions and differences may be rooted out.

2. To discover the light and power latent in man, the secret of all religion, the power of mysticism, and the essence of philosophy, without interfering with customs or belief.

3. To help to bring the world's two opposite poles, East and West, closer together by the interchange of thought and ideals; that the universal brotherhood may form of itself, and may meet with man beyond the narrow national and racial boundaries.

Glossary

akhlaq allah (Arabic): the divine manner of God.

artha (Sanskrit): acquisition of wealth.

bhakti yoga: (Sanskrit) the path of devotion.

dar-as-salam (Arabic): "door to peace."

dervish: Sufi practioner.

Hafiz: Khwaja Shams ad-Din Muhammad Hafiz Shirazi (d. 1326), Persian Sufi Poet.

jalal (Arabic): power.

jamal (Arabic): beauty.

Jami: Nur ad-Din 'Abd ar-Rahman Jami (1414–1492), Persian Sufi poet.

kamal (Arabic): "perfection," state of suspended activity.

khalif (Arabic: khalifa): successor or representative

Krishna: Hindu avatar of Vishnu

kun fayakun (Arabic): "Be and it became."

murid (Arabic): "willing," a Sufi initiate.

murshid(a) (Arabic): "guide," senior Sufi teacher.

musake (Arabic): "Moses listen."

Nada Brahma (Sanskrit): "Sound, the Creator."

nafs (Arabic): self, ego.

prakriti (Sanskrit): limitation.

purusha: (Sanskrit): cosmic consciousness, spirit.

qadr (Arabic): "power," personal will.

qaza' (Arabic): "determination," divine will.

Rumi: Jalal ad-Din Muhammad Balkhi Rumi (d. 1273), famed Persian Sufi poet of Konya and founder of the Mawlawi (Mevlevi) Order.

Sa'di: Shaikh Muslih ad-Din Sa'di (1210–1291) Persian Sufi poet.
saf (Arabic): "pure."
samsara (Sanskrit): worldly existence; the cycle of life and death.
sifat (Arabic): "qualities," manifestation.
sophia (Greek): "wisdom."
sulūk (Arabic): search for truth.
Vedanta (Sanskrit): the philosophy of the Upanishads.
zat (Persian; Arabic: dhat): essence.

Sources

Below are listed sources of the text within the volumes of *The Complete Works of Pir-o-Murshid Hazrat Inayat Khan, Source Edition* series.[1] Sources of other texts are cited within their section.

Social Gathekas

1	Sufism Not Pacifism	1922 vol. 2, 339–42
2	Our Work in the Line of Kinship	1922 vol. 1, 426–31
3	Optimism and Pessimism	1922 vol. 1, 432–36
4	Harmony	1922 vol. 2, 309–14
5	Happiness	1922 vol. 1, 502–04
6	The Mission of Sufism to the World	1922, vol.1, 267–69
7	Sufism	1922, vol. 1, 366–67
8	What the World Needs Today	1922, vol. 1, 347–49
9	Different Points of View	1922, vol. 1, 391–94
11	World Reconstruction, part 1	1923, vol. 2, 762–64
12	World Reconstruction, part 2	1923, vol. 2, 765–68
13	Kinship, part 1	1923, vol. 2, 777–79
14	Kinship, part 2	1923, vol. 2, 779–83
15	The Problem of the Day	1923, vol. 2, 64–69
18	Shaikh Muslih ad-Din Sa'di	1923, vol. 1, 162–65
19	Shaikh Muslih ad-Din Sa'di	1923, vol. 1, 166–68
20	The Solution of the Problem of the Day	1923, vol. 2, 811–13
21	Poetry, part 1	1922, vol. 2, 293–97
22	Poetry, part 2	1922, vol. 2, 297–99
23	Music	1922, vol. 2, 221–22
24	Harmony and Agitation	1924, vol. 2, 645–50
25	Art and Religion	1923, vol. 2, 909–14
26	Khwaja Shams ad-Din Muhammad Hafiz, part 1	1923, vol. 1, 186–89
27	Khwaja Shams ad-Din Muhammad Hafiz, part 2	1923, vol. 1, 190-92
28	The Sufi's Aim in Life	1922, vol. 2, 185–96

1 Omega Publications, New Lebanon, NY, www.omegapub.com. Free download available at www.nekbakhtfoundation.org.

29	Renunciation	1922, vol. 1, 84–91
30	Farid ad-Din 'Attar	1923, vol. 1, 206–12
31	Fate and Free Will	1923, vol. 2, 784–90
32	The Heart Quality	1925, vol. 2. 659–67
33	The Difference Between Will, Wish, and Desire	1926, vol. 3, forthcoming
34	The Power of Thought	1925, vol. 1, 147–53
35	East and West	1923, vol. 2, 901–06
36	The Awakening of the Soul	1924, vol. 2, 699–708
37	The Power of Silence	1924, vol. 2, 733–40
38	Humanity, the Seed of God	1923, vol. 2, 791–97
39	Our Activity Which Is Called the World Kinship	1923, vol. 2, 174–75
40	Art	1922, vol. 2, 272–80
41	The Divine Blood Circulation through the Veins of the Universe	1923, vol. 2, 880–85
42	The Power of the Word	1923, vol. 2, 825–830
43	Concentration	1925, vol. 1, 43–49
45	The Maturity of the Soul	1923, vol. 2, 836–41
46	Physical Control	1926, vol. 2, 159–65
47	Seeing	1925, vol. 2, 607–17
48	Sufi Mysticism	1926, vol. 2, 95–106
49	Cosmic Language	1924, vol. 2, 798–811
50	Spirituality, the Tuning of the Heart	1926, vol. 1, 533-–52
51	The Four Paths Which Lead to the Goal	1925, vol. 2, 557–65
52	Intellect and Wisdom	1924, vol. 1, 122–31
53	The Awakening of the World in the New Year	1926, vol. 1, 72–81
54	The Spiritual Significance of Sound and Color	1925, vol. 1, 8–18

Kinship

1	Universal Kinship of Humanity	1922, vol. 1, 33–5
2	The Problem of the Day	1922, vol. 2, 85–8
3	Ideal Among Nations	1923, vol. 1, 87–9
4	The Work of Our Movement in the Line of Kinship	1923, vol. 2, 114–17
5	A Kinship Meeting 1	1923, vol. 2, 743–45

6	Three Objects of Our Work	1923, vol. 2, 800–2
7	Religious Unity	1923, vol. 2, 842–43
8	Our Service to Humanity	1924, vol. 1, 25–9
9	A Kinship Meeting 2	1924, vol. 1, 196–202
10	Universal Language	1924, vol. 2, 93–8
11	A Few Words to the Workers in Kinship	1924, vol. 2, 146–52
12	Kinship Work in Prisons and Hospitals	1924, vol. 2, 201–2
13	Questions and Answers	1924, vol. 2, 239–45
14	Noiseless Working	1924, vol. 2, 286–93
15	Kinship Work	1924, vol. 2, 385–90
16	Wakening the Divine Spirit	1924, vol. 2, 444–52
17	Tolerance	1924, vol. 2, 510–14
18	The Importance of Kinship	1924, vol. 2, 569–72
19	The Message of God	1924, vol. 2, 614–19
20	Unity	1924, vol. 2, 829–33
21	Friendship	1925, vol. 2, 44–51
22	World Kinship	1926, vol. 2, 441–443

HAZRAT Inayat Khan was born in Baroda, India, in 1882. Trained in Hindustani classical music from childhood, he became a professor of music at an early age. In the course of extensive travels in the Indian subcontinent, he won high acclaim at the courts of the maharajas and received the title of Tansen-uz-Zaman from the Nizam of Hyderabad.

In Hyderabad Hazrat Inayat Khan became the disciple of Sayyid Abu Hashim Madani, who trained him in the traditions of the Chishtiyya, Suhrawardiyya, Qadiriyya, and Naqshbandiyya lineages of Sufism, and at last blessed him to "Fare forth into the world."

In 1910, accompanied by his brother Maheboob Khan and cousin Mohammed Ali Khan, Hazrat Inayat Khan sailed for the United States. Over the next sixteen years he traveled and taught widely throughout the United States and Europe, building up the first Sufi order ever established in the West.

In London Hazrat Inayat Khan married Ora Ray Baker. Four children were born to them, whom they raised in London during the First World War and afterward in Suresnes, France, where a little Sufi village sprung up around their home, Fazal Manzil.

The doors of Hazrat Inayat Khan's Sufi Order[1] were open to people of all faiths. Appealing to experience rather than belief, Hazrat Inayat Khan's discourses and spiritual instructions illuminated the twin themes of the presence of God in the depths of the human soul and the interconnectedness of all people. Numerous books were compiled from Hazrat Inayat Khan's teachings during his lifetime and posthumously. In September 1926, Hazrat Inayat Khan bade farewell to his family and disciples and returned to India. On February 5, 1927, he died and was buried in New Delhi.

1 Known today as the Inayatiyya.

Sulūk Press/Omega Publications is an independent publisher dedicated to issuing works of spirituality and cultural moment, with a focus on Sufism and, in particular, on the works of Hazrat Inayat Khan, his successors, and followers. For more information on the legacy of Hazrat Inayat Khan, please contact the Inayatiyya at 112 East Cary Street, Richmond, Virginia, 23219. www.inayatiorder.org.

Sulūk Press/Omega Publications
www.omegapub.com